Video Vision

Video Vision:
Changing the Culture of Social Science Research

Edited by

Martin J. Downing Jr. and Lauren J. Tenney

Cambridge Scholars Publishing

Video Vision: Changing the Culture of Social Science Research,
Edited by Martin J. Downing Jr. and Lauren J. Tenney

This book first published 2008

Cambridge Scholars Publishing

12 Back Chapman Street, Newcastle upon Tyne, NE6 2XX, UK

British Library Cataloguing in Publication Data
A catalogue record for this book is available from the British Library

ISBN (10): 1-4438-0001-5, ISBN (13): 978-1-4438-0001-3

H
61
.V44
2008

To Claude "Tommy" Downing, my parents (Dad and Betty), and Laura for their support and encouragement.

—MJD

In memory of Esmin Elizabeth Green, a mother of six and Jamaican immigrant, described by those who knew her as a "beautiful person."

Ms. Green's murder-by-neglect was captured on videotape at the Kings County Hospital Center Psychiatric Emergency Room and broadcast around the world. This videotape brought to light the falsification of documents, which read that she was up and to the bathroom while the videotape showed her writing on the floor dying. It has spurred an international effort for change in the psychiatric world and a caution to us all not to lose our humanity in this surveilled world.

—10e

TABLE OF CONTENTS

PREFACE

How did two students of environmental psychology come together to create a book about the use of video in social science research? This is a question for which we have continued to debate even as this book goes to press and our second annual conference on the subject is soon to take place. *Video Vision*, which began as an afternoon workshop intended for graduate students, has become an opportunity for us to reach a wider audience of researchers who may be considering or questioning the use of video in their own work. We of course would not be here without the efforts of early pioneers and dedicated academics in this field of visual research including Margaret Mead, Sol Worth, John Adair, Beryl Bellman, Bennetta Jules-Rosette, Paul Hockings, Marcus Banks, Sarah Pink, Gillian Rose, and David MacDougall. Therefore, we want to acknowledge them here and express our appreciation for influencing us in such positive ways. In deciding to contribute to this ever-growing literature, we wanted to write a book that tells a story of what it is like to be students of social science out in the field using a video camera. With any luck our volume has tapped into these powerful and personal experiences while introducing the empirical potential of this technology.

Rather than argue about the advantages of video, we would like to offer readers an ecological perspective that the editors of this compilation share in hopes of developing a useful theory with which to incorporate this methodology. We believe that video can act as a tool used, not for direct perception, but during direct perception. James Gibson depicts tool as an extension of one's hand or body, thereby pushing the boundary between person and environment beyond our skin (1987). As such, a camera would become part of one's being rather than a detached object of the environment (Gibson, 1987; Pink, 2001). Based on this connection, not only does the person perceive but so too does the camera. Now it would most likely be a fallacy to imply that our tool directly perceives objects in the environment in a similar manner as the human eye. So rather than push the envelope with regard to a radical empiricist approach to immediate experience, we propose a dual existence between Gibson's *tool* and Fritz Heider's *thing and medium* (1959). Harry Heft informs us that it is not clear whether Heider was in favor of the concept immediate experience,

ACKNOWLEDGEMENTS

Thank you so much to Professor David Chapin for introducing us to the idea of using video as a research tool and continuously supporting our efforts to explore this exciting medium. Without him we would not have been inspired to create our own Video Vision.

We would like to thank Professor Joe Glick for his support of the Video Vision conference as well as his contributions to our peer review process. We also appreciate his insightful comments regarding the final manuscript.

The peer review process was aided in part by Linda B. Loy and we thank her for her diligent editorial skill.

Our heartfelt thanks go to Dr. Justin Spinney at the University of Surrey for his motivating and pragmatic review of this manuscript.

Warmest regards and thanks to the Ph.D. program in Environmental Psychology at The Graduate School and University Center of The City University of New York for sponsoring the Video Vision Conference on September 10, 2007.

Special thanks to Judith Kubran and Jared Becker for their continuous support!

Finally, this book would not be without all of the exceptional contributions made by each author in our compilation. Our sincerest appreciation!

INTRODUCTION

Walter Benjamin, in his examination of authenticity being replaced by mechanical reproduction, comes so far as to suggest how film allows for the analysis of behavior (1969). It is a way of combining art with science to provide better insight into human life. David MacDougall recently suggested that films automatically portray complexities of social environment relationships, whereas writers must have the intent to do so (2006). This advancement of technology affords us a chance to, as Margaret Mead explains, "illuminate our growing knowledge and appreciation of mankind" (1975, p. 10). While this may be our ultimate goal as social scientists, we are perhaps accomplishing this at the expense of our informants. Susan Sontag, in her notes on photography, suggests that capturing people in a photo is a violation and it turns them into objects for our possession (1977). Researchers must try to resolve this dilemma by establishing rapport with participants, ensure their ethical protections, and use culturally relevant methods.

Decisions about whether or not to employ visual methods in a social science research endeavor are often made prior to arriving at the field site in order to satisfy human subjects protections requirements and funding proposals (Pink, 2001). But the usefulness of such methods will be dictated by the context. Researchers should determine the level of cultural familiarity with technology as well as obtain permission from authorities or informants before snapping a photo or recording a scene. This raises ethical questions including to what extent is consent informed and how will participants be represented through the medium. In Chapter two, Tenney and MacCubbin stress the importance of triangulating one of the Belmont Principles, *Respect for Persons*, amongst researcher, participants, and institutional review boards while underscoring the issue that informed consent is continuous throughout the research process and not a single introductory event. Libman and Fields, in Chapter three, describe the use of video messages to give participants more control over their filmed experience and the opportunity to determine audiences for such messages. Pink (2001) suggests that collaborating with informants can improve their awareness and ease anxieties. A collaborative project might consist of giving cameras to participants, using photo or video elicitation, or the joint editing of footage (Banks, 2001; Felstead, Jewson, & Walters, 2004; Pink, 2004; Tenney, 2006).

Early in the 1980's video was in greater demand than film by anthropologists because it was less expensive and had longer run times (Pink, 2001; Pink, 2004). This shift from film to video coincided with a breakdown in the art-science dichotomy, to which Benjamin had previously alluded. Pure objectivity, afforded by strict documentation and data recording, was being replaced with a more subjective approach for understanding social relationships. Building on this, researchers began to ask themselves what influences they bring to video, what benefits can be gained from reviewing footage with participants, what goals or intentions do participants bring to the project, and how should the video-making process be explained to audiences. These are questions for which we should still be asking of ourselves today. Ultimately, this leads us to a necessary discussion on reflexivity, which is the idea that social scientists should recognize and assess their role in the production of knowledge. An example of this comes based on reviewing the documentary *Silverlake Life* (1993). The filmmaker Tom Joslin records the last days and weeks of his intense struggle with AIDS, but feels compelled to evaluate this experience as both patient and director. In the first chapter of this volume, Downing reflects on his roles of recorder and interviewer behind the camera during the process of data collection.

Outline for Video Vision

In recent years the use of video to capture data has soared spurring debate about such concepts as reflexivity, participatory action, lived experiences, consciousness of the camera, role of the participant, role of the researcher, equipment selection, and the body-camera-environment connection. These issues have been addressed consistently throughout Video Vision. To begin this compilation, Downing makes a case for why video is a valuable tool for social scientists while using practical advice based on his personal experiences with this technology. Because his video interviewees could be considered part of a vulnerable population, persons living with HIV/AIDS, bringing the camera into their homes required additional safeguards to protect their privacy. This zooms into a section that addresses ethical responsibilities for using video in field research as well as methodological and analytical strategies.

Chapter two (Tenney & MacCubbin) presents readers with historical motivations for the creation of the Nuremberg Code, Declaration of Helsinki, and Institutional Review Boards and ethical guidelines for researchers working with human subjects in relation to video. They offer concrete insights into struggles researchers have faced when attempting to gain IRB approval for participatory action research, which used video as a research tool with populations who were considered vulnerable. So this chapter gives direction to IRB members, researchers, and participants about the challenges of protecting human subjects when using video. They address the need for various groups involved with the IRB process to educate themselves about new methods such as video.

In the third chapter (Libman and Fields), a feminist perspective is applied to introduce the significance of video messages as an instrument for homeowners to create housing policy discussion. The use of video messages as a technique to redistribute power to research participants offers an exciting way that video can alter the political landscape of power, educate individuals affected by a problem by individuals affected by that same problem, those who are in positions to help them, and the broader society.

This is followed by an in-depth examination of digital video-editing. Chapter four (Turan & Chapin) introduce us to the idea of video being first generation data and discuss the benefits of working with unaltered materials for analysis, while offering practical guidance on required skills such as creating bins to store data. Their work shows how video can zoom in on the humanity of research participants with the development of categories such as love and reverence. Additionally, Turan and Chapin offer a two-stage consent and release process to ensure that participants are comfortable with the imagery that has been created of them, and how it is being used – before it even becomes admissible as data.

Part II zooms out toward broader applications in the practice of using video in field research. Chapter five (Beaty) investigates the results of utilizing informant-made videos to better understand young people's perceptions of their school environments. She illustrates the power of video for capturing change. Looking specifically at how students interact with and within their school environments, this work transforms static research by creating a dynamic interplay between the person and the camera she is holding. Utilizing sociocultural theory, Beaty unmasks developmental processes of social identity and with a permanent record created by young informants, she opens up the scope of vision for how young people experience their worlds.

Following this in chapter six, Pine describes obstacles he faced when attempting to film meaning in everyday life and how this ultimately led to the adoption of an *aesthetics of use* for engaging "a secretive social world" (p. 146). His anthropological perspective is especially informative for the social scientist who wishes to introduce his or her method(s) on groups to which he or she is not yet an insider.

In chapter seven, Mausner presents readers with a look at how attaching video cameras to the heads of participants can be invaluable to understanding the experience of hikers – or any other experience where active use of the body is required. Beyond this, the author describes her process of creating a notation system, which has garnered wide acceptance as a means of analysis for units/elements found in natural environments.

Chapter eight (Beckman) explores the benefits of video methodology when working with survivors of Hurricane Katrina, concerning their decisions to either remain in New Orleans for rebuilding or to relocate. Her focus on social support networks and home opens up ways to combine psychological research with video and can be applied to a multitude of research endeavors. Beckman offers sound practical and experiential guidelines that should prove useful to both novice and professional video researchers.

Chapter nine is a collective effort to present two projects, *Red Flags* and *Easy Targets*, taken on by young people and researchers working in partnership with each other towards solving problems that affect them and us all. This evocative work grounded in participatory action research with young people who have been oppressed and discriminated against based on their race, ethnicity, and citizenship status is the crux of what the use of video in research is all about and has the potential to achieve.

Consistently, themes of power, agency, transformation, and change are found in these collected works leading us to believe there is something unique and real about the use of video as a research tool. Due to its constant flux and development, a researcher must be willing to adapt easily and view it as a craft. We believe it gets to the human experience in a way that a survey, interview, or even focus group alone cannot.

Despite cautions of the validity of self-report on camera and taking a moment in time that may become de-contextualized by the editing of phrases that can be used as a person may not have intended, video adds a truth and depth to research not previously attainable. This is especially true when participants have the opportunity to review, analyze, and present materials that were generated by themselves or in conjunction with researchers.

As the authors in this volume discuss the intricacies of using video-from obtaining IRB approval, to learning how to shoot a camera, to learning how to edit and present footage, to learning how to achieve an audience-we ask you to ask yourself: What is your Video Vision?

References

Banks, M. (2001). *Visual methods in social research.* London: Sage.
Benjamin, W. (1969). *Illuminations.* New York: Schocken Books.
Felstead, A., Jewson, N., & Walters, S. (2004). Images, interviews and interpretations: Making connections in visual research. In C. J. Pole (Ed.), *Seeing is believing? Approaches to visual research* (pp. 105-121). Oxford: Elsevier.
Friedman, P. (Director), & Joslin, T. (Director). (1993). *Silverlake life.* [Motion Picture]. United States: Zeitgeist Films.
MacDougall, D. (2006). *The corporeal image: Film, ethnography, and the senses.* New Jersey: Princeton University Press.
Mead, M. (1975). Visual anthropology in a discipline of words. In P. Hockings (Ed.), *Principles of visual anthropology.*
Pink, S. (2001). *Doing visual ethnography: Images, media and representation in research.* London: Sage.
—. (2004). Performance, self-representation, and narrative: Interviewing with video. In C. J. Pole (Ed.), *Seeing is believing? Approaches to visual research* (pp. 61-77). Oxford: Elsevier.
Sontag, S. (1977). *On photography.* New York: Picador.
Tenney, L. (2006). Who fancies to have a revolution here? The opal revisited (1851-1860). *Journal of Radical Psychology, 5.*

CHAPTER ONE

WHY VIDEO?
HOW TECHNOLOGY ADVANCES METHOD

MARTIN J. DOWNING, JR.

Advances in technology have improved our ability to capture lived experiences through visual means. I reflect on my previous work with individuals living with HIV/AIDS, the results of which are described in another paper, to evaluate the effectiveness of video as a medium that not only collects data, but also produces knowledge. I have provided strategies for confronting specific technological barriers and concerns in research. I made sure to consider my own role within this research, and have chosen to share the personal insights and revelations that occurred in light of using this visual method.

In this chapter[1] I describe how video technology can enhance qualitative research. Drawing on examples from my own work, which is reported in another paper (Downing, 2008), the value of this tool as a medium to produce knowledge is explored and evaluated. The possibility of collecting image-based data can lead to questions regarding ethics, role of researcher and camera, and analysis; as well as concerns about the proper use of video equipment. In what is to follow I have raised these issues and offered solutions based on actual experience. In doing so I want to stress that close attention has been paid to the concept of reflexivity, which is an awareness of the researcher's role in acquiring data (Lynn & Lea, 2005). My purpose here is to share with other qualitative researchers

---

[1] Reprinted with permission by *The Qualitative Report*. Original citation is Downing, M. J. (2008). Why video? How technology advances method. *The Qualitative Report, 13*(2), 173-177. Retrieved from http://www.nova.edu/ssss/QR/QR13-2/downing.pdf

the interesting, yet often surprising thoughts, reflections, and decision-making points I encountered as a result of incorporating video and ultimately having visual elements as a source of information. It has been deliberately written un-glossed so that my experiences with this technology will be more accessible and perhaps relatable.

The initial interest in video research occurred during the end of my first year as a Ph.D. student at the City University of New York. I was in the process of preparing a research proposal for my second-year field project, which was geared toward understanding the relationship between home environments and living with HIV/AIDS. I had already decided to collect survey data on sleep quality, perceived stress, medication adherence, and perceptions about urban residential environments. But I wanted to study home in the context of illness, so I realized that I would need to include a qualitative dimension to this project by visiting the residence of each participant. Interviewing participants in the comfort of their own home is essential for evoking emotional topics (Cooper-Marcus, 1995). But how might my efforts make a novel contribution to the literature? This was a question I would often refer to as I progressed toward a final proposal. Should I interview the participants about their experiences with home or was that too obvious a solution for such a problem?

I realized that it would be significant if each individual could describe to me the layout of his or her residence and what attention to HIV occurred in different spaces. So, I initially planned to write down this information as I heard it and hoped that a visual image could be reconstructed later during analysis. This, however, seemed entirely too complicated and virtually impossible for someone with my limited qualitative research experience. Fortunately for me, I had a colleague who was struggling at the same time with her own field project involving the use of video. Suddenly I had a viable option to collecting this valuable information.

My next question was not so simple to answer. How would I get consent from participants who were considered part of a vulnerable population to have a video camera inside their homes? It was already going to be a difficult situation explaining why I needed to conduct the study at their home rather than in a neutral or laboratory setting. Adding the use of video would make the research prospect even more threatening. I decided, somewhat regrettably, that all participants would be promised complete confidentiality where my eyes, as the principal investigator, would be the only set reviewing these tapes. This seemed to be the only ethical solution, despite the obvious benefits of having more than one viewer/rater during analysis. I came to this decision too quickly out of fear that no one would participate without the added security. As it turned out, I still had trouble finding a diverse and sufficiently sized sample.

This study received approval by the Institutional Review Board within the Graduate School and University Center of the City University of New York. However, since it was not a funded project I relied on my own 8mm video camera, which had the capability to display footage on a larger screen (i.e. television). This feature would become particularly important in the data analysis. For the purposes of my research proposal, I stated that participants would take me on a tour of the interior and exterior spaces within their residences. The video camera would capture the sights and sounds during the tour, leaving open the possibility of taping elements that were not explored by the individual. Initially, my only expectations for using this technology was to record the structure and layout of each home with the hope of uncovering some evidence of an interaction between the environment and illness. It would be an exceptional way of representing the physical space so that later I could revisit, reflect, and reconstruct the scene by simply watching the tapes. I had no idea how relevant that statement would become until months later.

During my first two home visits, I took on a much greater role than I had anticipated. I was working with two disabled participants who were not able to fill out the survey packet without my assistance. Given the number of surveys that I had included, I ended up spending close to an hour writing down answers for each participant. By the time I was ready for the video tour I felt mentally exhausted and unable to fully comprehend the situation at hand. I experienced technical difficulties during the first home tour despite having used this camera on several occasions. I was unaware that the nightshot effect had been turned on. I resolved this problem only after videotaping the tour in nightshot mode, and then awkwardly having to ask my participant if I could redo the experience. Fortunately I did not have any more equipment trouble with the remaining tours. However, those first two videos were very basic, emotionless, and lacked in dialogue. It was almost as if the camera had been attached to a remote control car and steered through the home. I also felt that the participants were shy about being recorded, even when it involved only their voices.

I arrived at the home of my third interviewee ambivalent about going through this process all over again. My mind was racing with concern that the project had taken on an entirely different face than I intended. Fortunately, this was the man who would turn it all around! Kaleb was a very outgoing and lively spirit who welcomed me into his home as if we had been friends for years. From the outset I could tell that he would be in charge of this whole encounter, and for once I was comfortable with stepping out of control. Once again I helped fill out the surveys, which gave Kaleb an opportunity to tell his story in between questions. I found that many of these participants wanted to tell the story of how HIV or AIDS came into their lives. I had not expected this during the design phase, but was quite receptive to it. I felt honored that these men and women wanted me to know about who they are and how they got to this point.

When it was time to do the video tour, Kaleb walked me over to his front door and turned into an actor playing for a full audience. As an experienced performer, this was nothing new for him. He took me through room after room showing me anything and everything about the home that he continued to create. At times I would stop and ask questions or make comments, to which he would further elaborate or show me something else. I was not only capturing the environment but his active life within it. What an experience this was turning out to be. From this point forward I approached each video tour as an opportunity to interview. While most of my questions were formed during these interviews, I did ask participants about any attempts they had made to improve overall health by altering the physical surroundings of their home. I also thought it was important to ask what adjustments to the interior and/or exterior spaces of each residence would be made if possible, and how these changes could affect a person's struggle with HIV/AIDS.

Thereafter, all I needed to do was probe a few times during a tour and participants would open up. As Pink suggests "Video invites informants to produce narratives that interweave visual and verbal representation" (2004, p. 62). It was as if my opportunity to meet them had become their opportunity to meet me, and subsequently anyone else I talked to about this. Sometimes I felt as though my video camera were being used as a weapon against landlords or housing policy. It was not uncommon for participants to remark on the difficulty in acquiring certain maintenance services (i.e. repairing of windows, smoke detectors, heating system, and bathroom drainage), or obtaining permission for particular amenities such as the installation of a washer and dryer or an extra door lock. But what I found more surprising was the positive reception that I received utilizing this tool. Instead of a threat to their security, it provided a voice for educating and even venting. Looking back after having developed some adeptness with the camera, I could see missed opportunities in the footage of my earlier tours.

I had promised everyone that their physical body would not be the focus of my filming in order to ease any fears. But how would I engage them in conversation if my eyes were constantly behind the camera? During Kaleb's video tour I found myself disconnected from him and the stories he was telling. There were times when I wanted to look him in the eye instead of being a mere extension of the camera, reminiscent of Gibson's "tool" in the person-environment relationship (1986). Unfortunately, I did not come to a solution that day, but on my next interview I made some adjustments to the filming process allowing me to be more personable with the remaining participants. At certain moments throughout the video tours movement would cease as objects were described, pictures were identified, or design modifications were explained. It was at these moments that I realized I could pull my head away from the camera and talk directly with the participants. I had managed to stay attached to the equipment while still filming, yet now I had joined the conversation.

This may seem like a simple concept, but for an amateur video researcher it made a world of difference. As a social scientist conducting these interviews, I needed to be a participant-observer (Willig, 2001). MacDougall (2006) reminds us to be aware of the bodies and images not in front of the camera. There are entire scenes taking place just outside the frame. My body and the participant's body were engaging in verbal communication to which the lens was not privy. Fortunately the built-in microphone was! When I began to review the footage in those early stages of analysis I remember being struck by the notion that my camera had captured more than just visual elements. Would this be information that I could use to effectively answer my initial question about how individuals living with HIV/AIDS relate to their home environments?

I decided to pursue an audiovisual analysis of the video footage with the hope of demonstrating relationships between home and illness. My first goal in this process was to view and transcribe all of the video tours. Once I had accomplished this I began to look for insights about any interactions between the participants, their homes, and HIV/AIDS. By extracting content from transcripts, I was able to focus on connecting participant words with visual elements. Specifically, I asked how these sights encouraged theme development within the interviews and text. What I found far surpassed my original intentions for this project. I discovered that the home serves as a place of security, self-expression, control, and restoration (Downing, 2008). But it was not just the participants' voice that led to these conclusions. The visual had provided essential support to the audio, thereby rendering both elements mutually reinforcing. At the outset, I may have forgotten that a video camera can hear as well as see; but never again will I underestimate the power that these two features might afford a qualitative research endeavor.

I have tried to stress in this discussion the unexpected qualities video afforded my research. Not only was I able to capture the physical environment of my participants, but also the camera provided a unique interviewing and analyzing opportunity. I found it to be a vehicle for capturing the lived experience of home and illness. While I certainly agree with Banks (2001) and Pink (2001) that not every situation warrants the use of a visual method, researchers should not be too quick to discount its potential. Video has long been considered a useful instrument for recording data, but this process is in itself knowledge producing. As such, social scientists must consider the possibilities of exploring human behavior with technologies that advance traditional methods. My advice for anyone considering video as an option in research is to be comfortable with your equipment and to have an open mind throughout the process.

References

Banks, M. (2001). *Visual methods in social research*. London: Sage.

Cooper-Marcus, C. (1995). *House as a mirror of self*. Berkeley, CA: Conari Press.

Downing, M. J., Jr. (2008). The role of home in HIV/AIDS: A visual approach to understanding human-environment interactions in the context of long-term illness. *Health & Place, 14*, 313-322.

Gibson, J. J. (1986). *The ecological approach to visual perception*. Hillsdale, NJ: Lawrence Erlbaum Associates.

Lynn, N., & Lea, S. J. (2005). Through the looking glass: considering the challenges visual methodologies raise for qualitative research. *Qualitative Research in Psychology, 2*, 213-225.

MacDougall, D. (2006). *The corporeal image: Film, ethnography, and the senses*. New Jersey: Princeton University Press.

Pink, S. (2001). *Doing visual ethnography: Images, media and representation in research.* London: Sage.

—. (2004). Performance, self-representation, and narrative: Interviewing with video. In C. J. Pole (Ed.), *Seeing is believing? Approaches to visual research* (pp. 61-77). Oxford: Elsevier.

Willig, C. (2001). *Introducing qualitative research in psychology. Adventures in theory and method.* Philadelphia, PA: Open University Press.

PART I

ZOOM IN: A FOCUS ON ETHICS, METHOD AND ANALYSIS

CHAPTER TWO

WHEN NO ONE WAS WATCHING: HUMAN SUBJECTS PROTECTIONS AND VIDEOTAPING (TAKE ONE)

LAUREN J. TENNEY AND PATRICIA MACCUBBIN

Introduction

The purpose of this chapter is to **embolden** and *underscore* the importance of human subject and participant protections in social science research when using video as a research tool. Authors not necessarily limited to the role of academics address issues of human participant protections and informed consent through many and varied lenses. Litigators, ethicists, patients, advocates, politicos, entertainers, educators, and members of the popular press and media have written extensively about fair warning of the risks and benefits of research to participants as well as obtaining true informed consent. What we present is just a snapshot of the breadth of work on the subject from the perspectives of ethics, regulation, and policy and we encourage you to further research these matters on your own. There is something uniquely invaluable about the level of access to information available to us today. If it were available in his time, the developmental psychologist Lev Vygotsky (1896-1934) might have said that the Internet allows for the conditions of an in-depth and personal activity-based experience of gathering information, which thereby furthers learning.

Beyond the simple fact that protecting people who are participating in research is the ethical thing to do, this work was inspired in multiple ways. First, Tenney's personal experiences as a doctoral student attempting to gain Institutional Review Board (IRB) approval for a research design, that included both the use of video and participatory action research with emancipatory underpinnings, highlighted for her certain problems researchers encounter when doing somewhat novel things.

Second, conflicts that other researchers have had obtaining IRB approval using video in the social sciences include a view that the IRB is "paternalistic" and maintains the status quo of "top down research" (Bradley, 2007 p. 341). Neither Tenney's nor Bradley's situations are unique as difficulties gaining IRB approval to begin social science research are so common that the Congress of Qualitative Inquiry published to the web, a draft position statement on qualitative research and IRBs with suggestions to improve the process (2006).

Third, Patricia MacCubbin, the Director of the City University of New York's Office of Research Conduct, has a sincere desire to work with researchers in finding ways to facilitate ethical research utilizing video. She kicked off the first annual Video Vision conference (September 10, 2007) with a presentation entitled, "Human Subject Protections & Videotaping: Take 1". MacCubbin's work offered us both the historical and ethical frameworks for the conference that spurred ongoing conversations about ethics addressed in this chapter.

Fourth, Michael Commons, Assistant Clinical Professor in the Program in Psychiatry and the Law at Harvard Medical School has engaged with Tenney in an e-mail interview offering his thoughts on the use of video in research. One of the most important points for consideration that he offered was the idea that researchers ought to consider using two or more video cameras to capture different angles of the situation. This is because with video, the angle in which one is shot can determine how the viewer perceives the situation, on a subconscious level. Commons, et al. (2006) use a "model of hierarchical complexity" (p. 431) in determining if the person who is said to have given informed consent is truly engaged in a process of both understanding the information that is being sought from them *and* is consenting to their role in the research process.

Fifth, and finally, questions of why the IRB is important and the depth to which one *really* has to have her/his work approved by an ethics committee are consistently heard when the name of this body is invoked. It is important for researchers to understand while it might seem an undue burden to them to have their work evaluated and scrutinized by an ethics committee, human lives have been lost and extreme psychological situations have been created when no one was watching. Having a disinterested, objective party review one's plans is a small price to pay, to ensure that *all* research truly meets the standards of Human Subject/Participant Protections.

We begin with an overview of why Human Subject Protections and Institutional Review Boards were established in the United States to add a sense of historical poignancy to "When No One Was Watching." We want to convey to you, the social scientist, why solutions to prevent further unethical behavior by scientists carry even more weight when the research tool one is using is a video camera. Guidelines for ethical conduct of research can be found in the Nuremburg Code (1947), Declaration of Helsinki (1964), Belmont Report (1979), and Institutional Review Boards themselves.

We then look at current practices concerning the informed consent process (Commons, et al., 2006) and how that process changes when you add video (Turan & Chapin, 2005). Next, we move into a discussion of how the different uses of video in research change the research landscape by augmenting privacy and confidentiality (Architecture-Research-Construction, Inc. 1985; Rivlin and Wolfe 1985; Sieber, 2007; Wolfe, 1975).

We conclude with strategies for approaching an IRB or ethics committee as a way of eliminating potential conflicts between researchers participants, and Institutional Review Boards (IRB). These strategies include:

Ensure that your research is well-designed;

Create a consent form that facilitates informed consent with informed choice for potential participants;

Demonstrate that you can identify when someone is giving true informed consent and that you have the ability to facilitate optimal conditions to meet the processes for obtaining informed consent outlined by Commons et al. (2006);

Create a separate consent and release process for your use of video in the form of an agreement between you and people you are working with;

Define how you will meet the standards set forth in the Nuremberg Code

(1947), Declaration of Helsinki (1964), and the Belmont Report (1979);

Create and give the IRB replications of the video techniques that you intend to employ by writing scripts and having actors perform scenarios;

Ensure that members of Institutional Review Boards keep abreast of cutting edge technologies—such as video; and,

Triangulate the principle of *Respect for Persons* from the Belmont Report (1979) to facilitate ethical research.

To reiterate, we write this chapter to reinforce that when using video in research, social scientists must heavily weigh the potential risks and benefits that the use of video presents to the participants of the research before one chooses video as a research tool.

When No One Was Watching

We mean this not to encourage surveillance but to point out how devastatingly unethical research and researchers can become when no one is watching.

For forty years (1932 - 1972) 399 African-American men were the study subjects of an investigation (N=600) that withheld medical treatment from them to understand the course of untreated syphilis - even after it was learned that penicillin was the "gold standard" for treatment. It took place in Tuskegee, Alabama (Fisher, 2007). The Center for Disease Prevention and Control's website[1], offers a fascinating timeline of the study beginning with Booker T. Washington's (1895) "dream for black economic development" and ending May 16, 1997 when President William Jefferson Clinton "apologizes on behalf of the nation" for the study. Often sited as a breakdown of ethics, the United States Public Health Service Syphilis Study at Tuskegee is often referred to as the Tuskegee Syphilis Study (Jones, 1983/1991; Cohen, Bankert, & Cooper, nd). The research in the study involved deception at such a monumental level. It is safe to say that a conspiracy was orchestrated to ensure that the men who thought they were doing all they could to obtain effective medical treatment - were not. Instead, those participants were watched so that "researchers" could learn what happens if Syphilis goes *un*treated. The information for the following scenario, which does not directly relate to video, but is the underpinning

---

[1] http://www.cdc.gov/tuskegee/timeline.htm

for the need of ethics in research, comes from the Centers for Disease Control and Prevention (CDC) timeline of the study.

Imagine This

It is 1932 - three years after the stock market has crashed and the American economic depression is in full swing. You are an African American man looking for medical help in Tuskegee, Alabama. It is thirty-two years before the Jim Crow Era ends, and the Civil Rights Act will be born in 1964. You agree to be a study participant in exchange for free medical care, free food, and paid funeral expenses. You go to doctors at local hospitals who do testing on you. You are told you have "bad blood". You do not know that the title of the study you have enrolled in is "Tuskegee Study of Untreated Syphilis in the Negro Male". Even after penicillin, the "gold standard" for treatment for Syphilis is confirmed in 1945 you are not advised of alternatives and you are not given proper medical treatment.

It is now 1962. You continue to see doctors in hospitals - many of them African American. This is because in 1932 at the experiment's inception Doctors Clark and Vondelehr promised hope to restore development funds that focused on the health of African Americans. Robert Motin, who continued Booker T. Washington's work after his death in 1915, agreed to support a six-month study if, "Tuskegee gets its full share of the credit" and "black professionals are involved[2]". Imagine how an un-invested third party could have altered the thirty-six and one half years of your life that followed, if someone had been watching.

However, no one was watching. For forty years - if you lived and had not died from the disease - this was your life as a medical research participant. Perhaps at some point you ask why a supposed six-month study grows to forty years. Over that time, some questioned the ethics of the work - but you do not know *this* is the study in which you are enrolled. Despite the ethical questions raised in 1968, the CDC and professional organizations such as the American Medical Association *supported* the need for the study and its continuation. You continue to go to licensed physicians believing you are doing all you can do to take care of the "bad blood" circulating through your body.

---

[2] http://www.cdc.gov/tuskegee/timeline.htm

Finally, public attention is drawn to the study in 1972 and subsequent outrage led to its end. An out-of-court settlement for $10,000,000 was awarded to the entire sample of participants. The award was scaled depending on whether you were in the "control" group or the "study" group and whether you were still living. This equated to $37,500 for you as a living participant with syphilis. If you died as a result of having medical treatment withheld from you, your spouse or offspring were also given small monetary settlements and medical treatment. Using an Internet inflation calculator, your award as a living participant in the study group equates today to $162,419.88[3]. It is important for you, the reader and social scientist, to pause and ask yourself, "How does this make me feel?"

There have consistently been ethical questions about using marginalized groups in research. Kurt Lewin (1946) urges the use of action research and notes:

> Recent research findings have indicated that the ideologies and stereotypes which govern inter-group relations should not be viewed as individual character traits but that they are anchored in cultural standards, that their stability and their change depend largely on happenings in groups as groups. (p. 208)

Jill Fisher's (2007) work also explores abuses of other marginalized groups in medical research including Native Americans, Latina/Latinos, and those who have been or are institutionalized in prisons and psychiatric facilities (pp. 117-120). She offers suggestions for ending these practices by moving solutions from an individual to systemic level. These concerns ought not be overlooked by social scientists - especially when using video as a research tool. This is because of the indelible imprint that video imagery leaves both on society and the individual participant who has been recorded with informed consent, and released the footage for use as data. As social scientists using video, we must make certain that the highest regard is taken for the people with whom we are interacting. We must prevent undue risk, and certainly uninformed risk, to any person, particularly when the participant may be considered as vulnerable or from a marginalized population. To implement these goals, the next section discusses several historical codes of conduct concerning the ethical practices of research.

---

[3] http://www.coinnews.net/tools/cpi-inflation-calculator

The Nuremberg Code

In 1949, nearly two decades into the Public Health Service Syphilis Study, The Nuremberg Trials produced ten "Directives for Human Experimentation" known as the "Nuremberg Code" for ensuring ethical research. The Public Health Service Syphilis Study clearly ignored the Nuremberg Code. Like most social change, legal intervention was the catalyst for the Nuremberg Code. In the "Doctors Trial" as it was referred to and is officially known as the *United States of America v. Karl Brandt et al* (Annas & Grodin, 1992; Weindling, 2001), there were twenty-three doctors who were tried for inhumane human experimentation after World War II. The lawsuit was spurred when the public learned about the barbaric experimentation that was being done on prisoners of Auschwitz. This inhumane experimentation included the Aktion (Action) T-4 program, where testing of the gas chambers on people with disabilities was conducted, killing more than 200,000 people as well as other atrocities (Heberer, 2002).

If you were the research participant, how would you like your informed consent process to be sought, explained, obtained, and coordinated before, during and after the research process? Consider how video plays into research as you read The Nuremberg Code[4] that follows and ask yourself, are you willing to have your most intimate thoughts videotaped?

1. "The voluntary consent of the human subject is absolutely essential. This means that the person involved should have legal capacity to give consent; should be so situated as to be able to exercise free power of choice, without the intervention of any element of force, fraud, deceit, duress, overreaching, or other ulterior form of constraint or coercion; and should have sufficient knowledge and comprehension of the elements of the subject matter involved as to enable him to make an understanding and enlightened decision. This latter element requires that before the acceptance of an affirmative decision by the experimental subject there should be made known to him the nature, duration, and purpose of the experiment; the method and means by which it is to be conducted; all inconveniences and hazards reasonably to be expected; and the effects upon his health or person which may possibly come from his participation

---

[4] Office of Human Subjects Research. *Directives for Human Experimentation. The Nuremberg Code.* Reprinted from Trials of War Criminals before the Nuremberg Military Tribunals under Control Council Law No. 10, Vol. 2, p. 181-182. Washington, D.C.: US Government Printing Office, 1949.
http://www.nihtraining.com/ohsrsite/guidelines/nuremberg.html

in the experiment. The duty and responsibility for ascertaining the quality of the consent rests upon each individual who initiates, directs, or engages in the experiment. It is a personal duty and responsibility, which may not be delegated to another with impunity.

2. The experiment should be such as to yield fruitful results for the good of society, unprocurable by other methods or means of study, and not random and unnecessary in nature.

3. The experiment should be so designed and based on the results of animal experimentation and a knowledge of the natural history of the disease or other problem under study that the anticipated results justify the performance of the experiment.

4. The experiment should be so conducted as to avoid all unnecessary physical and mental suffering and injury.

5. No experiment should be conducted where there is an a priori reason to believe that death or disabling injury will occur; except, perhaps, in those experiments where the experimental physicians also serve as subjects.

6. The degree of risk to be taken should never exceed that determined by the humanitarian importance of the problem to be solved by the experiment.

7. Proper preparations should be made and adequate facilities provided to protect the experimental subject against even remote possibilities of injury, disability or death.

8. The experiment should be conducted only by scientifically qualified persons. The highest degree of skill and care should be required through all stages of the experiment of those who conduct or engage in the experiment.

9. During the course of the experiment the human subject should be at liberty to bring the experiment to an end if he has reached the physical or mental state where continuation of the experiment seems to him to be impossible.

10. During the course of the experiment the scientist in charge must be prepared to terminate the experiment at any stage, if he has probable cause to believe, in the exercise of the good faith, superior skill and careful judgment required of him, that a continuation of the experiment is likely to result in injury, disability, or death to the experimental subject[5]"

---

[5] Office of Human Subjects Research. *Directives for Human Experimentation. The Nuremberg Code.* Reprinted from Trials of War Criminals before the Nuremberg

The Nuremberg Code offers us answers to some of the greatest ethical questions we face as researchers. Have we obtained true informed consent? Will this research benefit society? Is there a way to find answers to the problems we seek to fix without using humans? Have we made every attempt to minimize risk and unnecessary physical and mental suffering? Are we willing to be videotaped answering the same questions we ask of participants and publish those responses? Do the benefits outweigh the risks of using video? Have we created a safe space in which to record participants? Are we qualified to use video or teach someone how to use it if we are putting the camera in his or her hands? Are we prepared to immediately stop recording at the participant's request regardless of the participant's reason or for no reason at all, if continuation to the participant feels "impossible"? Are we prepared to stop the research protocol in total if someone is in jeopardy, even at the risk of losing data that might answer our research questions? If the answers to any of the above questions is anything but an emphatic "yes" our real answer is that we are not prepared to utilize video as a research tool. While the Nuremberg Code clearly outlined ethical conduct for researchers, there was still some ambiguity and continued unethical research which was the catalyst for the development of the Declaration of Helsinki (1964).

The Declaration of Helsinki (1964)

The World Medical Association's (WMA) webpage is worth exploring, and much of the following information was retrieved from it[6]. In 1964, the Declaration of Helsinki was created and adopted by the World Medical Association. Central to the declaration is the idea that the person must be respected and that the physician or researcher is in a position of power.

The Declaration of Geneva of the WMA: binds the physician with the words, "The health of my patient will be my first consideration," and the International Code of Medical Ethics declares that, "A physician shall act only in the patient's interest when providing medical care which might have the effect of weakening the physical and mental condition of the

---

Military Tribunals under Control Council Law No. 10, Vol. 2, p. 181-182. Washington, D.C.: US Government Printing Office, 1949. http://www.nihtraining.com/ohsrsite/guidelines/nuremberg.html
[6] http://www.wma.net/e/policy/b3.htm

patient" (Declaration of Helsinki, Section A. Number 3[7]).

The Declaration of Helsinki has been revised seven times since its creation in 1964, most recently with clarifications in 2002 and 2004, addressing concerns about the focus on the advances of science weakening the Nuremberg Code that Pelligrino (1997) outlined. To reform this, albeit in a clearly gendered way, the Declaration states,

> Each potential subject must be adequately informed of the aims, methods, anticipated benefits and potential hazards of the study and the discomfort it may entail. He should be informed that he is at liberty to abstain from participation in the study and that he is free to withdraw his consent to participation at any time. (Declaration of Helsinki, Section B. Number 22[8])

This is of the utmost importance for social science researchers to understand: science – even 'good science' - ought not ever outweigh the risk it may incur upon research participants. Underscoring the Nuremberg Code's ninth principle, this twenty-second principle of the Declaration of Helsinki holds researchers to the ideal that a participant can stop participation at any time for any reason or for no reason at all if continuation subjectively appears impossible to the participant.

Very often as social scientists, we relegate our studies to not needing the same level of protections as biomedical research because we are not directly altering the physical bodies of the people upon whom we are experimenting. However, the Declaration of Helsinki reminds us that this includes both "identifiable human material and identifiable data" (World Medical Association[9]). At the crux of concern IRB members when video is being used as a research tool is how the social scientist will protect identifiable data. If there is identifiable data, then this is considered 'high risk' research. In the IRB application, a program director must explain how s/he will protect the data. It is because all identifiable data must be adequately protected that researchers sometimes have such a struggle with getting video research approved and we discuss this in detail later in this chapter.

This Declaration also created protections for certain populations (pregnant women, fetuses, prisoners, and children) and protections to people who may be vulnerable and cannot give consent. It stresses that

---

[7] http://www.wma.net/e/policy/b3.htm
[8] http://www.wma.net/e/policy/b3.htm
[9] http://www.wma.net/e/policy/b3.htm

both the physical and mental well being of research subjects or participants must be protected at all times - even if that means ending the research protocol because people might be in danger.

In the section on *Students in Research* written by Maristela Cho (2006), of the CITI Program's course on Human Subject Protections, we are offered examples of how to limit coercion in accessing potential research participants[10]. Teachers or others in positions of power, like physicians or social scientists, might not realize the impact they are having on people they have asked to be involved in their research studies, and undue levels of coercion to participate might exist. Milgram (1963) proved this and we discuss how in this chapter. In order to avoid this, researchers ought not ask people over whom they exercise power to be involved in their research. MacCubbin suggests that in a doctor-patient relationship, the patient might agree to be in a study thinking 'this is my doctor, she would never put me in the placebo-control group and withhold treatment from me.' Yet we know, that very often this is *exactly* the case, as some participants have to be in the position of receiving placebos if the study calls for a placebo-control group.

It is important to note that in an editorial in the Annals of Internal Medicine, Pellegrino (1997) warned, "moral lessons are quickly forgotten" (p. 307). He argued that the Declaration at Helsinki weakened the Nuremberg Code by putting too much emphasis on the evolution of science and not enough emphasis on the "integrity of the subject" (p. 307). When using video, one has to ensure that the glamour and accessibility of research findings in a video format does not outweigh the ramifications an indelible imprint of intimate details about a person's life made available for public consumption, even if educational, can have on that person and her or his future life.

According to the Centers for Disease Control and Prevention (CDC), in 1974 the National Research Act was enacted. Its goal to require both the formation of Institutional Review Boards to ensure the ethics of government funded research and the necessity for researchers to obtain free, voluntary informed consent from research participants.[11] While the potential risks to participants who enter into biomedical research studies as subjects ingesting medications, undergoing operations, or having treatment

---

[10] www.citiprogram.org
[11] http://www.cdc.gov/tuskegee/after.htm

withheld from them if they are in the placebo group is apparent, the potential risks in social science research, particularly when using video, is somewhat more elusive.

The Milgram Experiment

Psychological danger can be as significant as physical danger. Stanley Milgram's work on obedience (1963; 1973; 1974) has raised ethical eyebrows for decades. Often described in a standard Introduction to Psychology textbook such as that by David Myers (2008), the experiment called for subjects to be deceived. Milgram's curiosity that motivated the study was to see if adults would harm other adults when commanded to do so.

The historical moment is important as it inspired Milgram's work. A short time before Milgram crafted his experiment, Adolf Eichmann, who is referenced as "the architect of the Holocaust" (Feinstein, 2005) was tried and charged with war crimes, crimes against humanity and hanged. Milgram questioned whether an adult would really listen to someone ordering him to capture, torture, and kill, or if all of the Nazis could be charged as willful accomplices (1974). However, to learn this would require the research subject not to know what was being tested. In a February 9, 1981 letter about his research, Milgram wrote, "The experiment only works if the subject does not know what it's about" (Milgram, 1981, p. 114).

There were three people involved in the experiment. The experiment (which did not have a control group) used the activity of teaching and learning to determine the level of obedience a research subject exhibits. The research subject is referred to as the "Teacher". The person the subject was teaching, was known as the Confederate to the researcher, as he was an "inside actor". To the research subject, however, he was just known as another research subject. The experimenter/authority figure monitored the situation to ensure that the participant carried out the experiment.

The Milgram Experiment was video recorded unbeknownst to participants. It involved even further deception in this way: research subjects were told that all of the participants would be paired with someone and that roles of either "Teacher" or "Learner" would be assigned *randomly*. In actuality, an actor would be paired with each research subject – rather than another research subject. The actor and research subject would pick a piece of paper that, as far as the subject knew, read either "Teacher" or "Learner". However, both pieces of paper read "Teacher" to ensure that the research subject was always in the Teacher role. The actor would act as if he got the slip of paper that read "Learner" and mention a heart condition to the participant.

Before beginning the experiment, the Teacher was told that every time the Learner was unable to produce a correct answer, he would have to flip a switch that would cause an electric shock to be delivered as a form of punishment for not learning. The research participant was given a 45-volt electric shock, so he would have first-hand knowledge of what the Learner would feel upon not being able to learn the assigned material.

During the experiment, the Teacher was to present the Learner with pairs of words he had to memorize. Every time the Learner gave a wrong answer, the Teacher was to give the Learner increasing doses of electric shock. The Teacher did not know that the electric shock he was giving the Learner was not really being delivered. While unknowingly being videotaped, the Teacher could not see, but could hear, the Learner, furthering the deception. Interestingly, the sounds of the Learner screaming in pain from the electric shocks administered by the Teacher, which the Teacher heard, were actually audiotaped, to provide for consistency.

Despite all of this, many research participants finished the entire experiment whereby three consecutive times they "shocked" Learners who got wrong answers. Some Subjects ended their participation as Teachers, but for the study to be stopped the subject had to object to four "prods" made by the experimenter: "1. Please continue; 2. The experiment requires that you continue; 3. It is absolutely essential that you continue; 4. You have no other choice, you *must* go on." According to the research design, it was only at the research participant's fifth rejection to continue participation that the study would be stopped (Milgram, 1974).

Milgram's conclusions (1973) are almost as shocking as his experiment:

This is, perhaps, the most fundamental lesson of our study: ordinary people, simply doing their jobs, and without any particular hostility on their part, can become agents in a terrible destructive process. Moreover, even when the destructive effects of their work become patently clear, and they are asked to carry out actions incompatible with fundamental standards of morality, relatively few people have the resources needed to resist authority. (p. 75-76)

The deception and coercion orchestrated by Milgram caused many of the research Subjects undue emotional stress and it is consistently cited as a breakdown of ethics. Remember that the research participants did not know that they were being recorded on film. However, to this day there are several videos available at no charge on the web that exhibit the Milgram Experiment that illustrate what psychological risk incurred by a research participant looks like. There is one video by Alex Gibney[12] that includes Doctor Stanley Milgram discussing the study and his findings. It is essential that we recognize the unethical research that was conducted by Milgram, as it involved deception and created great risk for the participants on a psychological level.

The psychological stress research participants experienced occurred both during and after the study. After the participant delivered the final shock of 450 volts for the third time the participant was debriefed and informed that the subject of study was not learning and memory, but that they, in fact, were the subject of study. Specifically, Milgram wanted to know how each individual, receiving $4.50 for one hour of work, would act when confronted with an authority figure to harm another. For participants who continued the experiment through to its end – to learn that about oneself – leaves a lasting impression, and creates a situation of undue psychological risk.

Milgram's study proved that people bow to authority with obedience but this is often not the subject of papers on his work because of his ethical misconduct. Let us pretend though, for a second, that Milgram's study was ethical. Perhaps he had used a "second order consent" (Wendler, 1996), informing potential research participants that there would be deception and filming involved in the study prior to engaging in an informed consent process to gain their assent to be involved in the study. Milgram found that 60-65% of participants were willing to deliver three consecutive jolts of 450 volts of electricity to a learner they did not know simply because they were commanded to do so at the insistence of a researcher/authority figure when the learner was unable to properly remember word pairs.

If environmental conditions are prime, how much influence do we as social scientists have when working with participants asking them to

---

[12] http://www.dailymotion.com/video/xlf851_presentation-de-lexperience-milgram_events

record intimate details of their lives on video for our use when such images are permanent and may make their way to the Internet or other databases for perpetuity? Is it not challenging to design research that will protect participants from this documented but disturbing side of human nature that allows us to bow so easily to authority? As Milgram exhibited, simple phrases such as "You must go on" are enough to prod behavior that individual participants knew was wrong. It is of the utmost importance for us as researchers to choose our words carefully and never, even unintentionally, use the position of power that the title Social Scientist affords us, in a way that limits a person's free will. If video images are part of a research project, will the social scientist insure that the participant's rights will be protected at all costs?

The idea of Milgram candidly filming participants brings us to issues of the use of video and what is appropriate or inappropriate behavior for a social scientist to be involved in. Certainly, issues of not complying with informed consent processes are apparent and they answer the questions of why the Belmont Report's (1979) principles of *respect for persons*, *beneficence*, and *justice* were developed.

The Belmont Report

The Belmont Report (1979) outlines the "Ethical Principles and Guidelines for the Protections of Human Subjects[13]" and was produced by the National Commission for the Protections of Human Subjects of Biomedical and Behavioral Research (National Institute of Health, 1979; Yoder, 2006). This report is of great importance to social scientists, as it specifies research encompassing not only medical procedures, but behavioral research as well.

There are three main principles found in Section C of the Belmont Report that all research must encompass, which include: *Respect for Persons*; *Beneficence*; and *Justice*. Discussed later in this chapter, we extend The Belmont Report to the entire research process. This includes interactions and transactions Research Participants, IRB Members, and Researchers have with each other by triangulating the principle of *Respect for Persons* as a way to facilitate ethical research.

---

[13] http://ohsr.od/nih.gov/guidelines/belmont.htm

Respect for Persons

Respect for Persons is the idea that no research ought to ever intentionally harm a person who has volunteered their body or experience to help Science better understand the human condition. Respect for Persons also brings to the forefront the requirement for **Informed Consent**. This is particularly true for what has been termed "protected populations" (pregnant women, fetuses, prisoners, and children) as well as people with diminished decision-making capacity or who are at greater risk for negative consequences of research. The informed consent process when using video as a research tool is discussed in depth later in this chapter.

Parental Permission with Child Assent is the type of consent process that is used with minors. Assent is simply agreeing to be involved as a willing participant in research. MacCubbin stresses that researchers understand when one is doing research with children one usually must get parental permission *and* child assent. A minor cannot give consent and a parent cannot give consent for a child to be involved with research; they can only give permission. If the child is old enough to understand what is happening to them, it is essential to explain the research protocol and obtain the young person's assent to be involved with the study. If the child says no, it means no and you cannot generally force a child to participate in a study if they do not wish to participate. Only in rare cases of therapeutic experiments with no other way to treat the child, such as a high risk medical procedure, would a parent and researcher be able to override the wishes of the child. If the child is able to assent, what the child says goes throughout the entire study. Parental permission with child assent, like informed consent, is a process, rather than an action.

For people assigned with diminished decision-making capacity, **surrogate consent** is the common procedure to enter a research protocol. A surrogate is someone who is designated ahead of time to make medical and other decisions for a person, such as a legally authorized representative or health care proxy. A person in the role of surrogate is never someone who has an interest in the study. A surrogate is concerned only with what is in the best interest of the person that the surrogate is representing. While there is no process of assent for people with diminished decision making capacity, once surrogate consent is obtained, it is essential for the researcher to respect the people that they are working with and if someone is actively objecting to involvement in the study, to end their involvement. This is true even when it means that the researcher will lose exactly the type of data being sought

MacCubbin urges program directors to understand that if the person has the ability to understand what is happening to them in the research process social scientists must keep the person informed and give the person respect. This is the essence of respect for persons. It is important for participants, surrogates, minors and their parents to know all of the details about the procedure and that researchers continue to give as much information about the process as exists. For people with diminished capacity this must be explicit.

MacCubbin's advice is, "It's best to be respectful and always tell participants what's happening next". An example she offers is that the person you are videotaping might be extremely sensitive to light. If you do not tell them you are going to use bright lighting to capture the shot, you may not find out this person can have an epileptic seizure from exposure to bright lights. If the potential subject or surrogate knows about the light, s/he could advise you about problems that might be encountered and avoided. In other words, the risks may be unrelated to the research, so keep participants informed to limit unanticipated problems. By telling participants and their surrogates what comes next, the researcher may be able to avert risk.

Privacy and Confidentiality are revered when you exercise due respect for research participants. Privacy concerns participants' expectations about what is happening to them. MacCubbin offers a scenario of someone talking on a phone in public. The person knows that others in close proximity can hear what s/he is saying, but there is an expectation that those nearby will not listen. Confidentiality, which is different than privacy, is concerned with what you as a researcher do with the data you have gathered and how you will protect identifying information. Confidentiality, MacCubbin stresses, is about how you as a researcher protect the data.

The use of video changes the dynamics of privacy and confidentiality, which are considered to be at the heart of most research studies, because with these factors, risk is minimized as no one can be identified. It is important for researchers to understand that the participants' recorded images create concern for Institutional Review Boards when reviewing the use of video in research. Video changes the parameters of research by eliminating a certain amount of privacy and confidentiality - especially if a goal of the research is to create an educational video with your findings, as participants are identified. The use of video transforms a previously unidentifiable statistic into an identifiable person perpetually linked to images that may range from being mildly embarrassing to expositions of matters deeply personal to that participant. With technology advancing so rapidly, it is common for such materials to potentially surface on the Internet or in other media and have a wider audience than the researcher originally anticipated. Participants ought to be well aware of what they are engaging in when consenting to be videotaped.

Can You Dig It?

In this section, we use Tenney's experiences of coordinating a participatory action research project with emancipatory underpinnings called "Can You Dig It?" to unpack the principles of the Belmont Report. A brief definition of Participatory Action Research is research that involves people who are affected by the problem in the design, implementation, and analysis of a research protocol (Bradley, 2007; Campbell, Ralph, & Glover, 1993; Fine, 2008; Lunch & Lunch, 2006; Odutola, 2003; Okahashi, 2000; Ralph, 1997; Tenney, 2006; Wadsworth, 1998). A brief definition of Emancipatory research is research conducted by the group affected by the problem. It desires to create change, with the goal of liberation from oppression (Cooper, 2007; Creswell, 2002; Tenney, 2006). Saul Alinsky (1971), David Chapin (Architecture- Research-Construction, Inc. 1975; 1985; Turan & Chapin, 2005, 2008), William Cross (1971), and Paolo Friere (1973) heavily influence Tenney's frame of reference.

After a lengthy IRB review process, the design was approved by the Graduate School and University Center of the City University of New York's Institutional Review Board (Tenney, 2006). Participants' perceptions of being video recorded ranged from discomfort with body image and how their voices sounded to excitement about having their likeness memorialized on videotape. This highlighted how necessary it is for researchers to prepare participants for what they are entering into when using video. As researchers, we have to be prepared to create a safe space for participants to explore themselves, and sometimes that means being supportive of participants who face themselves in uncomfortable ways, which, in turn, can make the researcher uncomfortable. This illustrated for Tenney that sometimes the risks of using video have little to do with the risks of the research being conducted.

In a research project Tenney (2006) coordinated "Can You Dig It?" she found that the use of video had plenty of evidence of its benefits. One of the greatest benefits was found in analyzing the data. This was expressed by many of the participants, as they were involved with the analysis (Pin, 2004). Further, one of the interview questions asked of participants was, "How do you feel about the use of video as a research tool?" Ultimately, even participants who felt uncomfortable and declined being videotaped due to their religious beliefs, perceptions about their physical appearance, or not wanting to publicly be 'outed' as a person with a psychiatric history, liked the idea of an educational video being produced. Some of these participants chose to only have their voice recorded on video, which was accomplished by leaving the cover on the lens, so that excerpts of their interviews could be added into a final product. Several participants who chose not to be videotaped chose to take footage of what interested them during their interview and this produced rich footage (Tenney, 2006).

Recruitment and the kick-off for "Can You Dig It?" (Tenney, 2006) was carried out during a 9-day protest and fast on the East Lawn of the Capitol building in New York State, to call attention to and stop the use of electroshock treatment (ECT) on children, which was organized by the Mental Patients Liberation Alliance. Formally known as Electroconvulsive treatment, ECT is a highly controversial medical procedure that requires anesthesia (which carries a risk of death). Its goal is to cause an epileptic seizure, technically called a grande mal seizure. For more than 70 years ECT has been used as a method of control and is still thought by popular psychiatry to be beneficial. So much so, that it is routinely court-ordered for hundreds of treatments at a time. ECT, in fact, causes brain damage, apathy, memory loss, and as reported by some of its survivors, destruction of life (George Ebert, Personal Communication).

Not all people involved in this study wanted to be identified. As in the example below, (Fig. 2-1) technology allows one to augment the features of the image, and there is equipment that allows one to manipulate the voice, etc., so that the person's identity remains private knowledge of the researcher as the individual's identity is kept confidential. Tenney heeded Banks' (2005) warning that the "'fuzzy face' effect" may "invoke associations with criminality for Euro-American viewers" (p. 130). As she was working with an already stigmatized population, people with psychiatric histories, she did not want to suggest to viewers, even on a subconscious level, that there was something criminal about the people they were watching. This is why in footage of those participants that wanted their confidentiality maintained she made efforts to not film their faces and in some cases, bodies, and then used digital effects such as blurring the edges of the moving imagery to further conceal participants' identity. It is important to note that images of people in this chapter were released by them for use (2006) and again, specifically for this work through individual communication (2008).

Fig. 2-1: Use of technology to blur video of participants from "Can You Dig It?" (2006) reading through *The Opal* (1851-1860) to protect their confidentiality.

Some participants, however, wanted to be known and decided to break their expectations for privacy and confidentiality while sharing their stories (Figure 2-1). Often scenarios of people wanting their likeness to be associated with them on videotape can be found when one is coordinating participatory action or emancipatory research. To reiterate, participatory action and emancipatory research is rooted in the idea of the group that is affected by the problem be the leaders in solving the problem (Bradley, 2007; Cooper, 2007; Creswell, 2002; Tenney, 2006). People wanting to break their own privacy and confidentiality, ought to be honored by the researcher and the Institutional Review Board. In Banks' (2005/2001) discussion of permissions for use of imagery (pp. 131-132), he noted the experience of one researcher who when given the opportunity to broadcast his work on television opted to decline the opportunity after he talked with participants about the opportunity. Banks reports that while most participants were excited by the opportunity, one person had moved on and had not disclosed that portion of his life in his new environments. This is a legitimate concern that social scientists ought to consider as sometimes publication of materials we produce takes some time. To honor this possibility, I contacted the participant in Figure 2 and asked him to re-consent to the use of his likeness. His response was, "Of course you can use it. I just wish you could see me a little better" (Personal communication with Participant).

Fig. 2-2: When asked for permission to use this photo from (2006) video in this chapter, this participant from "Can You Dig It?" responds, "Of course you can use it. I just wish you could see me a little better".

It is of the utmost importance that researchers not only understand the long term ramifications of having a moment memorialized on video, but that research participants must also know what you are planning to do with the video data. As in the case of Can You Dig It?, our modest footage has given many people involved with The Opal Project (the outcome of the research) hope that their perspectives will change mental health policy. Researchers and participants must agree on the use of the video on a continuous basis throughout the research, with the ability for the participant to opt out at any time for any reason. A two-staged consent and release process (Banks, 2005; Beckman, 2008; Bradley, 2007; Mausner, 2008; Turan & Chapin, 2005; 2008) helps to address this concern of the IRB when using video. It is discussed in greater detail in this chapter.

The language we use has a lot to do with the underpinnings of *Respect for Persons*, and in fact, the fields of biomedical and behavioral research often encourage a separation between "researcher" and "subject". In some of the social sciences, there is a move away from this explanation of the situation because many feel that there is too much power in the researcher when the experiment involves subjects of investigation. Many social scientists are moving toward working with people to examine a social condition or problem. Social scientists engaged in this new paradigm view the people they are working with as participants and in some cases, co-researchers (Bradley, 2007). If we view the research event as a social construction, we deeply understand that the method we use to construct the event determines, to a large degree, how we act in the event. Creating a situation where a research participant can act with agency as a participant in the process rather than being a subject or object of investigation improves the conditions of research for the participant, which should yield better results of the investigation.

Informed consent is central to the construction of how we as researchers carry out Respect for Persons. Below, we discuss in further detail that informed consent is an on-going process, rather than an action, as stressed by the Office for Human Research Protections (OHRP) but it is important to note here. If you are truly engaged in an informed consent process with the person you are researching, you acknowledge the power differential that exists between you and the participant and hold an inherent respect for them as another human, just as you are.

Some of the more ethical research practices prior to and including the Belmont Report suggest that the researchers use themselves as research subjects, if they were posing any potential great risks to the people upon whom they were experimenting (Principle 5, Nuremberg Code, 1949). This practice ought to be upheld. For social science researchers, this would include methods of participant observation as well as naturalistic observation. Conducting emancipatory and/or participatory action research fulfills Principle 5 in a very deep way, if the researcher, herself meets the recruitment criteria. Dating back to the 1920s, participation by those affected by the problem to solve the problem has been utilized by those in power (Aronovici, 1939; Lunch & Lunch, 2006; Singhal & Devi, 2003; Tomaselli, 2003).

Singhal and Devi (2003) write, "Whatever the mix of reasons, a new consensus has put participation at the center stage of social change initiatives of the 1990s" (p. 3) and Tenney can verify that this occurred within mental health policy in New York State. In the early 1990s, Tenney was the director of a youth-run organization that worked toward creating avenues of peer support, self help, and advocacy for young people involved with psychiatric systems, by young people in psychiatric systems (Tenney, 2000). This eventually became a statewide effort, which in 2008 is an International movement.

While Tenney was involved in the early days of the Youth Empowerment Movement, at 36 years old, she is simply a peer ally to the generations of young people that have followed and have since developed a statewide organization called, "YOUTH POWER!". Tenney was often asked to be involved in the development of research and programming by New York State from her perspectives of her experiences in the system. Stage 2! Youth Empowerment was a "pilot project" of the New York State Office of Mental Health concerning advocacy and empowerment programs, of which Tenney was a co-director and co-founder. This exposure to research and policy motivated her to go back to school, as she only received an Individualized Education Plan from a psychiatric outpatient program/high school in 1990 (she sees as a clear failure of the systems in which she was involved). Clearly, part of this article is written from an advocacy and participant perspective. This is also something practitioners of participatory action research ought to be cognizant of as a benefit of involving people in their research designs – many of the participants from the early 1990s went on to become scholars and it is evidence that liberation and emancipatory theories hold water.

As an activist researcher who uses participatory video methods (Lunch & Lunch, 2006), Tenney believes regardless of how uncomfortable it makes her feel, it is good practice for a social scientist to do with imagery and video what they would like participants and co-researchers to do and gets in front of the video camera, herself (Figure 2-3). It is important to note that Tenney met all of the recruitment criteria for this study that focused on advocates and activists who have psychiatric histories. She did have a consent agreement with herself.

Fig. 2-3: Video of 10e (Lauren Tenney) during a reading and interview session of "Can You Dig It?" (2006).

Tenney learned that some participants for varying reasons are terribly uncomfortable getting in front of the camera because of their perceptions of a poor body image. Other participants declined to be videotaped because they wanted their privacy to be preserved and still others held religious beliefs that forbade them from having their image captured on video. This created an opportunity for her to get creative about how these people could participate in the project. In "Can You Dig It?" individual participants could be involved in the research and decline to be involved in videotaping with no prejudice. What she did was offer to put the video camera in these individual's hands, asking them to take footage of material that they thought ought to be included in the final product. Participants who chose to take video footage as opposed to being videotaped personally, created imagery included video of someone signing one of the petitions to stop the use of shock treatment on children (Fig. 2-4), video of the encampment where individual petitions were hung (Fig. 2-5), and video of the protest signs that they made, sometimes with chalk drawings at the steps of the Capitol building (Fig. 2-6).

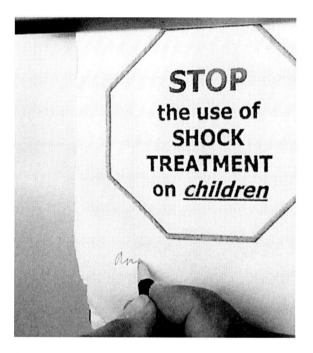

Fig. 2-4: Video of someone signing a petition to stop the use of Electroshock Treatment (ECT) on children in New York State. More than 1,100 petitions were gathered and presented to the New York State Office of Mental Health, to no avail, during the recruitment period of "Can You Dig It?"

The use of video and imagery enhances the need for *Respect for Persons*. Throughout history, we have seen time and again what (dis)respect for persons means and what terrible consequences it has on individual lives (Public Health Service Syphilis Study, 1932; Milgram Experiment, 1963; 1974). What does your list of possible scenarios for (dis)respect for persons entail? How will you eliminate scenarios that might create (dis)respect for persons while using video in your research?

Additional safeguards must be implemented when you are working with people who are considered part of a protected population or people who are considered vulnerable. It is very important to understand how power dynamics, further discussed in the principle of *Justice* below, influence a person's decision to be and remain involved in research.

Fig. 2-5: Video of the Encampment on the East Lawn of New York State's Capitol Building during a 9-day protest and fast calling attention to and attempting to stop the use of Electroshock Treatment (ECT) on children and other atrocities.

Finally, concerning *Respect for Persons*, Institutional Review Boards are concerned with the **incentives for participation**. Social exchange is important and shows that you respect the time and insight of those participating. However, and particularly if the incentives are enticing (i.e. hope of curing a terminal disease, a great monetary reward, or the opportunity to be in a video), participants might engage in research whereas otherwise they would not. While it is important to offer a social exchange to participants involved in research it is also important that the incentive is not so great that a person cannot refuse participation. There are many aspects to the call for *Respect for Persons* in the Belmont Report (1979) and it is essential in your research design that they are all accounted for and worked out. This is especially true when using video, which to a large degree alters the requirements of privacy and confidentiality (Beckman, 2008; Turan & Chapin, 2008) and eliminates the possibility of anonymity. At the heart of the principle of *respect for persons* one has to set up safe guards to prevent people from being harmed by video research because of its permanence and lack of anonymity.

Fig. 2-6: Chalk drawing at the foot of the New York State Capitol Building made by one of the participants of "Can You Dig It?" (2006) that reads, "Psychiatry is a fascist tool".

When one demonstrates respect for persons, one privileges the voices of the people they are working with. For some social scientists, who are receiving funding from state or other institutions to conduct the research, it is of the utmost importance that the funding does not get in the way of the findings. This means that even if the findings cause an uncomfortable situation for the funder, the findings *must* be released (Fig. 2-6). It is important to note that, "Can You Dig It?" was unfunded field research.

Beneficence

Beneficence is simply 'to do good' and 'to do no harm'. This is such a simple principle and yet such a hard practice. As social science researchers we want to understand the intricate underpinnings of human nature. We ask questions such as why people act and experience life the way they do; How to improve society; How to further humankind; How to eliminate or mitigate pain and suffering? We publish the answers to these questions so that others might learn from our participants. The social scientist must always put her or himself in the position s/he is asking another human being to be involved to get a true sense of what s/he is asking the participant to do. This is essential to meeting the principle of *Beneficence*.

In Tenney's many attempts at gaining IRB approval, she found herself repeating this statement over and again. "All I am doing is asking people who are advocates and activists with psychiatric histories to read through *The Opal* which are journals from 150 years ago that were written by people institutionalized at the Utica State Lunatic Asylum and tell me what they think of them, and what if anything ought to be done with them". She has spent years with some success attempting to gain approval to do research with video and whom some consider vulnerable (i.e. people with psychiatric histories). She routinely found herself saying, "I am not cutting anyone open nor am I asking them to ingest chemicals I do not know the effects of - and yet those types of studies are approved regularly". What Tenney has learned is that the concern of the IRB is that asking a person to reflect on troubling aspects of their lives which was seen by the IRB as something that can re-trigger the experience for a person, and perhaps damage their sense of wholeness. However, this sentiment flies in the face of emancipatory and participatory action research and is evidence of the deep stigma that society holds toward those with psychiatric histories.

The truth Tenney came to is that you never know how information is going to affect a person. What she learned through the IRB-approved study, "Can You Dig It?" is plentiful and not limited to the experience some participants had concerning uncensored thoughts they immediately regretted having had video recorded. When this issue came up, taping was immediately stopped and the information that the participants deemed unacceptable to have a record of was immediately deleted. This is a huge benefit of digital video recorders, which can be replicated in standard video cameras by rewinding the tape to the section the participant wishes to have removed and begin recording again, taping over the original material.

Issues concerning body image and identity that caused participants to feel mixed emotions also routinely came up. In one instance, a participant who had never seen herself on video asked for the entire tape to be deleted without even wanting to review past the first few seconds of the segment because of the way she perceived herself to look. Another participant was glad to get a copy of the DVD of her interview because she felt she never looked as good as she did in one of the segments. Yet a third participant asked for certain segments of his interview to be deleted because he felt that between the way he looked and what he was saying, he would further a certain stereotype and it was not what he intended.

While it is a protection for people to review and edit the video footage of themselves, it also is a valuable part of analysis. When you review the footage with participants you are able to get the perspective of the person you are working with on their answers. This review and release process allows for a discursive engagement of the researcher and participant as the investigated investigates the investigation with the investigator. In other words, as a social scientist, Tenney found it extremely valuable to have participants further explain the intention of their statements as they reviewed the recorded material together. It both clarified participant's intent and ensured that what she was hearing was what they were saying. This review process adds to the validity of studies that utilize video as a research tool.

How can one envision how another person will incorporate an invasive or intimate question into their frame of reference? How is a person with all of her or his specific cultural traditions, values, and beliefs going to respond to revelations they may express in a videotaped interview? Interviews, one of the social sciences' most acceptable methods of gathering data, are conducted with the belief that individual experiences are valued and ought to be explored. We must always take into account that individual experiences are as numerous as there are individuals and determine as many possibilities of risk and benefit as one can imagine.

We encourage social scientists to explore all possible positive and negative outcomes on the lives of people they are interacting with when determining the **risks and benefits analysis** of their research design. Tenney, having had personal experiences as a research subject herself states, "I have a keen understanding of what it means to be investigated". Researchers ought to realize that while your interview may last an hour, a day, or could happen at periods of time over years with participants, the conversations you have last with them, forever. Whether their experiences are good or bad, when drawing on personal experiences in a series of questions that when combined help lead to the answer of a social problem, often the very person comes to that answer as well and that can be a life transforming event. Being aware and sensitive about this will decrease the risk of harm.

Your **experimental design** is reviewed by the Institutional Review

Board to ensure *beneficence*. IRBs are charged with ensuring that good science is being done. MacCubbin explains that under the Federal interpretation of the regulation 45 CFR 46 it is assumed that you have to do good science to do no harm and that is why the IRB evaluates your design. When you discuss the use of video as a tool in your research design, it is important that you spell out exactly what your intentions are. This is particularly significant if you think that what you are doing is common knowledge because it may not be. Being as specific as you can in how, where, and why you are using video is as important as ensuring that your risk and benefit analysis is solid and reality-based. It is not uncommon for people to become emotional when you ask them personal questions about their lived experiences. It is important to understand the implications of your line of questioning and carry out the principle of beneficence in a very deep, meaningful, and concrete manner. It is equally important to demonstrate in your application to the IRB that you understand these aspects of research and will protect people involved in your design.

The education and training requirements for researchers to understand human subject protections have been evolving with the goal of providing more information to the researcher, IRB members, and project staff. In 1999 the Federal government increased the amount of training required for those involved with conducting funded research. Training in human subject protections can be obtained in several ways. For example, the CITI program is a subscription-based product. Each institution pays a flat fee for all their researchers to have access to the training without a charge being incurred by the individual researcher. It is cost effective for institutions to use because CITI program continually updates the modules and offerings with minimal increases in subscription rates. To accomplish the same thing on an individual institution basis would not be cost-effective at all. There are now over 900 institutions worldwide using CITI program as part of their training initiatives and we encourage modules on the use of video in social sciences to be created, to limit potential problems in obtaining IRB approval to use video as a research outlined in this chapter. To the best of our knowledge, training on the use of video research and human subject protections in social science research does not currently exist.

There is also a new web-based training course provided by the

National Institute of Health[14]. Issues of training are highly influenced by legislation, and government regulation and therefore, training is often political. MacCubbin explains the Office of Research Integrity instituted compulsory training in responsible conduct of research through an Executive Order from President William Jefferson Clinton at the end of 2000/beginning of 2001 which was rescinded by President George W. Bush in 2001. There was never any funding attached to the mandate. Currently, training continues to be an unfunded mandate in the United States. Training is currently mandated for those working on National Institute of Health (NIH) grants. The federal government recommends training for all researchers in human subject protections. Hence, most institutions require people to have human subject/participant protections training in their policies.

There is a long history to the requirements for training and education of researchers concerning human subject/participant protections. Most institutions require researchers to complete some type of training within their procedures. In the United States, it is essential that Principal Investigators and all people working on the study have taken a course on human subject research protections, such as the CITI program course. This relates back to the training strategy of the National Institute of Health to meet the policy requirements of the Responsible Conduct of Research (NIH, 2001; Thomas, 2001), discussed above.

Researchers ought to continuously **monitor and observe** their research process. Human subject research trainings make a point that this is important for the Principal Investigator to do, particularly if it is a large project with many investigators, study coordinators, and/or staff. All people who are working on a research project should be certified in human subject/participant protections. If you are the Principal Investigator, you want to make sure that the people working with and for you are carrying out the research protocol in an ethical way, because it is ultimately your responsibility to ensure that participants are protected. Sanctions researchers face for violating human subject protections can be career-halting and we describe them later in this chapter.

Also of concern to the IRB are the credentials and experiences of the Principal Investigator. This can be intimidating for someone just beginning in research. Tenney's experiences with the IRB left her feeling that if you

---

[14] http://oshr.od.nih.gov/cbt/

are doing something novel in your research, such as being a researcher who is 'out' as an activist psychiatric survivor using video in emancipatory and participatory action research, the IRB process can become even more intense. Tenney, with more than a decade of experience in her field, had to justify her past experiences with the psychiatric system and how that motivated her to engage in research on the experiences of others who have been involuntarily committed in psychiatric institutions as well as why she wanted to create an educational video about her findings. But even for a researcher using the most mundane methods, under deadlines of coursework, funding, and opportunities, awaiting approval to do research can be a frustrating and tumultuous process. Need we remind you of the mantra *Publish or Perish* that best illustrates this? A sound research design that answers anticipated questions about how you will promote and adhere to the principles of the Nuremberg Code (1947), Declaration of Helsinki (1964), and Belmont Report (1979) reduces potential re-submission processes that can postpone approval while clarifications of the research design are made.

Using video as a research tool, as we discussed, leaves a previously anonymous person with a firm identity in a format that may be saved in perpetuity. Ensuring that they are actively involved in an informed consent process, where they are informed of potential risks and benefits to them due to their participation in the study is essential. Imagine that you are a participant in a research study about personal experiences that creates an educational video about the findings. Many people will see this video if it is successful. Participants ought to understand this before giving their consent for involvement and be continually reminded of it throughout the process, again, highlighting the Office for Human Research Protections guidance.

It is important to make certain that the IRB understands that you recognize that researchers are required to immediately inform the IRB of any changes to their protocol throughout the research process as well as have participants re-consent, if necessary, to their involvement in the study once the amendment to your study has been approved. If at any point your research puts a person in jeopardy, you must immediately end the investigation. How could video put someone in danger, you might ask? Good. That is what you are supposed to explain to the IRB. Even if the risk is minimal, let the IRB understand how you are going to minimize any potential risk.

Finally, in general, IRB approval lasts for no more than one year. To continue multi-year research the **continued review** of the IRB-approved research takes place on an annual basis. These are the ways that the principle of *beneficence* is met. Once you know your research using video is respectful of the people and does good rather than harm, the third question you have to ask of your research design is whether or not it is just.

Justice

The third principle of the Belmont Report[15] (1979) encompasses *Justice* at both the Individual and Social realms of experience. Justice is carried out through "fair distribution from benefits and burdens of the research" (Belmont Report, 1979). **Subject Selection** and the **inclusion/exclusion** of potential research participants are also prime areas of interest for the principle of *Justice*. The Belmont Report eloquently and firmly explains the realities of institutional racism, gendered, sexist thinking, and cultural insensitivity in American society and how they impact selection and recruitment of potential research participants. Samples of Convenience are all too common in research and to all degrees possible, ought not be used. When participants are pregnant women or fetuses, people institutionalized in jails, psychiatric, health, or educational facilities, young, or at a socioeconomic disadvantage, they are likely to be in more jeopardy than those in the general population. This is why these groups are part of protected populations.

As argued by the Belmont Report, the overarching principle of *justice* is that if the outcome of the research will benefit the entire population, the entire population ought to bear the burden of risk to test the theory, procedure, or treatment under investigation. In other words, findings from which the rich will benefit ought not be researched using only poor or vulnerable research participants, because of "administrative convenience or because they are easy to manipulate as a result of their illness or socioeconomic condition[16]" (Belmont Report, 1979).

Allophilia[17] is the love of things and people different from you. Pittinsky

---

[15] http://ohsr.od.nih.gov/guidelines/belmont.html#gob3
[16] http://ohsr.od.nih.gov/guidelines/belmont.htm
[17] Daniel Fisher, MD, PhD. Executive Director of the National Empowerment Center Introduced Tenney to the concept of Allophilia (Pittinsky, 2005).

(2005) argues that tolerance is only the midpoint on a continuum between prejudice and allophilia. As a multicultural society, and a global world, we ought to strive for the love of attitudes, beliefs, traditions, values, and people who differ from us, not toleration. One of the trickiest aspects of cultural competence in practice is that if an experience is not within one's worldview or frame of reference to know, the chances of one even knowing the experience exists is slim. For example, "white skin" is an example of a privilege which many European Americans experience daily, (white privilege) but of which most appear unaware. Many refuse the idea of everyday prejudices those who do not look "white," "straight," "non-Muslim," or "normal" face, even though in 21st century America, racial, sexist, religious, and other prejudices are quite real. Because of this, issues of representation in video research are quite important (Beckman, 2008; Libman & Fields, 2008).

Stratifying research participants to ensure multicultural representation in one's research population is another part of the research design that comes under investigation by Institutional Review Boards. There has been great debate at what cost ensuring representation from groups that are in the minority and/or vulnerable populations ought to be included in research studies (Noah, 2003). Groups that are subject to coerced involvement due to power structures need additional safeguards and that is one of the factors the IRB works to ensure. If social exchange for the project meets unmet needs of participants, there may be a subtle or overt coercion to participate, whereas otherwise, participants would not provide informed consent. Granted, being involved in research that utilizes video is not the same as being involved in a clinical trial because participants are sick and cannot afford health insurance. However, for some participants, public and/or perpetual exposure can be a factor that researchers must weigh against the potential risks and benefits of having a public record of their experiences.

How one edits, analyzes and represents the material plays a role in this and many authors have offered strategies for ensuring the principle of *Justice* is carried out in the use of video (Banks, 2005; Beaty, 2008; Beckman, 2008; Libman & Fields, 2008; Lunch & Lunch, 2006; Odutala, 2003; Turan & Chapin, 2008). As discussed in detail above, Stanley Milgram's (1963, 1974) filming of participants in his study without their consent, for the world to see on the web today, also works against the principle of Justice. Of course, had Milgram envisioned the Internet, we would know him for different reasons and potential advances in technology should be thought out to all degrees possible. The Belmont Report offers the Public Health Service Syphilis Study/Tuskegee Experiment (1932) as an example of how researchers and organizations overseeing research commit social injustice (1979). The report urges that researchers must always guard against social injustice with the principle of *Justice*.

When using video as a research tool, the principle of *Justice* becomes even more important. This is because an indelible record of the research is captured often with the goal of publication and if not guarded in the proper way, video recording could expose participants in a way that simple audio recording or hand written notes could not. Also of concern is how onlookers will judge materials presented in video (Beckman, 2008; Libman & Fields, 2008; Odutala, 2003 Worth & Adair, 1972). It is impossible to curtail prejudices of the viewer. However, the IRB will want to know how you ensure that you protect participants from further stigmatization or discrimination. In a personal communication, Commons (2008) suggests that the researcher always use two video cameras, so that multiple perspectives of the situation are available as sometimes something as simple as the angle of the shot can influence perception (Worth & Adair, 1972).

Participatory Action Research is routinely grounded in the ideals of social justice. Bradley (2007) addresses the core of the concern for justice asking, how do we "amplify voice and self determination" (p. 346) if we are not allowed to give participants a blank slate to create the research? How can one have a truly participatory project if the IRB requires knowledge of what you are going to do prior to finding out from participants what they suggest ought to be done? How can one suggest questions, place, and space, if these are to be generated by participants? What are the benefits of research when generating academic knowledge is not the first goal of research? If the IRB is basing its decisions on a positivistic model, what role does eliminating social injustice and giving voice to those affected by social problems have (p. 345)? Referring to the fear of "bad stories" being told by participants explored by Fine et al. (2000, p. 115-117), Bradley explores the problems with assumptions and the unwarranted beliefs many researchers have encountered IRB's holding. A major concern about the IRB is its assumptions that participants will invariably tell "bad stories" and its subsequent concern for the impact these stories recorded on video can have on a participant's future life.

There may be a problem with an IRB (and not the researcher or the research design) if an IRB assumes that because people are "at-risk" or of "vulnerable" populations that they will tell stories that are driven by illegal or immoral activity. This is a reflection of the larger societal problems of discrimination and stigma associated with many of these groups, that because you are "at-risk" you must have done something wrong (Bradley, p. 343). Bradley also discusses the IRB's fear that the "portrait they [participants] paint" (p. 340) of their neighborhood might offend [rich] neighborhood dwellers.

Bradley's recount of the struggles to get IRB approval when using a Participatory Action Research model with video is worth reading and Tenney has shared many of his frustrations in the IRB process. He discusses the development of a multilayered consent process that included a media release and how the multiple consents seemed to "confuse" the IRB and that young people were not subjects or participants but "youth researchers/filmmakers" (p. 342).

MacCubbin suggests that when using participatory action research with video as a method for gathering data, it is a good practice for a researcher to consult with the 'neighborhood' or larger community/social group for their input into the design of the study. This is to ensure that the research has the cultural competency to work within that community or group. This is something Bradley (2007) acknowledges he wished he had done and wondered if it would have changed the IRB's perceptions of the young men he worked with (p. 348). Tenney (2006) uses this approach. She cannot say that it made the IRB process any easier, as the population she was working with, like Bradley's young men, have a social stigma attached to them. However, the process of including people affected by the problem being studied in the creation of the IRB proposal enhanced the design significantly. As one advisor to Tenney's project offered, two minds are always smarter than one. Tenney does ask researchers who are taking this approach of seeking advice from the community to prepare them for the long process of obtaining IRB approval, as sometimes their frustrations with the process can be as significant as the frustration the researcher experiences.

As much as social science research comes with its own set of potential psychological risks including undo stress and embarrassment that often go either unrecognized or diminished by researchers it is essential to understand as a researcher, that you really do not know what the person you are asking questions of has experienced. Asking people to draw on their experiences can cause them some level of psychological risk, especially if their experiences before meeting you have been negative.

For example, a research design utilizing video to understand young people's eating habits might include a question such as, "What did you have for breakfast this morning?" While this might not seem to be a question that could provoke embarrassment or humiliation, the person you were talking with however, might be part of the 10.9% of Americans who are food insecure - or part of its 4% subset who are extremely food insecure as published by the USDA (2006). Perhaps for breakfast the child got a beating. It is important for researchers to be cognizant of the prevalence of domestic violence when working with people.

Having this information documented on video presents several issues. While one could argue your simple question ultimately will help, as a researcher you may be a mandated reporter of child abuse and neglect, one also could argue that the researcher needs to fully weigh all of the potential risks they are asking other humans to engage in. One of the reasons video data are so powerful is that your audience can see what you see as the researcher. Video creates the conditions that allow an outsider to see joy, pain, and fear in people's faces, to see their expressions as they bear their souls. Video research changes everything and researchers need to be aware of potential pitfalls before they enter into it. Further, it is widely accepted that the validity of self-report is sometimes skewed due to embarrassment or other factors that prevent authentic answers. Video intensifies this as self-report captured on videotape is no longer a private and confidential communication between two people, but captured for varying audiences to see. Researchers can build the validity of their video data by ensuring the principles of the Belmont Report (1979) are being upheld with free informed choice and informed consent from the participants.

Researchers need to be prepared to deal with the consequences of their line of questioning. What members of IRBs want to see is that you, the researcher, have a firm hold on the potential risks and benefits of your design and how it may effect people you are investigating. Participatory Action Research that uses video complicates this and as Bradley (2007) points out, many IRBs are often unfamiliar with the method (p. 342).

As much as researchers need to be respectful of the IRB process, IRB members need to be respectful of alternative research methods – especially ones like participatory action research that utilizes video. This requires a *respect for persons* that includes the idea that participants are autonomous individuals that can in addition to create knowledge, change their realities and worlds. It is so important for IRB members not to fall prey to social stigmas. This includes that IRB members not assume that participants are not "smart" enough (Bradley, 2007) or because they have a psychiatric history, cannot make a decision to participate (Tenney, 2006) in creating and being participants in videos.

Some might say regardless of what research could come of it, inflicting undo physical or psychological harm flies in the face of human rights. Others might say there is sometimes a need that explicit conditions be met to have accurate data to analyze and work to come to an acceptable solution for potential research participants. Wendler (1996) offers a potential solution to the problem of needing deception in a study, as Milgram (1981) pointed out, by offering a "second order consent" where a potential research participant is informed that the study involves deception but is not told what that deception is, *before* the person enters into the informed consent process. We bring this in not to compare the use of video to the use of deception in research, but to illustrate that when one is doing research, to all degrees possible, one must mitigate and diminish potential risk while enhancing opportunities for its benefits.

There is good news. If in certain controlled and seemingly valid situations IRB approval can be obtained when using deception in research, then with valid reason and a well-thought out design, there is little reason that the use of video as a research tool should not be allowed to be used as a method. It is important to note that this method requires participants to be in an ongoing informed consent and release process (Chapin & Turan, 2005, 2008) and this is suggested by the Office for Human Research Protections (OHRP).

Privacy

"Private information is information which has been provided for specific purposes by an individual and which the individual can reasonably expect will not be made public (for example, a medical record)" (45 CFR 46, p, 3). Privacy is defined as an individual having control over the extent, timing, and circumstances of sharing oneself (physically, behaviorally, or intellectually) with others (45 CFR 46). Architecture-

Research-Construction, Inc. (ARC), a group of architects who conducted research on the settings in the psychiatric world such as mental institutions and group homes, rely on the concepts of Environmental Psychology. ARC (1985) emboldens the idea that "Privacy is essential to every person" (p. 57). This practice of protecting privacy reflects the principles of *respect for persons*, *beneficence*, and *justice* (Belmont Report, 1979). For the researcher using video to capture data, the issues of privacy and confidentiality in research are immense. As we indicated earlier in our discussion on *respect for persons*, an ethical requirement calls for researchers to protect the data they generate. This ordinarily means scrubbing all identifying information out of data generated by participants and respecting their right to maintain their choice to share their identities.

Video clearly changes this process particularly if the research calls for one to videotape a person's physical environment. ARC reminds us, "Since privacy means control over contact with others, the physical place must give us control over what we let others hear or see about ourselves" (p. 57). Downing (2008) found this in his study of people's homes when one participant took extra care to hide all of the different medications he had to take so visitors would not know of his medical condition. Additionally, privacy, according to ARC closely relates to territory or "control of a place" (p. 72). Suggestions for ensuring participants maintain control include, to all degrees possible, that participants ought to choose the place where videotaping occurs (Bradley, 2007; Beckman, 2008; Beaty, 2008; Tenney, 2006; Turan & Chapin, 2005).

Relying on Lewin's (1935) Dynamic Theory of Personality and Environmental Forces, a person has a "life-space" where one locomotes toward things they are attracted to and away from things which they are repulsed (pp. 67-113). Asking someone to explore the territories of their life intrudes on privacy. Particularly if the researcher is asking intimate questions or trying to understand inherently private spaces, such as the bedroom, bathroom, or home in general (Downing, 2008; Cooper-Marcus, 1995), it becomes even more pressing to respect the privacy of a person's space and place. Privacy and territory also closely relate to the concept of trust. Pointing to video surveillance of public places, ARC points out that "the environment reflects the fears of those who control it and use it" (p. 55) and reminds us of the importance of trust in any environment. Rivlin and Wolfe (1985) also indicate that surveillance is connected to trust in their exploration of institutions children are exposed to stating, "Teachers openly verbalized their need for surveillance and their lack of trust in children" (p. 207).

The bond of trust between researcher and participant must be strong. If the person you are obtaining data from is mistrustful of you, or what you are going to do with the information they are sharing with you, there are consequences for the authenticity of your research. This is true regardless of your use of video, but it becomes even more pronounced once the camera is turned on the participant. If there is mistrust, data are not going to be genuine because the person is not going to be completely forthright, and may not divulge information essential to your understanding, which they may see as more privileged content.

Though not discussed in detail in this chapter, there is a wealth of information about the use of video while obtaining informed consent. It is often discussed as a way of a researcher or provider of services, being able to prove that they did, in fact obtain informed consent prior to engaging with a person, as a way to limit liability and increase patient satisfaction and knowledge (Commons, 2006; Delaney, 2005; Enzenauer, 1986; Evans, et al., 2005; Evans, 2005; Rossi et al., 2005). This use of video, substantially different than using video to collect data, subconsciously provokes feelings of mistrust between researcher or provider and participant or patient and highlights issues of trust in research in a very deep way as liability is often a motivating factor for recording the consent process.

Confidentiality

Confidentiality according to Cohen (2006) includes methods used to ensure that information obtained by researchers about their participants is never improperly divulged. Cohen draws a distinction between private information and confidential information, defining identifiable information as information where the identity of the research subject is or may readily be ascertained by the investigator or associated with the information. It is important to understand that the breaking of confidentiality is the crux of how video augments conventional research. In 1972, Worth and Adair suggested that film (now video) was a "new research technique - another method for getting at the way people structure their own humanness" (p. 253). Humanness is something we ask researchers to tap into regularly - but how does one protect humanness? We believe maintaining confidentiality and privacy is part of the answer. However, respecting an individuals' choice to share their identity is another part of the answer, especially when participatory action research is being utilized.

It is of crucial importance to protect the rights of research participants when using video and allow them to determine what they are comfortable with sharing with the world beyond the researcher. Social scientists using video as a research method have offered strategies on how to ensure proper representation of people when the use of video research breaks confidentiality. These strategies include video messages (Libman & Fields, 2008; Lunch & Lunch, 2006), employing informant-made videos (Beaty, 2008; Worth & Adair, 1972), participatory video techniques (Bradley, 2007; Gui SLC, 2008; Lunch & Lunch, 2006; Snowden, 1967; Tenney, 2006) and narratives (Turan & Chapin, 2008).

It is important for the researcher to give the participant time to mull over the decision of what aspects of their video they would like to share, particularly if sensitive private information, such as medical conditions or past behaviors are memorialized on video. In the event of a successfully published and widely utilized research study, the public may come to know individual participants and participants ought to be aware of this and not have an expectation of privacy or confidentiality if you choose to not employ technologies that augment their likeness. Participants in video research must understand that their information, if they assent to this informed consent and release process, will not be held confidential and they will loose their anonymity and privacy.

Time absolutely plays a role in this process: a person's developmental stage, role in society, or current perspective, can make certain information that seems perfectly acceptable to release at one point in life extremely exposing years later. Let us not kid ourselves. Researchers love little tidbits of information that make a point. Very often these poignant moments when captured on film are later translated to a sound byte by the researcher to drive home a point. However, the captured phrase may be the last thing the participant wanted to see him or herself saying to the world. It is important, in the informed consent and release process to ask research participants to have this forward thinking when they release the use of data. This is to ensure that they are aware of long-term ramifications of having an indelible exposure of their humanness for all to see memorialized through the use of video research (Banks, 2005).

After addressing the risks of video research, participants also need to understand the benefits of their participation to the research process and the possibility to empower their lives and situations by participating. These benefits include the opportunity to have an effect on their community (Bradley, 2007); influence government policy and regulation (Libman & Fields, 2008; Tenney, 2006; Odutula, 2003; Okahashi, 2000) learning how to make videos (Beaty, 2008; Bradley, 2007; Gui SLC, 2008; Worth & Adair, 1972); and better understanding how people perceive the world they are engaged in (Mausner, 2008). Bradley (2007) points out that sometimes IRBs do not necessarily see these outcomes or processes as benefits and must begin to recognize them as such (p. 343).

Cohen (2006) reminds us that anonymity and confidentiality are not two different sides of the same coin - they are in fact, two separate things. Anonymous means that no one, anywhere or ever, including the researcher, can identify individual participants. Utilizing an anonymous survey is generally the only type of research that is truly anonymous. Interviews are not anonymous because the researcher knows who the person is. One maintains confidentiality in non-anonymous research by removing all identifying information, which is not limited to simply removing a person's name.

Using video that does not capture the faces of participants does not render it anonymous. MacCubbin offers a situation in the use of video that involved the response rate of giving medical attention in the birthing process. A female medical professional who had shaky hands was inadvertently able to be identified by her medical disorder, putting her at greater risk than others in the video for being sued for malpractice or discipline because she was identifiable as her medical condition broke her confidentiality.

A participant's participation in research may need to be kept confidential, as well as their private information (Cohen, 2006). Researchers need to understand this and illustrate to the IRB that they recognize this requirement by offering strategies for how they will communicate to participants the limitations of protections for their privacy, confidentiality, and anonymity through the informed consent process. Even if your goal is not to produce public material, you cannot guarantee complete privacy and confidentiality to potential participants. For example, short of using an anonymous survey, if your data are seized, people who otherwise would be unidentifiable become identifiable and this could potentially present unintended consequences for them. The informed consent process ought to detail this in a concrete way, to allow potential participants to ground their decisions about participation in true informed consent and informed choice, discussed below.

The Informed Consent Process

An eloquent analysis of what it means to obtain informed consent for mental health treatment can be found in Commons et al (2006) paper, "Informed Consent: Do you know it when you see it?" While this work discusses informed consent in treatment, we extend its principles to the concepts of informed consent in research. Commons and his colleagues first explain that in its very nature informed consent is a process that entails a "hierarchical complexity", which relies on what they term adult developmental theory, which reflects Vygotsky's activity based theories of learning. This is consistent with the Office for Human Research Protections call that "informed consent is a process, not just a form" (http://www.hhs.gov/ohrp/humansubjects/guidance/ictips.htm).

Informed consent is an activity based learning process that requires assent or agreement of the participant to be involved in the study. This is where the idea of hierarchical complexity shines through. First, the model of hierarchical complexity insists that some of the tasks involved in the process must be more complicated than other tasks in the process. Second, the more complicated tasks give way to the less complicated tasks. Finally, hierarchical complexity requires that the series of tasks must be interdependent of each other, and take place in a specific order, requiring one event to be met before going on to the next event (p. 431).

Echoing the Office for Human Research Protections, Informed Consent is not an action or event, and certainly not a signed piece of paper (http://www.hhs.gov/ohrp/humansubjects/guidance/ictips.htm). Informed Consent is a multi-staged process that needs to be met at every point of the research to ensure that coercion is not involved in a person engaging in treatment or research. Informed Consent is continuous throughout the research process and in addition to informing the IRB if the study changes in any way, people participating in the research may need to re-consent as the study changes.

Commons et al. (2006) suggest that informed consent actually requires two activities, each with its own processes. The first process is concerned with the act of informing. "Informing" is the act of the researcher or provider giving the potential client or research participant information about the research or treatment protocol they are entering into so that the potential participant has enough information to make an educated decision about the risks and benefits of participation. The second process, "consenting" is the act of the research participant giving her or his assent or consent to be involved with the treatment or research protocol. However, Commons et al explain that each of these activities, informing and consenting, have their own steps that need to be met to ensure completion.

For Commons et al, the act of informing requires several aspects: First, the researcher must give the potential client or research participant all available information about the protocol and time to digest that information. Second, the researcher must detail all of the known potential risks and benefits of engaging in the protocol. Third, the researcher must determine whether the participant truly understands the information that the researcher has shared. Following the ideals of hierarchical complexity, once the person has been informed of what their participation in your study means, such as being in a video that will be shown to audiences as an educational tool, the next process is the act of the researcher obtaining consent, which for Commons et al (2006) requires four tasks:

> Obtaining 'consent' includes four abstract propositions: offering the patient choice of the treatment plan; giving the patient time to decide on a treatment plan; determining that the patient is competent; and obtaining the patients assent to the execution of the chosen treatment plan. (p. 431)

The use of video in social science research requires the researcher to complicate the hierarchical complexity because the addition of video requires another aspect of the research a participant must give assent to in order to be involved. So, relying on Commons and his colleagues (2006), the informed consent process for the use of video requires the researcher to first go through the three processes to inform a person of their research plans as detailed above and then gain assent from the potential participant through the four tasks of consent to enter the research protocol. Second, the researcher must inform the potential participant of the risks and benefits of the use of video through the three phases of 'inform' and obtain assent through the four phases of 'consent'.

For all of the difficulty researchers face in obtaining IRB approval to use video as a research tool, on informed consent forms, there is usually only a small reference to the use of video. For example, there may be a line stating, "you may choose to have your interview audio or video recorded or not recorded at all" with only a line simply stating, "I give my permission to be video recorded" with the options of circling "yes" or "no" to prove the person was engaged and assented to give consent. Just because only a small piece of the actual consent form addresses the use of video in research does not imply that it is a small piece of the ethical considerations of research. The social scientist ought to always realize the weight of having segments of one's life, with limited privacy and broken anonymity and confidentiality, analyzed and edited for public consumption.

It is because we see the inherent value of the use of video in social science research that we are so demanding of the researcher ensuring that participants are protected from undo harm. Models of a dual consent and release process are essential for the social science researcher to follow (Beckman, 2008; Bradley, 2007; Turan & Chapin, 2005, 2008).

It is in this informed consent and release process that trust between researcher and potential participant is established. In the Turan and Chapin model, first, there is a form entailing both an agreement between the researcher and participant stating that the researcher will not utilize the footage without the prior review of the footage by the participant. Both the researcher and participant sign this agreement. This gives the participant more power to determine what happens with the footage than the researcher has. After the participant has reviewed the footage, they are asked to review a release form and either agree or decline to release the footage. Release forms typically detail how the video will be used, who will see it, issues of ownership, the amount of time that the video will be kept, and if, when and how the videotape will be destroyed (Lunch & Lunch, 2006). If participants agree with the material set forth in the release form, they are asked to sign it and "release" the footage for use.

Some researchers go one step further (Turan & Chapin, 2005) by asking participants to review the final product and again release or refuse to release the use of their identifiable information once the editing process has been completed. This is to ensure that micro-clips of a person's experiences, edited into many other micro-clips of experience have fidelity to the person's intention and lived experience. The length of time a researcher may use video has always had some level of question, attempts at resolving this include disclaimers indicating of the destruction of the film after its use or having it explicitly stated in the consent form that the footage may be used again at some future point.

The Notes Toward Division 7 Input to the APA's Project Work Group (Berenbaum, Cauffman, & Newcombe, 2003) include the idea that IRBs allow researchers to store videotapes indeterminately for possible future research as the information is both extremely valuable and literally costly. They suggest the storage of videotapes be allowed as long as it specified on the informed consent form and detailed in the process of informing and gaining assent from potential research participants that the videotape will not be destroyed and may at a future date be utilized for other research (p. 3). However, MacCubbin explains that usually there is a re-consent process for use of video footage in another (or "further") research project. Blanket consent to use the data forever in any type of research is rarely approved unless it is truly anonymous and as we have discussed, video eliminates anonymity.

Participatory Action Research brings a whole new aspect to the use of video including the ideas of participant created and directed video in places and spaces of their choosing. As with any type of collective, collaborative research effort anonymity is impossible. With a permanent memory imprinted on video, the idea of anonymity in research must be revisited. Matt Bradley (2007) calls into question how IRBs are "relegating them [participants] to the status of anonymous objects of study," (p. 346) and how this is diametrically opposed to Participatory Action Research, which positions participants with the same amount of power as researchers.

The Congress of Qualitative Inquiry (2006) begins their discussion draft position paper on Institutional Review Boards and Qualitative Research with this quote:

> Qualitative research is a situated activity that locates the observer in the world. It consists of a set of interpretive, material practices that make the world visible…Qualitative researchers study things in their natural settings, attempting to make sense of, or to interpret, phenomena in terms of the meanings people bring to them. (Denzin & Lincoln, 2003, p. 4-5 as cited by Congress of Qualitative Inquiry, 2006, p. 1).

Remembering Bradley's (2007) inquiry, how do we "amplify voice and self determination" (p. 345) if we are not allowed to give participants a blank slate to create the research? How can you have a truly participatory project using video if the IRB requires knowledge of what the researcher intends to do? How can a researcher suggest questions and places, and spaces research is to take place in, if these are to be generated by participants? Bradley asks, what are the benefits of research? When generating academic knowledge is not the first goal of research and the IRB is basing its decisions on a positivistic model - what role does eliminating social injustice and giving voice to those affected by social problems have? Unfortunately, the progress of social science and the refinement and greater acceptance of qualitative methods creates unforeseen problems for Institutional Review Boards – and researchers attempting to gain IRB approval.

The Problem Statement of the Congress of Qualitative Inquiry includes, "Our primary concern is the lack of fit between self- delineated standards of qualitative research and IRB procedures grounded in a narrow model of science" (Berenbaum, Cauffman, & Newcombe, 2003). These discussion notes also suggest that there is an ongoing general concern for behavioral researchers attempting to gain IRB approval stating, "The need of the separation of behavioral and medical research in the IRB review process" (p. 3). One of the most important points Bradley makes is the need to have separate IRB applications for the Social Sciences and Biomedical studies. Tenney echoes these calls.

The institutionalization of the IRB is one of the most important things that happened to protect the welfare of potential research participants. It deserves full respect, as people have lost their lives and experienced psychological harm due to unethical research. However, asking someone to read a book and tell you what they think about it or make a video about the environment in which they live is quite different than cutting open someone's brain and taking a look inside. For reasons we have outlined throughout this chapter, we ask researchers to understand the sordid history that led us to this point and have patience with the IRB. We ask IRB members to ensure that social stigmas are not guiding their decision making processes. We want IRB members to expand their knowledge base about cutting edge methods in the social sciences, such as the use of video, to eliminate some of these problems that cause IRB applications to need multiple refinements or be rejected.

We must honor the spirit of human participant protections. As video becomes more commonplace in social science research tough questions concerning the long-term ramifications of enduring imagery need to be taken into consideration. For some time, the Office for Human Research Protections (2003) slogan was, "Doing it Right . . . Together!" and perhaps that is how we ought to be thinking about the relationship between the social scientist, Institutional Review Board and Research Participant when video is being used as a research tool.

Sanctions

In "Big Brother or Allies: In Defense of IRBs and RCRs. Jim Thomas (2001), a sociologist, explores the relevance of training on ethics for social science researchers. Particularly for many of us who are just beginning to do research, it is important to understand where some of the hesitation to approach Institutional Review Boards comes from. Remember that human subject research protections were instituted to some degree with the Nuremberg Code (1947), the Declaration of Helsinki (1964) and were further refined by the Belmont Report (1979). However, it was not until the turn of the 21st century that the Office of Research Integrity, which is part of the Department of Health and Human Services, created a policy on the Responsible Conduct of Research (Thomas, 2001; NIH, 2001), which remains strongly recommended but unfunded.

While the responsible conduct of research spans issues such as learning about and avoiding plagiarism, verification, and conflicts of interest, one often employed strategy to achieve the responsible conduct of research is to have researchers trained in ethics and human subject research protections. Most institutions require training in research and ethics to help achieve the responsible conduct of research. If uncertified in human subject research protections, a researcher may be in noncompliance with his or her institution's policies. This may create serious consequences for the researcher and her/his affiliated institution.

Possible consequences of noncompliance with ethical regulations are plentiful. These include the potential suspension of an individual research project, potential investigations into the IRB practices of the entire institution, potential suspension of all research of the researcher in question or potential suspension of all research occurring in the entire institution that gave assurance[18] for the researcher through IRB approval, if an investigation is being conducted. The consequences may be severe and career-halting. It is best for the purpose of good research and a fruitful, respectable career in the social sciences to avert the need for experiencing these or other sanctions by always conducting ethical research. There is not one set of rules for what ethical research means because IRB members

---

[18] http://www.hhs.gov/ohrp/FWAfaq.html#q2

look at each protocol on an individual basis. If you think there might be an ethical issue in your research, it is best to approach your IRB Administrator or Chair for clarification to avert unwanted potential future problems.

The American system of Institutional Review Boards is somewhat of a complicated system. In brief, each University or Research Institution is certified, or has assurances[19], that they act in compliance with the principles of the Nuremberg Code (1947), Declaration of Helsinki (1964), and Belmont Report (1979). For IRBs this includes at least three things. First, IRBs must assure that individual research protocols warrant approval. Second, IRBs must assure that all researchers are engaged in an informed consent process with participants in their research. Third, IRBs must assure that researchers are actually doing *exactly* what is outlined in the consent form and design. This includes informing the IRB of any changes, reasons for these changes, and if found necessary by the IRB, complying with the IRB requirements for revisal and amendments to the informed consent, including having participants re-consent to their involvement in the research.

Noncompliance with IRB regulations may have serious consequences. If it becomes known that a researcher is in noncompliance with IRB requirements and immediate corrections are not made to remedy the situation, the institution could lose its assurances. "Serious and continuing noncompliance," which is reportable, could trigger a "for cause" site visit (see Office for Human Research Protections). If, during a site visit, the Office for Human Research Protections finds other serious problems in the administration of an institution's IRB, then the following consequences could very likely occur. First, funding for the project could be immediately frozen and/or terminated. Second, the IRB could have no choice but to stop your study and seize your data. Third, for the researcher, suspension from school or employment is possible. Fourth, the researcher's name and information about their unethical behavior may be posted in a "Determination Letter" on the Federal Government's Office for Human Research Protections website[20]. Fifth, if you are the subject of a Determination Letter, you could be essentially blacklisted in the research community as someone who is unethical and unable to do research.

---

[19] http://www.hhs.gov/ohrp/FWAfaq.html#q2
[20] http://www.hhs.gov/ohrp/compliance/letters/index.html

In the following section, we address ways that social scientists can strengthen human subject and participant protections in practice as well as techniques for approaching IRBs and other ethics committees to use video as a research tool.

Gold Standard Practices for Approaching Institutional Review Boards and other Ethics Committees when Using Video in Social Science Research

We write this section to further demystify the IRB process when using video as a research tool. It is important to note that for some countries, such as Australia, the use of video in research is seen as commonplace, and Australia's (2007) National Statement on Ethical Conduct in Human Research simply acknowledges that "Interviews are usually recorded by audio- or video-tape or notes" (p. 26). Tenney calls for a goal for replication of this affirmation by the United States in this article.

Note that the IRB takes each research application individually and evaluates the design on its merit and how the program director intends to handle and mitigate risks to participants. We encourage you to be aware of the composition of IRB members as this will help determine what their areas of expertise are. If the committee is made up of people who are unfamiliar with innovative techniques that go beyond positivistic sciences, such as using video, it is important that you are even more detailed in your descriptions of your intended plans. Marcus Banks (1995) discuses issues of documentation, representation, and collaboration in the use of visual methods, writing:

> Images are no more 'transparent' than written accounts and while film, video and photography do stand in an indexical relationship to that which they represent they are still representations of reality, not a direct encoding of it. As representations they are therefore subject to the influences of their social, cultural and historical contexts of production and consumption[21].

The editing process and analysis of video data are essential parts of the concern for human participant protections. Consider social, cultural, and historical contexts throughout this process. As researchers we must be acutely aware of the power we have to create and augment reality as we add generalizable knowledge to the literature in our respective fields, often addressing issues of social (in)justices. To address issues of power, we

---

[21] http://sru.soc.surrey.ac.uk/SRU11/SRU11.html

wish for researchers, IRB members, and participants to triangulate one of the principles of the Belmont Report, *Respect for Persons*, throughout the entire research process. We stress that this includes the process of approaching your Institutional Review Board for approval to conduct human participant research when using video.

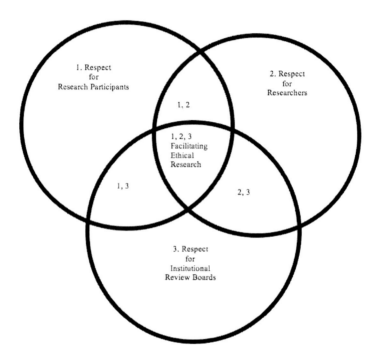

Fig. 2-7: Triangulate the Belmont Report (1979) Principle of *Respect for Persons* to facilitate ethical research: Respect for Participant, Researcher, and IRB.

We use the Venn diagram above (Figure 2-7) to illustrate that when the principle of *respect for persons* is triangulated amongst the three groups, we set conditions to facilitate ethical research. In the overlapping circles of the Venn diagram, (1,2, 1,3, 2,3) we find respectful interactions between the Participant and the Researcher, the Participant and the IRB, and the Researcher and the IRB. It is in the space where all three entities come in contact with each other (1, 2, 3) that is the space all social scientists, IRB members and participants ought to aspire to be engaged in as it is the space where people are working together, echoing Office for Human Research Protections' (2003) slogan of "Doing it Right . . . Together!". We believe that if IRB members, researchers, and participants are all actively engaged in the principle of respect for persons that this will facilitate ethical research.

We convey to you that IRBs by their nature are designed to be judgmental bodies. The people on those bodies, however, critical they are in inspecting your research design ought to be respectful. In other words, there are ways to evaluate proposals while giving respect to the researcher and potential participants, particularly if they are doing something novel, and IRBs ought to do all that they can to ensure that this is happening.

IRB members ought to hold the same respect for persons for researchers that it holds for participants. This means IRB members must believe that researchers do not intentionally set out to harm people and communications ought to be respectful. It also means that IRB members have to respect the rights of the person who wants to break her or his privacy and confidentiality to further the creation of generalizable knowledge and put a human face on the situation. IRB members need to do all they can to become familiar with cutting-edge techniques such as the use of video as a research tool and participatory action and emancipatory research.

When IRB members continually expand their knowledge about various qualitative methods and approaches, such as video, and are open minded about advances in participatory action and emancipatory research, they are both showing respect to the researchers they work with as well as potential participants, furthering the protection of human participants in research.

The researcher ought to hold the same respect for the IRB that it holds for participants. This respect to the IRB can be shown simply by creating the most solid research design you can. For the researcher who may be more creative than technical, more interested in action than paperwork, the IRB process can be un-nerving. If the IRB Administrator or Chair informs you that your application has been rejected with revisions, it is essential that your dealings with the IRB remain respectful. By the time you are waiting to learn of the status of your application, you should already have developed a relationship with this person. As Tenney has heard many times, "The IRB Administrator is just the messenger", You know the old adage, 'Don't shoot the messenger,' yes? However, we believe that the person in this role is more than the messenger. The IRB Administrator or Chair can truly assist you in understanding what IRB members' concerns about your design are so that you may better address them in your revisions. Particularly for those frustrated by the process, look at the process of gaining IRB approval to use video in research as a necessary safeguard to ensure that *no* researcher can put *any* person in potential harms way without their full informed consent and informed choice.

Respect for participants, especially when utilizing video, means ensuring that he or she fully understands the recording and editing process and the possibilities of showing footage to many audiences and agrees to be involved with it. Engaging in a consent and release process mitigates this as it shows respect for the person to be able to make decisions about the use of his or her likeness, with the ability to stop participation at any time, for any reason, without prejudice – even if it means you lose the exact types of data you have been hoping for.

Participants must also have a *healthy* respect for the researcher and as Milgram's Experiment (1963; 1974) showed, sometimes a participant can feel undue, unhealthy pressure to comply with requests of a researcher. We must all work to safeguard against this happening. Additionally, research participants ought to have a clear understanding that the goal of the IRB and the researcher is to protect the participant from undue risk and harm. The participant ought to always feel free to contact the IRB or researcher with questions about their participation.

This respect, as addressed above, is deeply grounded in trust and open communication. When there is a free flow of information, the process is less likely to stall from confusion. We believe that no researcher wants to potentially put another individual in harms way without their informed consent and informed choice – and then, will do everything possible to minimize potential risk.

Perhaps, if there was ever a valid reason for professional distance, it is in the space of a researcher who is in the IRB approval process. As a researcher using video, one ought not hold back explanations of the ways in which the researcher intends to protect people participating in their research protocol, or in the means of obtaining a participant's informed consent.

There is an advantage for the researcher to communicate with the IRB early. This means submitting the IRB application long before you need approval, as video might extend the review process, particularly if you are intending to work with protected populations or carry out participatory action or emancipatory research. It is important to develop a relationship with the IRB Administrator or Chair. MacCubbin suggests that there seems to be a trend in high-powered researchers meeting with the IRB before they choose to join a University, to ensure that they will be able to do their research. The relationship a researcher has with an IRB is critical. From the point of original contact through the continued review process, the IRB Administrator or Chair can play a crucial role in furthering the success of your ability to begin and continue research. Cultivating these relationships can take time but it is time well spent. We believe you will find that not only can IRB Administrators or Chairs give you deep insights into the needs of the IRB members before submitting your application, which can greatly reduce the need for clarification during the initial review of your proposal, but also they are often happy to help.

Process participants can become enthralled quite easily with the assigned roles of Researcher, Participant, Administrator, and IRB Member. Cross (1971) discusses how sometimes we label people because it helps us better define ourselves. Zimbardo's (2007) Stanford Prison Experiment from 1971, which has had its own set of ethical questions, ought be a staunch reminder of how quickly we fall into roles and the power that they assume or lack – and how dangerous that can be. The IRB process can be incredibly intimidating for a new researcher, particularly when using a method, such as video, that may not yet be commonplace in your institution. It is important to remember that like you, those on the IRB are people and therefore, approachable. Seeking out guidance for how to approach the IRB about your design from the IRB Administrator or Chair early in the process will only help guide you to securing IRB approval in the future.

Include a literature review of the use of video in your research protocol, so IRB members can see how well thought out your design is and have evidence of its benefits in research. To mitigate the risk of hearing "rejection with revisions" from your IRB Administrator or Chair, add plenty of examples of other research that has used methods you would like to employ to your literature review in your IRB application. This research helps IRB members from various disciplines that might be grounded in quantitative monomethodic or positivistic methods to understand your qualitative approach and why it is essential that you gather data using video to understand the problem at hand (Congress of Qualitative Inquiry, 2006).

It is important for you to understand that IRB members may not be accustomed to dealing with all of the various ways researchers are using video. These are not limited to taking video of participants (Beckman, 2008; Turan & Chapin, 2005, 2008) or their homes (Downing, 2008); using video messages (Libman & Fields, 2008; Lunch & Lunch, 2006; Odutola, 2003; Okahashi, 2000); or giving video cameras to participants to have them take video of their chosen footage (Beaty, 2008; Bradley, 2007; Gui SLC, 2008; Mausner; 2008; Worth & Adair, 1972).

The goal for those involved in the creation and oversight of research is to do "good science." At the heart of that venture is to both protect the people who are participants in our studies from undue physical and psychological harm and to ensure that people who are entering situations that have potential risk with free informed choice and informed consent. Therefore, we must take every avenue available to us to show that we are minimizing risk; prepared to handle potentially risky situations; and explain how we will debrief participants after the study. This strategy of a solid research design and proposal will enhance IRB members understanding of our work and ability to facilitate ethical research in the field. IRB members and researchers are all overworked. It is essential that all parties are "Doing it Right . . . Together" (OHRP, 2003) because when we are not we put the people we come in contact with at risk and it just does not work.

Concerning Other Issues of Informed Consent

Issues of consent for people who are not the research participant are also of concern for the Institutional Review Board. If someone mentions another person in their answers to a research question, this brings up issues of consent because a third party could potentially be at risk. To clarify this concern of the IRB acknowledge this very real possibility in your informed consent form to the potential participant. Prepare a small script to offer IRB members what you would say to a person who is a potential participant before starting research. An example is simply to ask participants not to disclose to whom they refer. That is asking participants to keep people they are referring to anonymous and not name any one. Explain to the potential participant the same way s/he is giving consent to be involved in research, that you ethically, could not include something about an identifiable person without their consent. Be proactive. The IRB seeks research protections of subjects – and secondary subjects or third party subjects. To limit the need for IRB proposal revision make sure that

IRB members know that you will not ever identify secondary subjects or third party subjects in your research proposal.

To further limit the need for proposal revisions, in addition to the informed consent form which spells out how data will be recorded, your informed consent process ought to include a clear informed consenting strategy concerning the editing of the videotape. This is especially important when anonymity will not be granted to participants, and privacy, and confidentiality might be compromised. Concerns that IRB members have about undue risk to research participants can be averted by using the informed consent and release process outlined above (Banks, 2005; Bradley, 2007; Turan & Chapin, 2008).

Address the following questions for IRB members in your proposal: Will the participant see the video before it is accepted as data for the research? Will the participant be able to edit the video before it is accepted as data? Will you review the material with the participant immediately after the interview? Will you send a final DVD of the material to the participant to have them "release" its use? Will you send a DVD of the final product to the participant to have them "release" the use of their likeness in your work? These types of questions help the IRB determine the level of risk in the study.

MacCubbin offers a checklist to researchers of issues to address concerning video that need to be detailed for the IRB and they include:

Research participants should be informed of the intent to video.

Research participants should be informed of the reasons for the use of video.

Research participants should be informed of whether participation depends on being videotaped.

Research participants should understand the circumstances of video.

How will the videotaping be done?

Will the participant be identifiable in any way? (i.e. face, unique features, voice, name, etc.)

Who will do the videotaping?

Who else will be in the video?

Research participants should understand the possible consequences of video.

What are the circumstances of the destruction of the videotape?

How long will the videotape be kept?

What will be done with the videotape before its destruction?

Who will have access to the videotape?

When using new, innovative techniques for gathering data such as video, you might want to include as an appendix to your application a DVD of what you are suggesting to do, using actors. For new and innovative techniques, it is necessary to spell out exactly what the technique is. If there are devices you are using such as head-cameras (Mausner, 2008), then bring the device in to the IRB so that IRB members can see how it works and test it out for themselves to gain a better understanding of what you are doing. If you are using a voice disguise system (Gui SLC, 2008), using actors, create a DVD to show IRB members the method so they have a sense of what it looks like and what is happening, to help them determine the level of risk.

While you cannot pilot your technique without IRB approval, you can write a script and hire actors to play out the scenario to help the IRB understand your method. Remember that IRB members come from many different fields. Despite the advances in using film and video over the last 40 years as discussed above, if using video as a method to collect data is not common within the disciplines IRB members are involved, it is going to present questions. Successfully anticipating IRB members concerns and desires to facilitate ethical research can be accomplished by meeting the principles of the Nuremberg Code (1947), Declaration of Helsinki (1964), and the Belmont Report (1979)

Another strategy social scientists can consider using is obtaining background information on your techniques. Discuss the methods with experts in the field and request testimony from them to be included in your

IRB application. This approach not only gives validity to your proposed study, but in these conversations with experts, our own methods can become refined. We learn new techniques to guard against undue risk to participants, and we become aware of issues we may not ever have even imagined come into light, as the tales of experts' experiences in the field are often quite enlightening. Further, we have learned that while some are intimidated to contact high-powered researchers, many are eager to discuss their approaches with newcomers to both the method and the field, so we encourage you to reach out to those who can give us further insight into the process.

Just because you are doing something that might be novel or explicit does not immediately negate your ability to do it, if you can soundly create your argument to go forth with your design. Simon Rosser at Minnesota University has investigated ways of increasing prevention of HIV/STI in Gay men using websites to survey people. Rosser used sexually explicit visuals to keep people interested in the survey and successfully argued that it is what is typical within the targeted population (2008). As with the development of a "second order consent" (Wendler, 1996) in the use of deception in studies discussed earlier, when a researcher makes a sound argument, and makes every effort to protect participants, IRB members are more likely to support the work, even if at first it seems to be a project for which they would never take responsibility.

Finally, use the resources available to you through the government and non-profit organizations that have oversight over human subject protections. The Office for Human Research Protections (2004) offers eleven "Human Subject Regulation Decision Making Charts" to determine whether the researcher's proposal actually meets the definition of research, whether an expedited review will be possible, and addresses concerns around informed consent[22]. These charts can seem overwhelming at first but they are actually quite thorough. We recommend that you print them out to review them as many of the decisions lead you between different charts in the set. There is a wealth of information available to researchers on this website to guide people through the creation of the IRB application, development of consent forms, and information about protecting people in research studies.

The City University of New York also has an electronic "research

---

[22] http://www.hhs.gov/ohrp/humansubjects/guidance/decisioncharts.htm#c1

determination" form[23] which helps project directors make decisions about whether your research actually meets the regulatory definition of human subjects research.

The Association for the Accreditation of Human Research Protections Programs (AAHRPP) also is a valuable resource to social scientists that details the process of assurances and how institutions become accredited to approve research and explains research standards. The AAHRPP also has a section on their website[24] specifically to give information to research participants and includes one participant's perspectives of being involved in research.

According to the National Patient Safety Agency in England, the National Research Ethics Service was founded in 2007 combining the previous Central Office for Research Ethics Committees and Research Ethics Committees. Their website[25] offers guidance to researchers and a range of publications on ethical research.

There is little standard information about IRBs and video from a policy or regulatory perspective. We hope that as more people get involved with utilizing video as a research tool more institutions and government regulatory agencies will follow Australia's (2007) lead and add videotaping in to the general procedures in which one documents research interviews.

Conclusion

A long history has spurred the need for human subject research protections. As we have seen, promoting ethical conduct in social science research is as complex and time-consuming as it is urgent and unyielding. The use of video to record data complicates an already complex process. Video complicates the research participant's protection process by removing the key factors of anonymity, privacy, and confidentiality research participants are ordinarily granted.

We ask researchers to view the Institutional Review Board approval process as an opportunity to have a disinterested third party review their

---

[23] http://www.cuny.edu
[24] http://www.aahrpp.org/www.aspx?PageID=24
[25] http://www.nres.npsa.nhs.uk/

proposed work. Through a solid preparation and review, the research design invariably becomes more defined and less random, furthering protections of research participants from unforeseen risk of harm and allowing them to make decisions about the level of risk they are willing to incur in the name of social science. The IRB is suppose to look at proposed research designs not from the perspective of an institution or with concern for grant money or coursework requirements - but from the perspective of what it is the social scientist is doing with the research participants.

Of the deepest concern to IRB members is: how are social scientists informing potential participants about the risks and benefits of their participation and minimizing those risks? What are the benefits of the method? How will the researcher increase opportunities for benefits of the research protocol? The goal of the IRB is to facilitate ethical research. We triangulate the principle of the Belmont Report's (1979) *respect for persons* to achieve this goal.

Ethical research that produces controversial findings cannot be eliminated for its ethics and its findings will stand. Better tools for researchers such as video cameras that are often still a novel idea to many IRB members need to be introduced with thought in meaningful ways. Anticipate and answer potential questions that IRB members will have utilizing strategies outlined above to exhibit that you have thought out potential risks and developed methods to limit unnecessary risks to participants. Limit concerns IRB members have about your research design by ensuring that you use a multi-stage consent and release process along with your informed consent process (Bradley, 2007; Banks, 2005; Turan & Chapin, 2005, 2008). The works in this volume offer exemplars of how to obtain IRB approval and carry out cutting-edge ethical research. We encourage you, as you read the other chapters, to see how well thought out research designs unfold in practice from multiple perspectives, challenges and successes.

There is a long history in American Research of people suffering at the hands of unethical researchers when no one was watching. Conflict management skills are required by all parties involved to successfully obtain approval to do research. We ask Social Scientists, IRB Members, and Research Participants to treat research - and each other – with respect. By triangulating the principle of *respect for persons* (Belmont Report, 1979) we can further facilitate ethical research, which ought to be the goal for us all.

References

Alinsky, S. (1971). *Rules for radicals: A pragmatic primer.* New York: Random House.

Annas, G. J., & Grodin, M. A. (1992). *The Nazi doctors and the Nuremberg code: Human rights in human experimentation.* New York: Oxford University Press.

Architecture Research Construction, Inc. (1975). Places and settings. Handbook. Ohio: Ohio Department of Mental Health.

—. (1985). *Community group homes: An environmental approach.*

Aronovici, C. (1939). *Housing the masses.* New York: John Wiley and Sons Inc.

Banks, M. (1995). Visual research methods. *Social Research Update.* Department of Sociology, University of Surrey. Retrieved May 12, 2008 from http://sru.soc.surrey.ac.uk/SRU11/SRU11.html

Banks, M. (2005/2001). *Visual methods in social research.* London: Sage.

Beaty, L. M. (2008). Watching transformation in student-made videos. In M. Downing & L. Tenney (Eds.), *Video Vision: Changing the culture of social science research* (pp. 111-133). UK: Cambridge Scholars Publishing.

Beckman, A. (2008). Remember to press record: A practical guide for using video in research. In M. Downing & L. Tenney (Eds.), *Video Vision: Changing the culture of social science research* (pp. 179-194). UK: Cambridge Scholars Publishing.

Berenbaum, S., Cauffman, E., & Newcombe, N. (2003). Notes toward division 7 input to the APA's project work group" *APA Division Seven Newsletter Developmental Psychologist.* Retrieved on May 12, 2008 from http://www.apa/org/divisions/div7/newsletter/div7newsletter112002.pdf

Bradley, M. (2007). Silenced for their own protection: How the IRB marginalizes those it feigns to protect. *ACME Editorial Collective.* Retrieved May 31, 2008 from http://www.acme-journal.org/vol6/MB.pdf.

Campbell, J., Ralph, R. Glover, R. (1993). From lab rat to research: The history, models, and implications of consumer/survivor involvement in research. Paper presented at the fourth annual National Conference of State Mental Health Agency Services Research and Program Evaluation, Annapolis, MD.

Cho, E. (2006). Students in research. Rose, S. (editor), In CITI Human

Subject Protections course (Ed.). Retrieved May 12, 2008 from www.citiprogram.org.

Cohen, J. (2006). IRB review criteria. Presentation at the 2006 City University of New York IRB Symposium Presentation. Retrieved on June 4, 2008 from www1.cuny.edu/academics/research-scholarship/human- subjects-research/rsources/hipaaslides.html.

Cohen, J., Bankart, E., Cooper, J. (n.d.). History and Ethics. Collaborative Institutional Training Initiative. (retrieved on July 22, 2008 from www.citi.org).

Commons, M. L., Rodriguez, J. A., Adams, K. M., Goodhear, E. A., Gutheil, T. G., & Cyr, E. D. (2006). Informed Consent: Do you know it when you see it? Evaluating the adequacy of patient consent and the value of a lawsuit. *Psychiatric Annals, 36*(6), 430-435.

Commons, M. L. (2008). E-mail interview. Personal Communication.

Congress of Qualitative Inquiry. (2006) Position Statement on Qualitative Research and IRBs Discussion Draft May 4-6, 2006. Retrieved from http://www.c4qi.org/PositionStatement.pdf on May 12, 2008.

Cooper-Marcus, C. (1995). *House as a mirror of self.* Berkeley, CA: Canari Press.

Creswell, J. W. (2002). *Research design: Qualitative, quantitative, and mixed methods approaches* (2nd ed.). Thousand Oaks, CA: Sage.

Cross, W. (1971). The negro to black conversion: Toward a black liberation psychology, *Black World, 20*(9), 13-27.

Delany, C. M. (2005). Informed consent: Ethical theory, legal obligations and the physiotherapy clinical encounter. Unpublished doctoral dissertation, University of Melbourne. Retrieved May 12, 2008 from http://eprints.infodiv.unimelb.edu.au/archive/00001865/01/DelanyFINAL.pdf

Department of Health and Human Services. *Title 45 Part Code of Federal Regulations Title 46 Protection of Human Subjects, 45CFR46.* Retrieved on June 14, 2008 from http://www.hhs.gov/ohrp/documents/OHRPRegulations.pdf

Downing, M. J., Jr. (2008). The role of home in HIV/AIDS: A visual approach to understanding human-environment interactions in the context of long-term illness. *Health & Place, 14*, 313-322.

Enzenauer, R. W., Powell, J. M., Wiswell, T. E., Bass, J. W. (1986), Decreased Circumcision Rate With Videotaped Counseling. *Southern Medical Journal. 79 (6), 717-720.*

Evans, D., Smith, M., & Willen, L. (2005). Human guinea pigs pay for lax FDA rules. *The Seattle TImes.* Retrieved May 12, 2008 from http://seattletimes.nwsource.com/html/businesstechnology/2002606640

_drugtesting06.html

Evans D. (2005) Big pharma's shameful secret. *Alliance for Human Research Protection.* Retrieved May 12, 2008 from http://www.ahrp.org/cms/content/view/335/29/

Feinstein, T. (Ed.). (2005). Uncovering the architect of the Holocaust: The CIA names file on Adolf Eichmann. National Security Archive Electronic Briefing Book No. 150. Retrieved on May 12, 2008 from http://www.gwu.edu/~nsarchiv/NSAEBB/NSAEBB150/index.htm

Fine, M., Weis, L., Weseen, S., & Wong, L. (2000). For whom? Qualitative research, representations and social responsibilities. In, N. Denzin & Y. Lincoln (Eds.), *The handbook of qualitative research* (pp. 107-132). Thousand Oaks, CA: Sage.

Fisher, J. A. (2007). Governing human subjects research in the USA: individualized ethics and structural inequalities. *Science and Public Policy.* 34 (2), 117-126.

Friere, P. (1973). *Pedagogy of the oppressed.* New York: Seabury.

Heberer, P. (2002). Targeting the "unfit" and radical public health strategies in Nazi, Germany. In D. F. Ryan & J. S. Schuchman (Eds.) *Deaf people in Hitler's Europe* (pp. 49-72). Gallaudet University Press.

Jones, J. H. (1983/1991). Bad blood: The Tuskegee syphilis experiment. New York: The Free Press.

Libman, K., & Fields, D. (2008). Video messages in social science research: methodological and ethical considerations. In M. Downing & L. Tenney (Eds.), *Video Vision: Changing the culture of social science research* (pp. 73-92). UK: Cambridge Scholars Publishing.

MacCubbin, P. (2007, September). Institutional Review Boards & Video Taping: Take One. Presentation at the first annual Video Vision Conference, New York, NY.

Mausner, C. (2008). Capturing the hike experience on video: An alternative framework for studying human response to nature. In M. Downing & L. Tenney (Eds.), *Video Vision: Changing the culture of social science research* (pp. 163-178). UK: Cambridge Scholars Publishing.

Milgram, S. (1963). Behavioral study of obedience. *Journal of Abnormal Social Psychology, 67,* 371-378.

—. (1973). Perils of obedience. *Harper's Magazine, 247,* 62-77, December 6.

—. (1974). Obedience to authority: An experimental view. New York: Harper and Row.

—. (1981). This week's citation classic. *Citation Classics, 5*(114).

Mitscherlich A, Mielke F. (1949). *Doctors of infamy: the story of the*

Nazi medical crimes. New York: Schuman.

National Institutes of Health. (1979). *The belmont report.* Retrieved May 12, 2008 from http://ohsr.od.nih.gov/guidelines/belmont.html

National Institutes of Health, Office for Human Research Protections. (2003). Doing it right . . . together. Retrieved May 31, 2008 from http://www.litbang.depkes.go.id/ethics/knepk/download%20dokumen/presentasi/OHRP%20-%20tutorial%202003.ppt

National Health and Medical Research Council, Australian Research Council, & Australian Vice Chancellor's Committee. (2007) National Statement on Ethical Conduct in Human Research. Australia. http://www.nhmrc.gov.au/publications/synopses/_files/e72.pdf

National Patient Safety Agency in England, National Research Ethics Service, England. Retrieved May 12, 2008 from http://www.nres.npsa.nhs.uk/.

Noah, B. (2003). The participation of underrepresented minorities in clinical research. *American Journal of Law and Medicine, 29*(2-3), 221-245.

Odutola, K. (2003). Participatory use of video: A case study of community involvement in story construction. *Global Media Journal, 2*(2), Article 11.

Office for Human Subjects Research Protections. *Directives for Human Experimentation. The Nuremberg Code.* Reprinted from Trials of War Criminals before the Nuremberg Military Tribunals under Control Council Law No. 10, Vol. 2, pp. 181-182. Washington, DC: US Government Printing Office, 1949. Retrieved May 12, 2008 from http://www.nihtraining.com/ohsrsite/guidelines/nuremberg.html

—. (2003). Doing it right . . . together. Retrieved May 31, 2008, from www.litbang.depkes.go.id/ethics/knepk/download%20dokumen/presentasi/OHRP%20-%20tutorial%202003.ppt

—. (1993). Office for Protection from Research Risks. Tips on informed consent. Retrieved on May 31, 2008 from http://www.hhs.gov/ohrp/humansubjects/guidance/ictips.htm

Okahashi, P. (2000). The potential of participatory video. *Rehabilitation Review, 11*(1).

Pellegrino, E. (1997). The Nazi doctors and Nuremberg: Some moral lessons revisited. *Annals of Internal Medicine, 127*(4), 307-308.

Pittinsky, T. L. (2005). Allophila and intergroup leadership. In N. Huber & M. Walker (Eds.). *Building leadership bridges: Emergent models of global leadership.* College Park, Maryland: International Leadership Association.

Ralph, R. O. (1997). Participatory research and stakeholder involvement in community mental health evaluation research. Workshop in participatory research. *Seventh annual conference on state mental health agency services research, program evaluation and policy.* University of Southern Maine.

Rivlin, L. G. & Wolfe, M. (1985). *Institutional settings in children's lives.* New York: John Wiley & Sons.

Rosser, B.R.S. (2008). Internet research vulnerabilities and solutions. Presentation at the 2008 Association for the Accreditation of Human Subject Research Programs annual conference: Quality Human Research Protection Programs, Minneapolis, MN.

Rossi M., Guttmann, D., Megan J. MacLennan M. and Lubowitz, J. (2005).

Video informed consent improves knee arthroscopy patient comprehension. *Arthroscopy: The Journal of Arthroscopic & Related Surgery.* 21(6): 739-743

Sieber, J. (2007, May 25). Privacy and Confidentiality: As Related to Human Research in Social and Behavioral Science (Research Involving Human Participants V2)" Retrieved May 31, 2008 from www.onlineethics.org/CMS/research/resref/nbacindex/nbachindex/hsieber.aspx.

Singhal, A., & Devi, K. (2003). Visual voices in participatory communication. *Communicator, XXXVIII*(2), 1-15.

Snowden, D. (1967). Eyes see, ears hear. Memorial University, Newfounland Canada. Retrieved from www,fao.org/waicent/faoinfo/sustdev/cdirect/cdre0038.htm

Tenney, L. (2006). Who fancies to have a Revolution here? *The Opal* Revisited (1851-1860). *Journal of Radial Psychology. 5.*

—. (in press). Psychiatric slave no more: Parallels to a black liberation psychology. *Journal of Radical Psychology.*

The Nuremberg Code (1947) In: Mitscherlich, A, and Mielke F. *Doctors of infamy: The story of the Nazi medical crimes.* New York: Schuman, 1949: xxiii-xxv.

The Opal. (1851-1860). Edited by the patients. Utica, NY: Utica State Lunatic Asylum.

Thomas, J. (2002). "Big Brother" or Allies? In defense of IRBs and RCR. *SSSI Notes, 29* (March), 4-6.

Tomaselli, K. (1989). Transferring video skills to the community of power. *Culture, Communication and Media Studies.* University of Kwa-Zulu-Natal, South Africa. Retrieved on August 30, 2008, from http://ccms.ukzn.ac.za/index.php?option=com_content&task=view&id=505&Itemid=69

Turan, Z. & Chapin, D. (Directors). (2005). *Living Salk Institute*. [Motion Picture]. New York.

Turan, Z. & Chapin, D. (2008). How we learned to love the immersion of digital video editing. In M. Downing & L. Tenney (Eds.), *Video Vision: Changing the culture of social science research* (pp. 93-109). UK: Cambridge Scholars Publishing.

United States Department of Agriculture. (n.d.). 2007. Food Security in the United States. Retrieved May 12, 2008 from http://www.ers.usda.gov/Briefing/FoodSecurity.

Weindling, P. (2001). The international scientific commission on war crimes and the Nuremberg Code. *Bulletin of the History of Medicine, 75*(1), 37-71.

Wendler, D. (1996). Deception in medical and behavioral research: is it ever acceptable? *The Milbank Quarterly, 74*(1), 87-114.

Wolfe, M. (1975). Room size, group size, and density: Behavior patterns in a children's psychiatric facility. *Environment and Behavior*, 7, 199-224.

Wadsworth, Y. (1998). What is participatory action research? *Action Research International*, Paper 2. Retrieved May 12, 2008 from http://www.scu.edu.au/schools/gcm/ar/ari/p-ywadsworth98.html

World Medical Association. (1964). *Declaration of Helsinki*. Retrieved May 12, 2008 from http://www.wma.net/e/policy/b3.htm

Yoder, L, (2006, April). The basics of human subjects protection. *MedSurg Nursing*. Retrieved May 12, 2008, from http://findarticles.com/p/articles/mi_m0FSS/is_2_15/ai_n17212612

Zimbardo, P. G. (2007). *The lucifer effect: understanding how good people turn evil*. New York: Random House.

CHAPTER THREE

VIDEO MESSAGES IN SOCIAL SCIENCE RESEARCH: METHODOLOGICAL AND ETHICAL CONSIDERATIONS

KIMBERLY LIBMAN AND DESIREE FIELDS

Introduction

In the summer of 2006, before the housing foreclosure and lending crisis hit the mass media, the Housing Environments Research Group (HERG) was charged by an advisory board of regulators, economic and community development officers and other representatives from the lending industry with the task of investigating why low- and moderate-income homeowners fail to reach out to their mortgage lenders and nonprofit organizations for assistance when they fell behind on their mortgages. As graduate students working within HERG we traveled to five cities and spoke to groups of homeowners in order to answer this question. However, in our conversations with homeowners it became clear that people did call for help and that this 'problem' needed to be reframed. In this research, we used video messages and focus groups as our methods. In developing, conducting, and disseminating this work we encountered entwined methodological, ethical, and political dilemmas. These, in part, stemmed from our role as student researchers coming from different race and class positions than the homeowners we spoke to. They also came from our desire to use this research to promote social justice. Victoria Lawson (2007) argues that the same neoliberal forces that shaped the context of the foreclosure crisis—an expanded discourse of personal responsibility, the withdrawal of public support for collectively consumed social goods, and the extension of the market--are also reasons researchers should seriously attend to the ethics of care. She argues that a feminist ethics of care is not about fixing the flawed and needy, but rather about the centrality of social relationships built around trust and mutuality, and extending our thinking beyond theoretical notions of justice and into the day-to-day contexts that express our ethics (Lawson, 2007). With this chapter we hope to make visible, and situate, the ethical concerns and dilemmas we negotiated in the context of this research. We hope this critical reflexivity will both be useful to other researchers, and support our argument that ethics in video research is an iterative series of considerations that extends far beyond obtaining IRB approval.

The social justice dimension of this research centers on the reframing of the relative roles of homeowners, lenders, and regulators in the creating of the foreclosure crisis away from the neoliberal strategy of emphasizing individual responsibility and thus, blaming the victims of this crisis for its inception. Within the social sciences framing refers to the ways that messages are constructed to influence our interpretations of them, so reframing an issue entails changing the definition of a problem, its causes, and remedies (Entman, 1993). Rather than developing strategies to encourage delinquent borrowers to seek help, we concluded that nonprofit organizations and mortgage lenders need to acknowledge and better understand the ways that such borrowers already seek help. As our understanding of the nature of the problem we were researching evolved, our video methodology, which we term "video messages", took on a new significance. In a research context that started from a point where prevailing knowledge held that half of homeowners in default on mortgage payments were "non help seekers" who failed to communicate with their mortgage lenders or to seek nonprofit assistance when they met with financial difficulties (Roper Public Affairs and Freddie Mac, 2005), our use of video messages may be seen as an effort to create an opportunity for low-income homeowners to use the research process to communicate from a position of strength and a stance buoyed by the experiences they shared with others (Fine, 2006). We hold that by using video to allow these homeowners to send a message to the very institutions that defined the problem in terms of their not reaching out to communicate, video messages constitute a means of gathering "counter-hegemonic perspectives and standpoints that challenge dominant views" (Fine, 2006, p. 90). However, the meanings that such messages take on outside of the context in which they were made can be a source of ethical dilemmas for video researchers (Odutola, 2003). In this chapter we will first provide some background on the research context and describe a video message methodology, then briefly review literature on visual research and video methodologies in the

social sciences and the feminist and participatory stances on ethics that
inform our approach to video research before finally discussing the ethical
and methodological concerns that led us to devise the video message
methodology, and the ensuing conflicts we faced as researchers around
representation, ownership, and uses of these video research products.

Research Context

When we began this research the mortgage foreclosure crisis in the
United States had yet to dominate newspaper headlines, though early
warning signs were evident in the form of homeownership preservation
initiatives and working groups on foreclosure at community development
organizations[1], and efforts by states to pass anti-predatory lending laws
(efforts successfully challenged by the federal government with claims that
subsidiaries of national banks were exempt from regulations by state
banking authorities) (Morgenthau, 2007). Indeed, the precursor to this
research was a 2004-2005 national survey by HERG conducted among
low-income homeowners who received nonprofit pre-purchase
homeownership education, which showed troubling trends including fear
of foreclosure, a high incidence of making mortgage payments 30 and 90
days late, and many homeowners failing to return to nonprofits for
assistance and intervention when they encountered financial difficulty
(Saegert, Justa, & Winkel, 2005). While all of these pointed at the crisis to
come, prevailing knowledge among the advisory board to this study,
comprised of regulators, economic and community development officers
and other representatives from the lending industry at the time we began
this research was that most mortgage delinquencies "self-cured" before
going into default (i.e. delinquent homeowners were able to resolve the
delinquency on their own without assistance or intervention by their
mortgage lender). Research conducted in 2005 at Freddie Mac, a
government-sponsored enterprise that works to expand the secondary
market for mortgages, indicated that half of homeowners in delinquency
on mortgage payments were not in contact with their mortgage lenders,
and suggested ways to encourage these homeowners to contact their
lenders (Roper Public Affairs and Freddie Mac, 2005). Taken together
these suggest a troubling pattern whereby lenders and other players in the
mortgage industry viewed their own intervention in mortgage delinquency
as unnecessary, yet sought to bring about this very behavior among

---

[1] C.f. the Homeownership Preservation Initiative (HOPI) in Chicago, a coalition of
Neighborhood Housing Services of Chicago and the city of Chicago

delinquent homeowners.

It was in this context of growing unease about the sustainability of the American Dream among low- and moderate-income Americans, and popular wisdom that simultaneously downplayed early mortgage delinquency as an indicator of later default and foreclosure and shouldered delinquent homeowners with the responsibility of communicating and negotiating with their lenders to resolve mortgage delinquency, that we traveled to five cities around the country as graduate research assistants for HERG in July and August of 2006.

The sites for the focus groups were selected to represent a mix of market, geographic, economic, and demographic factors to yield locally and nationally relevant results about the experience of mortgage delinquency among low- and moderate-income homeowners. In combination with census data, state per-capita foreclosure rates and the prevalence of high-interest subprime loans by Metropolitan Service Area (MSA), evidence from HERG's 2004-2005 survey documenting incidence of ever being behind on mortgage payments or making late payments, and fear of foreclosure guided the site selection process. Together these indicators helped us identify sites where low- and moderate-income homeowners might be especially vulnerable to becoming delinquent on their mortgages. The availability of nonprofit foreclosure intervention and other homeowner education resources and anti-predatory lending campaigns was an additional selection criterion used to narrow potential study sites to those where delinquent homeowners had the opportunity to seek assistance for their financial difficulties.

The final sites for the focus group research were:

New York, NY
St. Louis, MO
Hamilton, OH
Duluth, GA
Waco, TX

To learn about how low-income homeowners responded to mortgage delinquency and their experiences with seeking assistance for this problem we used mixed and multiple methods which included focus groups, video, questionnaires and field notes. We conducted nine focus groups and two individual interviews with a total of 88 homeowners and five focus groups with a total of 39 nonprofit professionals; in all 127 people participated in this study. The majority of participants (70%) were female. Across all groups, the majority of participants were African-American, with English-speaking Latinos (30%) and whites (16%) representing small portions of our sample. Homeowner participants may be characterized as moderate- or low-income people, most of who had experienced difficulty with health problems of their own or of a member of their support network; problems with underemployment and unemployment; or other unsustainable debt in addition to having experienced difficulties making mortgage payments. All expressed being challenged by the demands of homeownership.

Our use of focus groups as our chief research methodology helped us to develop a unique understanding of the issues at hand. Focus groups are a socially grounded research method with the potential to create situations that can offer more insight into a topic than survey or interview methodologies (Morgan, 1997). Whereas social scientific inquiry often entails exploitation and artificiality, feminist psychologist Sue Wilkinson (1999) notes that focus groups can serve as an empowering and non-exploitative mode of investigation, qualities that we felt were critical to our research. We found that the use of focus groups yielded a deep understanding of the emotions, stories, and different viewpoints involved in the issues of mortgage delinquency and foreclosure. As a feminist method, focus groups have the potential to move participants' understanding of issues that impact their lives out of individualistic frames and, as a result, gain a more politicized and critical collective consciousness about the forces that influence their lives (Wilkinson, 1999). This shift can lead research participants into undertaking previously unimaginable action toward addressing problems in their lives and communities.

In our use of video on this project we adopted a critical and reflexive approach (Lomax & Casey, 1998; Rose, 2006) to the twin concerns of methodology and research ethics as we came to recognize that rather than questions asked and answered at the outset of research, these issues might be better understood as a series of conflicts that shift and evolve throughout the research process. Thus while we entered the field with a video methodology that addressed a set of initial ethical and methodological concerns we had around our use of video, this "solution" of video messages later gave rise to other conflicts about the politics of representation, ownership of video research products and the ethics of packaging and circulating as a product the sentiments shared by research participants in a moment of empowerment and catharsis. Initially our concerns centered on ethical questions of balancing risk to participants against the project's aims and the expectations of an advisory board, and methodological challenges related to the potential impact of video recording on the validity of our data and a desire to use video as a source of complementary data rather than a visual transcript of the research. In response to these issues we devised a method of video messaging.

Video Messages

Video messages have been used in business to do collaborative work (Takada & Harada, 2006) and are popular in mainstream culture for purposes as varied as activism (OneWorld, 2005), communicating with military troops and personnel stationed overseas (Gilmore, 2002), and affirmations of religious faith (Fathers Glory Ministries, 2008). Visual methodologies are also gaining steam in the social sciences--our use of video in this research is part of a larger movement in the social sciences toward the use of such methodologies, more specifically where researchers (co)create rather than simply interpret visual texts (Rose, 2006). The video messages were co-created by the focus group participants and us. We used the last question in the focus group as a prelude to the creation of video messages:

> If you could communicate a message to researchers, policymakers, financial counseling staff lenders or homebuyers about preventing foreclosure who would you send it to and what would you say?

This provided an opportunity for personal reflection at the close of groups, and gave participants time to first formulate and then share their messages in the space of the focus group. Although our methodology differs from approaches to participatory video in that participants were not educated about how to use video equipment and did not direct or film the messages themselves, we shared with such approaches an aim to strengthen communication with decision makers (Lunch & Lunch, 2006). To this end we told participants that their messages would become part of a nationally collected pool of messages to be used in a video that would educate the lending and nonprofit community (our project advisory board) on how to prevent and remediate mortgage delinquency and foreclosure. Immediately after the conclusion of each focus group those who wanted to had the opportunity to go on video with their message. Before each group began we created a setting for video recording these messages outside the room in which the group was conducted, to facilitate an efficient rollover from the focus group to video data production. Our basic considerations in arranging such spaces included adequate lighting, privacy, and site-specific visual interest such as murals and plants within the offices. In addition to addressing many of our initial ethical and methodological concerns we feel video messaging was particularly well-suited to pair with focus groups because the opportunity to create a message served as a platform for focus group participants to express a critical consciousness arrived at during the focus group, thus becoming an outlet for them to act on the impetus to address the problems affecting them and their communities.

We ended up with 18 messages: 10 from homeowners and 8 from professionals; roughly 11% of homeowners and 20% of professionals created a video message. Among the ten homeowners who chose to create a video message, six were Black females, three were Black males, and one was a white female. Five white male, two Black female, and one Latino female professionals chose to create video messages. Homeowners sent messages to other homeowners, lenders, and nonprofit staff. Messages from homeowners to other owners or potential homeowners emphasized seeking help for mortgage delinquency in order to prevent foreclosure, provided moral reassurance to others who might be experiencing financial difficulty, and encouraged potential homeowners to educate themselves about loan products before purchasing. Messages from homeowners to lenders noted the importance of lenders providing options early on in mortgage delinquency, providing professional and courteous servicing, and asking for honesty about loan terms and affordability. Messages from homeowners to nonprofit organizations highlighted the need for ongoing post-purchase outreach, counseling, and education.

Critical Visual Methodologies, Reflexivity in Video Research and Feminist Ethics

Our reflections on the use of video messages in social science research are grounded in critical theories of representation and visual methodologies; the notion of reflexivity in video research; a feminist ethics of care; and social justice as an ethical imperative in participatory/democratic research.

Gillian Rose (2006) advocates a critical visual methodology where researchers use approaches that acknowledge the significance of the particular social and cultural milieu in which their work is situated. Rather than objective data, still photos, video and audio recordings used for research purposes[2], as with other forms of representation, serve to privilege certain cultural forms over others (Hall, 1997; Rose, 2006; Said, 1978). Because visual methodologies give meaning to research subjects through representation (Hall, 1997), questions of power relations in video research are by necessity a discussion of research ethics (Rose, 2006). As such researchers working with video need to consider the power relations their work is articulated through, communicates, challenges and reproduces (Rose, 2006). In particular we must concern ourselves with the social effects of images, especially how our video data and research products depict difference (Rose, 2006), because these images are read in terms of belonging and exclusion (Hall, 1997).

Echoing this concern for the social context in which video research is done and seen, John Berger's (1972) work in critical visual studies argues that the site of meaning lies not in the image, but rather in the relation between the image and the viewer. In this sense images produced by visual research are not an objective truth so much as an exchange among the researcher, the researched, the image and the audience/spectators (Hall, 1997; Rose, 2006) and must be situated thusly in the social context in which they are created and viewed (Berger, 1980).

As researchers need to take into account how the broader social context of their work shapes video research products and their interpretation by viewers, so too must they recognize that doing video research entails a consideration of how their work is constituted in and through a context created by their contributions and those of research participants, and the camera itself. Rather than engaging in questions of video data of social phenomenon as *either* objective *or* distorted by the presence of the camera then, Lomax and Casey (1998) point to a reflexive approach that addresses how the process of data collection socially constructs and produces the data when studying social phenomenon with video research methods. According to this methodological stance neither the camera nor video researchers are detached observers, but active participants in the activity being recorded and the phenomenon of study (Lomax & Casey, 1998). Such an approach to video research acknowledges that the choices we make about filming in performing the role of researcher, and the self-awareness research participants demonstrate around their role as objects of research and as to the documentation of their activities (Lomax & Casey,

---

[2] Rosenstein (2002) holds that these are objective data.

1998) all help constitute the form that video data takes. The interactions required to set up equipment and begin taping, and the spatial and verbal organization which researcher and participants must undertake before data collection begins, lead to questions about when, in field work, research begins and ends and the role of the researcher in this process along a continuum ranging from invisible to active participant (Lomax & Casey, 1998). A reflexive approach to video research recognizes how researcher involvement contributes to the research process and how this process produces video research data and products (Lomax & Casey, 1998).

Conceiving of video research in the social sciences as situated in particular social and cultural contexts; laden with power relations; and shaped by the contributions of the camera, the researchers and participants is a stance that encourages visual researchers to recognize the positionalities with which our work is loaded. This approach has much in common with Sandra Harding's (1995) notion of "strong objectivity", which argues that the ideal of neutrality in research presents a barrier to objectivity because it fails to acknowledge the positions and values researchers bring to their knowledge-seeking efforts. Instead of masking what we bring to the research process with the cloak of neutrality, strong objectivity is achieved by actively working through these, "gathering as much evidence as possible, from many distinct vantage points, all in an effort not to be guided, unwittingly, by predispositions and the pull of biography" (Fine, 2006, p. 89).

Cahill et al.'s (2007) notion of participatory ethics addresses institutional policies, research practice, and politics, dimensions of ethics in research practice that, together with Lawson's (2007) work, call for us to conduct "research informed by an 'ethic of care' in its most profound sense as a deep respect for relationships and humanity" (Cahill et al., 2007, p. 306). This position highlights the overlap between the ethical concerns of research practice and the politics of representation for researchers using visual methodologies.

In the context of this project the video messages were used as a tool for creating social change toward justice by providing a platform for the very homeowners who were excluded from designing the research, framing its questions, or shaping its analysis to speak back to the lenders and regulators that collaborated to initiate this work. While our project was not participatory in its development and implementation there are a number of concerns we share with writers/researchers on feminist and participatory ethics. These are rooted both in a shared commitment to using research to work toward social justice, as well as the simultaneously exclusive and collaborative nature of this research project. Here the project grew out of a collaboration between researchers, regulators, and nonprofit professionals, but excluded homeowners from participating outside their role as focus group 'subjects' and video message makers. As our field work progressed and we recognized the need to reframe foreclosure as a collective issue that is not just about personal responsibility for spending or calling for help, we came to see the potential for this study to share stories that challenged the status quo and push for a new understanding of the issues we set out to investigate (Harris et al., 2001).

The video message methodology provided us with a visual record of the ways homeowners framed these issues while attending to the need to minimize risk to participants, balancing this imperative with concerns as to the fruitfulness and utility of our video research products, and creating a source of complementary video data that would move beyond a visual transcript of the focus group proceedings. In the remainder of this chapter we discuss in more detail these initial ethical and methodological considerations which we addressed by devising a video message methodology, then turn to the considerations around representation, ownership and use of these video research products to which our methodology gave rise.

Initial Ethical and Methodological Concerns: Risk and Validity, Utility and Fruitfulness

Although our initial research plan called for video recording the focus groups in their entirety we worried that the topic of financial difficulty, especially unresolved issues like the ones many participants were contending with, might create an emotionally charged situation during the focus groups. So while the project's advisory board of funders expected us to deliver videos of the groups, we felt that doing so might actually compromise the ability of participants to speak openly and honestly about their experiences. This tension carried both an ethical concern about the potential for distress created by the possibility of capturing emotionally disturbing moments on video and thus increasing risk of harm to participants, and a methodological concern that video recording the groups in their entirety might threaten the validity of the data by preventing participants from speaking fully and openly about their experiences due to the presence of the camera. In addition to these other issues, the reality of the project's funding and advisory structure added a level of concern about how the video data we generated could be the most fruitful and useful. Several of the funders were interested in the kinds of messages that might reach homeowners at risk of foreclosure and encourage them to seek nonprofit assistance. The expectations built into the project forced us to consider how we could use video in a way that minimized harm to participants and threats to validity while fulfilling the expectations of the project's sponsors.

We emphasize the ethical conflicts raised by the use of video in social science research because the difficulty of ensuring confidentiality when not only interactions but faces and contexts are visually recorded makes video data especially vulnerable to (perhaps unwitting) abuse (Rosenstein, 2002). In the interest of engaging in critical visual and social research, we pushed ourselves to be present to the relations of vulnerability that unfolded as we crafted our video methodology, "understanding that social researchers should always be the most vulnerable--not those being studied or 'left' behind once the research is complete" (Fine, 2006, p. 88). We also wanted to attend to both the ethical obligation to respect that communities and individuals have 'sacred' stories they may not want shared beyond the research context, and the politics of research that brings private experience to the public as part of the task of producing evidence of oppression and injustice (Fine et al., 2007). These concerns, in part, prompted us to use video messages instead of video recording the focus groups because the video message methodology allowed participants to have control over what they chose to take public.

The choice to go on camera and deliver a previously formulated message is an essential component of the ethics of this method because it ensures that no one is on film that does not expressly want to be and represents an embodied and active form of consent. In this way our ethical choice also addressed the potential threats to validity associated with holding back important facets of the experience of mortgage delinquency among focus group participants because of discomfort about being video recorded.

By placing control over what the camera captured in the hands of the research participants this methodology represents a reflexive engagement with the process of video data production because it recognized and responded to the ways that the camera, researchers and participants influence this process (Lomax & Casey, 1998). With video messaging we hoped to create a more direct and intentional relationship between participants and the video camera, instead of simply aiming for objective and representational video data achieved through participants becoming accustomed to the presence of the video camera as a silent observer. This method also had the advantage of creating a source of complementary data to accompany the focus group recordings and transcripts, our field notes and the closed-ended questionnaire, rather than simply serving as a visual transcript. Thus we were able to engage in a process of triangulation, considering the content of the video messages alongside these other records of the research process (Rosenstein, 2002) to identify concepts, check validity, narrow findings and draw conclusions (Miles & Huberman, 1994).

The format of video messages draws many parallels to well-recognized forms of media representation of people, events and social issues like broadcast news and public service announcements. By placing the people experiencing this issue at the center, the similarities between video messages and broadcast news give this method the potential to recast the power of the news media to frame issues. The methodology of the video messages was structured so as to acknowledge the ways participants had come to define and understand their experience through discussing it with similar others. By leaving the contents and recipient of the message up to the sender participants were able to craft video messages that spoke to those they identified as key figures in questions of foreclosure, be they other homeowners, nonprofit organizations, mortgage brokers or lenders. Still, critical social research must be a means not simply of engaging critical consciousness among the oppressed, but of awakening the privileged (Apfelbaum, 2001), thus calling for us "to theorize not only the speaking but the listening; to think through the conditions under which relatively privileged people are willing to hear and act on oppression" (Fine, 2006, p. 87). One way we used our role as researchers to co-create the video products that came out of this research was to encourage participants to think of video messages as akin to public service announcements. The brief format of public service announcements is accessible, familiar to many, and a media communication that people tend to recognize as speaking on important social issues. In this sense video messages might be seen as a method that not only provides a forum for homeowners to voice their experiences and critical consciousness but a way to engage those to whom the messages were directed.

Reconsidering Method and Ethics:
Analysis and Dissemination

In addition to being a potential means of engaging the privileged in a discourse around oppression, video messages offer advantages for data analysis. The brevity and compact nature of the messages succinctly suggested themes for analysis and pointed to the ways participants framed their experiences with mortgage delinquency and foreclosure. Furthermore, these characteristics made the units of meaning within each message clear and easy to recognize. By constructing a case-ordered matrix (Miles & Huberman, 1994) that detailed the sequence of units of meaning and key phrases in each message we were able to observe consistent patterns in these messages. Because we used video to create a source of complementary data rather than a visual transcript, the video messages have facilitated a process of triangulation among the other types of data we collected (Rosenstein, 2002), including field notes, site summary analysis, and focus group transcripts and audio. This process entails making connections across the data types to identify themes and concepts that maintain significance across the various data sources, giving us a deeper understanding of the issues involved in our analysis.

While the succinct nature of the video message simplified the analysis of the discourses of foreclosure, we went on to negotiate a series of ethical challenges as we edited and disseminated our findings. Because our findings called into question prevailing stereotypes and representations of homeowners facing foreclosure, issues of representation and the ways in which the video messages might be used were pivotal in the ethical and methodological choices we made as video researchers in data analysis, presentation and dissemination. Video data raises questions not only about confidentiality but about ownership, where and to whom it may be shown, and when a waiver might be required before sharing the data (Rosenstein, 2002). Like others we questioned how, and with whom, to share the research so that it could lead to action toward justice (Cahill & Torre 2007). This led us to struggle with selecting messages to share with funders, and whether or not to share them with the nonprofit organizations that also sponsored the research.

In part this struggle stemmed from how the combination of the focus group methodology and the subject matter of financial hardship led to a critical consciousness among participants. While focus groups may serve as a naturalistic social context where meaning is made by groups of people discussing their common experiences (Wilkinson, 1999), financial struggles are rarely discussed openly. Thus the space of the focus group was one where participants could talk about their individual experiences collectively in a manner that was not always available to them in their day to day lives. We found that this format encouraged participants to think reflexively, placing their experiences of economic hardship and oppression and homeownership in a broader context. Often, participants expressed a sense of awareness that others in their community were facing similar issues, but at the same time most had yet to discuss their financial difficulties openly with others outside of the focus group. Many expressed a feeling of relief at unburdening themselves and drew strength from the realization that they were not alone in their struggles.

Coming out of this social exchange, participants used video messages to share their personal experience in one of two ways. Some depersonalized it as a means of sharing information and expressing new understandings of the issues while controlling their level of vulnerability. One man, who during the focus group cast his experience of mortgage delinquency in terms of how it reflected on his status as husband and caretaker of his family,

> There's nothing worse than a man feeling like he can't provide for his family…that was the biggest thing I had to struggle with,

went on to create a video message that spoke to the feelings of self-blame that others might experience in a similar situation. In it, he emphasized that:

> Bad things happen to good people. Mortgage delinquency doesn't mean that you're a bad or irresponsible person.

Another example of safe disclosure came from a woman who bought a multi-family dwelling in New York City, hoping to rely on rental income to sustain her mortgage, but encountered problems with tenants not paying rent that contributed to her mortgage delinquency. In her video message to first time homeowners purchasing multi-family dwellings, this woman highlighted the importance of ensuring that the homeowner's income would be enough to pay the mortgage rather than depending on rental income, noting that this could lead to stress on homeowners and their families should tenants be unable to pay rent. In both of these cases the video message served as a forum where delinquent homeowners were able to draw on their personal experiences to encourage and educate other homeowners or potential homeowners without relating the details of their own connection to these issues.

Others were able to use video messages in an empowered way, as an outlet for expressing the meaning they were taking away from the group. The collective and critical consciousness arrived at in a number of groups centered on the often disrespectful and unprofessional treatment homeowners encountered in their attempts to resolve their mortgage delinquency over the phone with their lenders. Hearing others share stories of being insulted, steered toward risky solutions to clear their debt, or harassed by mortgage lenders appeared to allow individual homeowners to reframe their experiences, moving out of shame and hurt into anger and demands for justice. Thus one man used his video message as an opportunity to communicate to his mortgage lender, whom he named in the message:

> This message is to my lender [company name redacted] I would like to thank you for giving me an opportunity to buy a home from you, but at this time I am not satisfied with the [way] that you treat me, the way that you hang up in my face, I don't like it, I think that you could be more professional.

In a message to her mortgage lender, another participant contested the notion that the responsibility for resolving mortgage delinquency lies solely with the borrower, stating:

> A lot of things if you don't know you just try to figure it out on your own, and you kind of end up going in circles. It seems like the mortgage company doesn't call you until you're right at foreclosure.

This last message in particular challenged dominant views in the lending industry about expectations for communication between mortgage lenders and homeowners.

Both the safe disclosure and the empowered appeal modes of video messaging addressed earlier ethical concerns we had around giving participants control over the level of disclosure of their experience captured on video and of speaking to the goal, which emerged with our findings, of using this research to question characterizations of delinquent homeowners. At the same time, the iterative ethics we employed in this work led us to recognize that collecting these messages at the end of our focus groups, when some participants were feeling highly charged, has both strengths and limits. It is a strength because the messages communicated the reflexivity and broader consciousness participants developed in the focus groups. For some the message seemed to capture a cathartic moment. As an anecdote, one man left the groups saying he felt he had shared more than he planned to because he felt safe and supported with the group. We felt concerned that people may have said things in their video messages that felt good to share in this kind of moment; but questioned whether they would still want that moment shared later on. This question, and our experiences sharing some of these messages with our advisors, led us to see the power of these moments also as a potential limitation to sharing the messages in more broadly disseminated products of the research.

In using this material to communicate our research findings to the project's advisory board, we faced a set of practical and ethical issues associated with the visual dimensions of video messages. In the context of meetings with our advisors from the lending community and the staff at participating sites we shared video messages to elicit feedback from the advisory board on our preliminary findings and data analysis strategies, and to share the content of messages with lenders and regulators of the lending industry. Sharing Berger (1972; 1980) and Rose's (2006) concern for the relationship between image, context and meaning, Lynn and Lea (2005) use the concepts of internal and external narrative to consider the meanings attached to visual research products. Internal narrative describes the content of the image on film, while the external narrative is the context in which the image or film is viewed, with these narrative strands interacting to co-create meaning (Lynn & Lea, 2005).

In sharing video messages with advisors from the lending community, we were transporting them from the safely empowered moment in which they were created to a context where the external narrative was one where discussions of mortgage delinquency and foreclosure were understood and discussed in completely different terms. Recall that we went into the field to learn why homeowners fail to seek the assistance of their lender or a nonprofit organization when they encounter financial difficulties, and that we actually found that rather than getting these homeowners to seek help, the issue was one of better supporting the ways they already sought assistance to increase the effectiveness of these strategies. So in sharing video messages with our advisors, we were situating them in an external narrative where assumptions of individual irresponsibility among delinquent homeowners prevailed.

Although sharing the messages in this forum seemed ethically sound because we had the informed consent of participants who voluntarily delivered them, and addressed the imperative to bring into the open experiences of oppression (Fine et al., 2007) by delivering to the lenders and nonprofits the messages people directed to them, this external narrative set up a conflict around the politics of representation. We felt concerned about representing the research participants both as they were and chose to represent themselves and in a way that would not reinforce or support negative stereotypes about low-income homeowners as irresponsible spenders, or, as some non-profit professionals said "people with Champagne tastes on beer budgets." We also share a concern for representing communities or collectives' points of disjuncture, rather than generalizing these in the interest of presenting consensus (Torre & Fine, 2007). Not all of the homeowners we spoke to were critical of the neoliberal ideology, and as researchers who are critical of neoliberalism, it was ethically challenging to present this particular disjuncture. Our dilemma here lay in our simultaneous inclinations to use our research and findings to challenge, rather than support, the neoliberal agenda and also to represent the range of perspectives held by our participants. In our analysis and dissemination we emphasized the mixed views of participants on issues related to neoliberalism, such as individual responsibility. We created a montage of messages that highlighted this tension. This montage included messages to lenders and loan officers that implicated them in the foreclosure crisis, as well as messages to other homeowners stressing the ability to budget and avoid foreclosure through individual behavior. Thus, the selectivity of the editorial process is one place where video researchers can, and should, literally work through the political and ethical concerns of representation.

One Black participant, who spoke powerfully in the focus group about redlining, racial profiling, and the lack of regulation and enforcement of the lending industry went on to create a video message directed at potential homeowners. This message exhorted potential homeowners to avoid being victimized by predators by researching their mortgage company before purchasing, getting all the details about their loan and not allowing themselves to be rushed at closing, stating that:

> You don't want any hidden surprises, because those hidden surprises can cause you to lose your home.

We felt his message conveyed a sense of the vulnerability to victimization that many participants expressed, and decided to share it with our advisors. In sharing it, the focus of our advisors was not on the message about foreclosure which this man conveyed, but on his shirt, which was printed with the words: *'I'm not drunk, I'm still drinking"*. This created a tension between the internal narrative of the message and the external narrative, which we hoped to create through presenting this video in the context of our early findings, that recast the issue of mortgage delinquency and help seeking.

The extreme power differential between our advisors and participants contributed to our subsequent ethical dilemma, which centered on the politics of representation. After viewing this message one advisor criticized our choice to not edit out the text from this mans t-shirt. This made us rethink our choice to not edit this image and represent this homeowner as he chose to present himself on film. The internal narrative of this clip, specifically the text on the t-shirt reinforced the very stereotypes we were attempting to dispel in the external narrative of sharing our early findings.

Our choice to collect video messages from nonprofit professionals and financially challenged homeowners facilitated their "talking back" to the lending community. This also allowed professionals and homeowners to contextualize their experiences, think reflexively, and voice this new understanding. bell hooks (1989) discusses talking back as a means of liberation, of moving from object to subject. In this way our methodological choice to use video messages had positive ethical implications with regard to the politics of representation embedded in research. However as the example above illustrates, these positive implications are contingent on our editing choices.

As non-Black video researchers we need to acknowledge that as we analyze and edit, we selectively shape the racial narrative of our work. In a global cultural context that has commodified Black popular culture, self-representation serves as cultural capital (Hall, 1993). In turn, our representation of participants' identities shapes the [mis]appropriation of this capital by the research audience. We hoped to create representations that went beyond binaries of high/low (Hall, 1993), deserving/undeserving. In the context of video work this may entail presenting video images that embody differences, which do not "coalesce around a single axis of differentiation (Hall, 1993, p. 112), but exist rather in tension with one another. By electing not to obscure the text on the man's shirt, we avoided creating a neatly packaged video research product that conformed to notions of the deserving and undeserving poor.

While sharing video messages with our advisory board prompted us to reflect on the politics of representation to which we adhere and the racial narratives we create in the use of visual research, the prospect of sharing these video research products with the nonprofits who collaborated with us in organizing the focus groups brought up more traditional ethical concerns about maintaining confidentiality of research participants. We hoped to bolster the validity of our analysis by soliciting feedback on our interpretations of early emerging themes from nonprofit staff, however doing so also meant potentially revealing the identity of participants in a context they may not have expected when signing their consent forms. Finally, the seemingly simple act of putting the messages on DVD and mailing them to advisors with an interim research report created the potential for the messages to find their way into the broader public.

Conclusions

This chapter reflects on the development and use of video messages as a research methodology and the ethical concerns that shaped this process. We reflect on this process as a way of calling attention to the situated nature of ethical and methodological concerns in the research process, particularly as they are made more complex by the representational dimensions of video research. In so do doing we demonstrate both the reciprocal relationship, and tensions between, the considerations of rigorous investigation, ethics and care, as well as the responsibility to use research to promote social justice.

Our experiences using video in conjunction with focus groups to understand low-income homeowner's responses to threat of foreclosure led us to reconsider the relative roles of ourselves as researchers, video as a research tool, and our participants. At the outset of this work we were challenged to include video methods in a way that would not force focus group participants to be filmed and thus began an iterative process of thinking through the ethical implications of collecting, analyzing, and sharing this data. We feel that video messages have potential as a methodological tool for researchers working toward social justice because they allow participants to talk back to policy makers and others with more power. This method also goes beyond the traditional concerns of an IRB with regard to ethics by adding an embodied active consent process where participants have greater control over what they put on film. Still, as with all visual methodologies there are ethical challenges regarding the editing/analysis and consequent politics of representing others. Here we wish we could have included the message makers in the analysis and decisions we had to make about how and with whom to share this material. We found that the IRB procedure of not collecting personal information such as addresses and phone numbers in conjunction with data impeded our ability to go back to participants with such questions. Importantly we did not encounter this dilemma until a year after our data had been collected. Again, we note this to stress that ethics in video research are situated and iterative, and are difficult to plan for--the interdependent nature of methodological and ethical decisions--each have implications for the other.

References

Apfelbaum, E. (2001). The dread: An essay on communication across cultural boundaries. *International Journal of Critical Psychology, 4*, 19-34.

Berger, J. (1980). *About Looking*. New York: Pantheon Books.

—. (1972). *Ways of Seeing*. London: Penguin.

Cahill, C., Sultana, F., & Pain, R. (2007). Participatory ethics: Policies, practices, institutions. *ACME: An International Journal for Critical Geographies, 6*(3), 304-318.

Cahill, C., & Torre, M. (2007). Beyond the journal article: Representations, audience, and the presentation of participatory research. In S. Kindon, R. Pain, & M. Kesby (Eds.), *Connecting people, participation and lace: Participatory action research approaches and methods* (pp. 196-205). London: Routledge.

Entman, R. (1993). Framing: Towards clarification of a fractured paradigm. *Journal of Communication, 43*(4), 51-58.

Fathers Glory Minstries. (2008). Recordings of Heidi Baker of Iris Ministries, Retrieved May 26, 2008 from http://www.fathersglory.com/insp/Roland_&_Heidi_Baker.htm

Fine, M. (2006). Bearing witness: Methods for researching oppression and resistance--A textbook for critical research. *Social Justice Research, 19*(1), 83-108.

Fine, M., Tuck, E., & Zeller-Berkman, S. (2007). Do you believe in Geneva? In C. McCarthy, A. Durham, L. Engel, A. Filmer, M. Giardina, & M. Malagreca (Eds.), *Globalizing cultural studies* (pp. 493-525). New York: Peter Lang.

Gilmore, G. (2002, September 6). Pentagon kiosk showcases video e-mail sent to deployed service members. American Forces Press Service.

Hall, S. (1993). What is this "Black" in black popular culture? *Social Justice, 20*(1-2), 104-114.

—. (Ed.). (1997). *Representation: Cultural representations and signifying practices.* London: Sage Publications.

Harding, S. (1995). "Strong objectivity": A response to the new objectivity question. *Synthese, 104*(3), 331-349.

Harris, A., Carney, S., & Fine, M. (2001). Counter work: Introduction to 'under the covers: Theorizing the politics of counter stories'. *International Journal of Critical Psychology, 4*(1) 6-18.

hooks, bell. (1989). *Talking back: Thinking feminist, thinking black.* Boston: South End Press.

Lawson, V. (2007). Geographies of care and responsibility. *Annals of the Association of American Geographers, 97*(1), 1-11.

Lomax, H., & Casey, N. (1998). Recording social life: Reflexivity and video methodology. *Sociological Research Online, 3*(2).

Lunch, N., & Lunch, C. (2006). *Insights into participatory video: A handbook for the field.* Oxford: Insight.

Lynn, N., & Lea, S. J. (2005). Through the looking glass: considering the challenges visual methodologies raise for qualitative research. *Qualitative Research in Psychology, 2,* 213-225.

Miles, M., & Huberman, M. (1994). *Qualitative data analysis: An expanded sourcebook.* London: Sage Publications.

Morgan, D. (1997). *Focus groups as qualitative research.* London: Sage Publications.

Morgenthau, R. (2007, April 30). Who's watching your money? The New York Times.

Odutola, K. A. (2003). Participatory use of Video: A case study of community involvement in story construction Global Media Journal, 2(2).

OneWorld. (2005). Campaigners to send video messages for G8 leaders using mobile phones. Retrieved May 26, 2008, from http://us.oneworld.net/article/view/78959/1/

Roper Public Affairs and Freddie Mac. (2005). *Foreclosure avoidance research.* Freddie Mac. Accessed on April 15, 2008 at: http://www.freddiemac.com/service/msp/pdf/foreclosure_avoidance_d ec2005.pdf

Rose, G. (2006). *Visual methodologies: An introduction to the interpretation of visual methods.* London: Sage Publications.

Rosenstein, B. (2002). Video Use in Social Science Research and Program Evaluation. *International Journal of Qualitative Methods, 1*(3), Article 2.

Saegert, S., Justa, F., & Winkel, G. (2005). *Successes of homeowner education and emerging challenges: Evidence from a national survey of neighborworks organizations clients*: The Housing Environments Research Group at the Center for Human Environments.

Said, E. (1978). *Orientalism*. Harmondsworth: Penguin.

Takada, T., & Harada, Y. (2006). Citation-capable video messages: overcoming time differences without sacrificing interactivity, I3: Information Spaces and Visual Interfaces. Kalmar, Sweden.

Wilkinson, S. (1999). Focus groups: A feminist method. *Psychology of Women Quarterly, 23*(2), 221-244.

CHAPTER FOUR

HOW WE LEARNED TO LOVE THE IMMERSION OF DIGITAL VIDEO EDITING

ZEYNEP TURAN AND DAVID CHAPIN

Editing Video is Like Making Soup

For the Video Vision conference that formed the basis of this book, we made a short video about making soup as a metaphor for doing video editing. Our metaphor is that to be good at making soup requires that the cook get really close to the ingredients by selecting, chopping, tasting, and by using more of this or less of that. Making good soup comes from letting both the quality and quantity of what is at hand influence the texture and taste of the soup. The experience of making soup exceeds simply eating soup. Similar to soup making, video editing requires getting close to one's data. A good edit also comes from looking, selecting, chopping, and using more of this or less of that. Our video piece tried to convey the experience of video editing using visual language to claim the doing is as engrossing as the consuming. In this chapter we use words rather than images to convey and advocate for the experience of video editing for the sake of the experience, itself.

Speaking of Video in Everyday Life

There is a way of thinking about video in the pages of this book that is "in the world." Most everyone nowadays participates and performs in the production of the video vision in everyday life; we have come to know ourselves as we act with and for and before and through an active camera; we have come to use this knowledge in how we make video, how we watch it and how we interpret it. This contemporary person is perfectly comfortable with everyday technologies of imagery. A five-year old now expects to see what she looks like right after her picture is taken, and demands that pictures she does not like be deleted from the digital camera. She understands that she is performing to create an appearance. "Delete" was not part of the everyday vocabulary ten years ago and yet "Delete" today is a powerful way to control appearance.

Sarah Pink writes about this sense of video in everyday life as the camera participates in setting up familiar roles. She makes a case for how easily people are willing to slip into roles—to play the right game—with a camera present, happily becoming the "[real] estate agent" in leading the interviewer (Sarah Pink, herself) about the apartment, describing its attractive and salable features (Pink, 2004, p. 72). In this volume, Lara Beaty (Chapter 5) describes her sense of the camera becoming an "Actant" with high school videographers. She sees the camera as an active participant in the scene. As for a larger, cultural sense of the work of participating in a visual culture, we like the work of Marita Sturken and Lisa Cartwright (2001). Sturken and Cartwright unpack the highly interactive process in which we all, in this very visual culture, engage in creating and interpreting imagery. We share an enthusiasm for being part of this approach.

Speaking of Video in Field Research

But there is another position here of speaking as field researchers in the social sciences asking the question: How do people create meaning in their lives? How does the world work for people and how do people work in the world? Beyond the mechanical sense of knowledge, we researchers in this position are interested in the felt, sensual, appreciated, emotionally reacted-to aspects of our everyday lives. We are troubled by the paradigm of social science based on the logical positivist tradition, which claims that only that which can be measured can be subjected to hypothesis testing and therefore only the measurable can finally be made into valid science. This is an old battle that has spanned several decades now. Still, even though field researchers have been able to move out of laboratories into the everyday (the "real") world, and even though we have been able to hope that we are affecting social justice and think we can see beauty in the potentials and possibilities of our world, many of us have not been able to move out from under the shadow of positivist processes.

There is nothing new about challenging logical positivism or about proposing alternative paradigms in the social sciences. Karl Popper

(2002/1956) led this challenge after being appalled at the contributions made by social science to the European Nazi regimes of the 1930s and 1940s. Especially he challenged the notion that any science is concerned with "proof" and suggested that science consists of good stories about that which is not yet disproved. Feminists starting in the 1960s criticized the inability of logical positivism to effect social change, especially because of its own structural relationship to power, it could not dispute the very power relationships that kept women "in their place." Our purpose is not to make the challenge itself, but to record the fact that the challenge has been with us for a very long time. The positions of current alternative paradigms, including feminist paradigms, are discussed in detail by Guba and Lincoln (2005). Their thoughtful article provides a framework to distinguish different paradigms based on issues of Ontology, Epistemology, and Methodology. These distinctions are in the world and well made and yet still we feel the shadow of logical positivism hovering about our research work using video.

Many field researchers have moved towards narrative as an approach to inquiry in the world. But it is difficult to be satisfied with "just" telling stories. For one thing, in some milieus—a university social *science* department, for instance, or in an academic book chapter—just telling stories leaves the storyteller with a vulnerable feeling. This seems often to lead researchers into freighting on processes of generating and analyzing data that have the trappings of science.

At Home with Video Cameras

A good example of a scientized representation of video data is Relieu, Zouinar, and La Valle (2007). This is characterized as a video ethnography, which "seeks to inform the design of home technology" (p. 45). The study was accomplished by placing recording cameras in several homes over large chunks of time. Here, extensive use is made of a conversational analysis technique attributed to Gail Jefferson (Relieu, Zouinar, & La Valle, 2007, p. 65) in which transcriptions are written out line by line, using many conventions and added symbols. This technique is interlaced with video clip stills overlaid with arrows and squiggly lines. Here is an example of dialogue between Justine and Simon (Fig. 4-1):

```
    37 just.: why is it always at mealtime that
it doesn't go on
    38          well?  that's [(incredible)
    39 simon:             [wa*it  hey:    #8
you'll* be able to watch &
    40                      *looks at camera
*points to camera
```

Fig. 4-1: Sample dialogue (Relieu, Zouinar & La Valle, 2007, p. 58).

The authors then carefully analyze the transcriptions in several paragraphs following each fragment of transcription. Their method revels in detail. Their method also distances the reader by requiring a separate code for the data to be understood. Nevertheless, the details serve to underpin three very informative substantive categories: "Playful Orientations to the Recording Equipment: Performance vs Ordinariness," "The Video Camera as an Overhearer: Making Apologies," and "The Video Recording: A Resource Constituted as an 'Arbitrator.'"

About half of the article's 23 pages are devoted to just the sort of analysis as we have described above; in addition there are also three pages which explain the conversational analysis technique which is being used. In other words, a good deal of this article is devoted to method. While we actually like and appreciate this article, we cannot help but feel that it is giving two messages which we find off the mark.

A first message of the article is that this scientification of data (transcriptions to words and symbols subjected to conversational analysis presented with links to gestures indicated in video clips) is useful, proper and ought to be the norm in analyzing video data. To be fair, the authors state none of this; it is our reading of the presentation. A second message is that methodological technique is significant for the fact that it is a way of achieving an outcome—in this case the legitimatization of an analysis which justifies the writing of a journal article.

There is another way of seeing the use of this or any other methodological technique. Technique is a process—a process that requires getting and being immersed in data. This immersion is the crux of what we wish to say. It is important, we think, to not see whatever techniques of analysis we use as mere bath-water. The bath-water is what immerses the baby.

To illustrate this process of immersion, we will describe our experiences with past projects as both working as a team and as individuals.

Objects of Legacy

One of the methods Zeynep used in her dissertation fieldwork was video-ethnography (Turan, 2008). Her dissertation focused on the material objects of displaced people and analyzed how people used objects of legacy to claim their collective identity following loss of their homeland and in some cases their families. The study explores how personal objects were used as a form of resistance—a tactic against the destruction of cultures as well as memory of peoples, and for remembrance and reenactments of past social mechanisms—by populations dislocated in the wake of the collapse of the Ottoman Empire. The three groups studied were the descendants of those who were victimized by the mass killings of Ottoman Armenians in 1915, the Greek-Turkish Population Exchange of 1923, and the Israeli occupation of Palestine in 1948. The Armenian and Palestinian participants live in New York City and the Greek participants in New York City, Athens, and Salonica.

The dissertation dealt with the following questions, and formulated answers to: "How is culture contained, represented, passed on, and reenacted in objects in the aftermath of displacement?" and "What is the relationship between self, personal objects, memory, and collective identity?" The research questions guided the selection of a qualitative research methodology that is exploratory in nature. Zeynep designed a comparative multi-method study based on ethnographic analysis using audio or video interviews. The interview transcripts were used as a source of oral history of experiences of forced relocation, cultural trauma, and the use of material objects to aid in the collective re-building after trauma.

From 2002 to 2006 Zeynep completed 41 interviews. She interviewed 13 Greeks of Asia Minor origin in Salonica, Athens, and New York City in 2002, 14 Armenian Americans and 14 Palestinian Americans in New York City in 2005 and 2006 in their homes. She asked questions regarding the meaning of the objects they identify with being respectively Greek, Armenian, or Palestinian, their degree of attachment to these objects, and the degree of significance of their collective identity in their daily lives.

The research spans over four years and the methodology evolved in this period from audio interviews to video interviews. For the project, Zeynep transcribed all the interviews—two thirds of them video and a third of them were audio interviews. Was there any difference between two methods in terms of the material? Not really. What was said was recorded the same way on both the video and the audio. Reading transcriptions makes no distinction between one technique or the other. However, the act of watching the video over and over again, and paying attention to all sorts of details in the background, the researcher develops an intimacy to the material, which involves all her senses. For example, a participant's bookcase captured on the video made it clear that she kept many books in her shelves on her ethnic background, which was an indicator of her intellectual involvement in her background as well as her behavioral involvement, which was confirmed by her answers to the interview questions. Zeynep was able to make the connection only after watching her interview several times.

Same Person, Different Environment

In the early 1970s David was part of the ARC (Architecture-Research-Construction) Group in Cleveland, Ohio, doing work in mental hospitals and other total institutions intended to change physical environments. ARC was dedicated to showing that much of what was considered to be non-conforming behavior was in fact a very reasonable reaction to disorienting environments. Recently, David came across some material on the SONY AVC 3400, one of the very first portable video setups available on the consumer market. He recalls a tape made using this equipment showing the same person in two very different environments. The first environment was a noisy, chaotic, hard-surfaced eating area with perhaps two-dozen people literally bouncing off each other. On the tape, the camera focused on one person and recorded her behavior. She shrieked, cursed, and complained. At another time the same person was sitting in a room with David in a stuffed chair and low lighting talking about how if she were ever to get out of the institution she would have to get a job. David asked her to talk about how she would approach a job interview. She thoughtfully described some her limited skills but said that she was a good worker she would do her best. The video was edited to show the contrast between the two different situations. It was barely possible for viewers to believe that it was the same person! Editing the videotapes made the contrast vivid simply by juxtaposing action in one place (wildly noisy, obnoxious) with action in another place (quiet, thoughtful) and thus created a narrative of a person interacting with the environment.

Editing Video was Not Enjoyable—Then

However, it was no easy task to produce this edited video. First, consider what "portable" equipment looked like then. It was weighty and cumbersome, required intricate threading of reel to reel 1/2" video tape, shot only in black and white, and was expensive. But, at the time it seemed miraculous! Editing was another matter. To edit a tape one had to have essentially two very large reel to reel tape consoles, one a "source" tape and the other a "target" tape. There was no way to know exactly where anything was on the source tape other than to run through the material, using a not-very-accurate counter, getting approximately closer and closer to where one wished to start a scene. Then the two tapes had to be electronically synchronized, essentially by running the tape backwards for 5 seconds and then again forwards and at the precise moment cue the source tape by "rolling" it ahead or back so that it started recording into the target tape. Then one had to tinker with the target tape to cue the exact point into which the next scene would enter. Then the whole process was done again. And again... And again... And if there was a "mistake," one essentially started over, having to redo everything at least from the point of the mistake forward.

The changes since the early 1970s SONY AVC 3400 are stunning. The revolution has been in the electronics of video—more compact, more automatically point and shoot, more computer based—but the place to realize these changes is in what we now can do with video. In contemporary society, each of us is better schooled and experienced in sophisticated visual languages than we may imagine—and the digital video technology that is so easily available makes creators of us all. People everywhere are doing video; video cameras are everywhere before every tourist's eye. But there is another, unseen aspect of this technological shift: digital video editing. It is also suddenly common for everyone to do video editing. Think YouTube!

These changes one might say have crept up on us, hardly noticed. Anyone who has done any video fieldwork is liable to have read John Collier's classic book on visual anthropology (1986). There is nothing easy about the techniques advocated in this book. But suddenly technological changes have made the process of digital video editing quite a different matter. We think these technological changes have not only changed digital video editing to make it easier and more intuitive, but also have changed the very nature of what editing is.

People Making Meaning in an Icon of Modern Architecture

We will narrate the steps we, Zeynep and David, went through in editing a joint project at the Salk Institute for Biological Studies in 2004. The Salk Institute for Biological Studies, overlooking the Pacific Ocean in La Jolla, California, is justly famous as an icon of modern architecture. It was designed and built in the early 1960s under an inspired set of circumstances involving two great figures of the mid 20th century: Louis I. Kahn, Architect, and Jonas Salk, Biologist and creator of the first successful polio vaccine. For us, this place was also compelling for the apparent sense of "Place Attachment"—a seminal concept in our field of environmental psychology—amongst people who inhabit this building. It was our desire to learn more about the nature of this attachment to place that led us to create our 54-minute video research documentary, *Living Salk Institute* (Turan & Chapin, 2005).

The moment we start to describe the process of editing digital video, we are on changing grounds. We will describe at this writing in 2008 using video tape but even now current developments in media include cameras with internal hard drives or solid state chips for storage. We assume that readers will make the leap to whatever media is currently in use and smile with us for being so out of date.

Experiencing Editing

In our *Living Salk Institute* project we shot 33 hours of videotape and interviewed 18 people. Our "interviews" might better be called "narratives." They were very open ended in that we asked each person to tell us their own story in their own way. People often chose a particular place in the Salk Institute building that they liked and where they would want to tell their story. Because we were interested in how people make meaning in a place, we occasionally pushed them a bit to explain why they had said what they had said. And we sometimes asked a particular question intended to invite them to delve deeper into a particular issue. For the most part, though, the narratives flowed freely. What is critical is that once we had shot the material and captured it into an editing program, we had to identify it in some way. For instance, we might label the tape with the name of the person being interviewed. (We note that in this work, participants were fine with being identified by name and so we had no need to worry about keeping names confidential.) This very first act of identification becomes the first act of "Categorizing." This first categorization takes place before any processing is done with the tape; before any decisions are made about what will contribute to the narrative or what will not.

Before anything can be done with this tape it must be "captured" into the computer hard drive. In other words, we move the videotape from the camera into the computer so that it is accessible for editing. Remember, we are considering the tape itself as first generation of data. Even inside the computer, it is still the digital original, unaltered first generation!

At this point we want to make sure it is clear that even though we are claiming that we are working with "First Generation," we are *not* claiming that video is inherently more valid than audio or otherwise somehow more true. In any medium whether video, audio, still photographs, or even simply taking notes, we get what we record and this is a selective process. The point we are making here is that in working with video, even after we have "captured" our material into the computer, we still have our first generation of data. The same could be said for digital audio—unless or until it is transcribed into typescript. A transcription or typescript, however, is *not* any longer first generation. The same material might look very different depending on who types it, using what conventions.

In doing social science research, everyone engages in processes that help one to get close to one's data. There are many ways that this takes place. We have already mentioned transcribing recorded interviews. Why is this done? In order to produce a record of an interview which can be manipulated and analyzed. A tape recording is typed out on a computer, word for word (sometimes by the researcher herself, sometimes by a hired assistant). At this point we want to repeat that a transcription of "First Generation" data (the audio recording) is already a "Second Generation." Punctuation is wildly different depending on how the material is heard. Anyone who has done this also knows that it is a process open not only to interpretation but also to outright errors. The transcription is *not* the data; it is a second generation representation of the data.

Given that we are not claiming video as superior per se to audio, we still want to point to the difference between using a video camera in an interview and an audio tape recorder. With a camera it is clear that there is a desire for action. Not so with audio tape. A video camera suggests performance (See Pink, 2004). An audiotape suggests recitation. While there may be situations where one would consider a recitation more to the point (members of an ethnic group recalling their ancestor's social practices, for example), at the Salk Institute we were interested in place and running narration and how people performed their roles.

The Immersive Pleasure of Looking Again

Once the video is captured it is compelling and interesting to watch and hear. One of the handy qualities of working with video in an editing program is that it is possible to "scrub" forward, backward, from any point to any other point. "Scrub" is simply a representation on the computer screen of a "control" that is moved along a timeline with a mouse. So a first claim we want to make about the efficacy of working with video in a computer is how easy it is to access any part of an interview or recording. It is actually a pleasure to sit and watch an interview repeatedly; to notice nuances, to begin to think about what it represents. We sometimes did this together, discussing what we were seeing. But who would want to view 33 hours of raw video? It is interesting, but at the same time tiresome, hard-work, and makes for red eyes. For one thing, this is raw data, which doesn't mean much of anything without some sort of analysis. Once we have looked and listened, we can begin to cut clips. Cutting clips into bins is the initial step of doing an analysis.

Clips in Bins are Fundamental to Video Editing

Making clips is a necessary step to create order. For the 18 Salk Institute interviews, we named clips using first the initials of the participant and then a brief excerpt of what the person was saying at the time, for example, "K.M. He was our spiritual guide." The word "clips" comes from film editing, where a scissors is used to physically clip one piece of film from another. For digital video editing the word is a metaphor. It also is represented with both a title and a visual image.

To organize clips we categorize them in "Bins" which are also folders. Each bin gets a name. To name something means reflecting on what it is, what it represents, who is in it, what is being said or done… Order comes from sorting into the bins that which is similar and that which is different. What is there just some of and what is there a lot of? What can be folded together and what needs to be separated apart? The act of labeling and sorting is a continuation of an analysis.

Categories Form the Basis of an Analysis

Naming the bins is not so simple. We often named a bin something which we thought would be a significant theme and then later as we collected more clips we found that we had to either eliminate the bin or change the name of the bin. And then, changing the name made us take some clips out of one bin and put them into another. Step by step our analysis evolved.

It seems perfectly reasonable to think that all data analysis in social science research is about forming categories. Categories are essential structuring elements in analyzing data. We will use some examples from *Living Salk Institute*.

One of our Analytical Categories: "Love"

The repeated emotional portrayal of people's affection for this place led us to create a category called "Love." This category is directly connected to the concepts of "Place Attachment," central to our interests, which was mentioned in the introduction to the *Living Salk Institute* project (See Altman & Low, 1992). In fact, the strength of the expression of this sense of connection was intense. For instance, a member of the Salk family recalled his own childhood memories by saying while standing on the roof of the building and referring to it, "Things sort of fade and you end up forgetting a lot of the stuff... It's nice just to have one place that stays stable that you can sort of come and reconnect with."

Another Analytical Category: "Reverence for Jonas Salk"

During an interview our attention may be scattered or fragmented. We are in a new environment, concerned about finding the good existing light, and that whether or not the camera is aiming at a right angle to make a good composition (or follow and anticipate action) and that sound we want to hear is being recorded above whatever background ambient sound we want to exclude. But feeding the interview into the computer and sitting and working away at it provides a more direct relation to the material. We can stop the material at any point and look closer. We can go back and forth. We can give the same clip several different names if we see several different ways of seeing it. It was in this state of immersion that we began to see something that we had not anticipated in how emotionally connected our participants seemed to be when they spoke of Jonas Salk. It was as if he were part of the building. In fact, he was quoted to us as having said "If you touch this building, you touch my dream." It was from comprehending this, only after repeated viewings, that we formed the category, "Reverence for Jonas Salk."

We want to take the reader more deeply into this experience. Several of the people we interviewed had been personally close to Jonas Salk. The word "legacy" appeared in most all the interviews. But it was not until after we had looked at one particular interview repeatedly on the screen that we noticed the glint of a tear in an eye. As we repeatedly watched this part of the interview we had a new appreciation of how powerfully meaningful this moment was for recalling Jonas Salk's acts. By moving one frame at a time through an enlarged sequence of still frames it dawned on us that we were seeing a tear appear and then disappear. Seeing the tear caused us to reexamine all the other interviews, looking for enactments of deep emotion. Because of immersion we found this same emotional connection expressed in different ways, over and over. Of course both this clip and the clip mentioned earlier ("K.M. He was our spiritual guide") were placed in the bin that we named "Reverence for Jonas Salk."

The 54-minute video documentary that we constructed out of this process was in a sense, "our" narrative. We went through a process of analysis that involved cutting clips and creating bins and categories, and yet we never lost touch with the narratives of our participants. We always worked with first generation data.

Another Project: How Kids Deal with Chaos

David is currently working with "Project Stretch," a complicated set of programs, computers, teachers, and middle school level kids, all directed towards introducing collaborative work and critical thinking into schools. Videotaping a particular example of this program in action at a middle school in the Bedford Stuyvesant neighborhood of Brooklyn, New York, it was obvious from the first session that chaos (in the form of harsh surfaces reflecting noise, high energy levels of kids, occasional school personnel wandering through, neighborhood traffic noises) was an issue. Video taped material here was first cut into events through the course of about five months of taping. Then cuts were named by who appeared in them, using names of teachers and kids. Next, the same material was re-cut into categories formed to describe what was happening within the clip. Example of these categories are, "Focusing Intently," "Collaborating," "Gaming," and "Explaining." This video is now being edited into a brief exposition of how kids deal with the chaos mentioned earlier. In particular, by crossing categories the possibility has emerged of depicting different styles of learning. "Styles of learning" include creating a local personal space (humming, drumming, using earphones, talking to oneself, or wearing a hat with earflaps), body postures (sitting, standing and reclining way back horizontally), and roles (novice, expert, adept at one knowledge but not another). One revelatory moment in the video is a clip depicting a young computer user apparently deep into an interaction with a project, eyes focused intently, suddenly responding in thoughtful detail to a question asked by a teacher to another student at a distance. Obviously this person was quite capable of both concentrating intensely and still being tuned into his surroundings. The chaos was obvious from the start but what editing video has helped to reveal is the multiple ways kids have developed to deal with their surroundings.

What's Different about Doing Video from a Participant's Perspective?

Participants know how to perform in a situation with a video camera present. Performance and contemplation are significant aspects of a person's developmental narrative, especially if they can see their performance and reflect on it. Individuals understand the world and locate themselves through filters of familial, community, and cultural narratives (Rajiva, 2006, p. 168). Narratives give form to one's self-perception, and they lay the groundwork for how one is perceived. The reflexive character of research is designed to improve the richness of the analysis, while maximizing the participant involvement. Reflexivity, a source of insight and critical examination of the research process, is a significant aspect of feminist research, and it has been an integral part of the data analysis in terms of locating the researcher within the research. As Elizabeth Wheatley observes: Ethnographic relations, practices and representations, as well as the metaphors we use to make sense of them, are contextually contingent—their character is shaped by who we look at, from where we look, and why we are looking in the first place (Wheatley, 1994, p. 422).

This idea about the participant's perspective is true regarding video in general. How can we think about this in relation to editing and the point that we have been trying to make about immersion? Editing is a process that happens over time and moves generally from the grosser level (all the footage shot) to the more refined level. This iterative process is an opening for participants to be involved. In our practice we always prepare rough cuts for each participant's interview and distribute these DVDs for review (This is inherent to the two-part consent process that we describe in Appendix A). We wish that we could say that this has been a rich, interactive process, but it has not. What we have gotten is an occasional objection to a particular statement by the participant, usually something said in an unguarded moment that the participant would now find embarrassing. We have always complied with the participants' wishes and removed unwanted statement or moments.

Next time we hope to get more active participation with wide open discussing of ideas. It is easy, for instance, to imagine sitting with a participant and her or his rough cut video, seeking discussion and comment all the way through. This might even be done with a group. Wouldn't it be interesting to video tape this process and then do it all over again—the participant comments on the participant commenting on the participant's performance... Well, you get the idea.

What's Different about Doing Video from a Researcher's Perspective?

Video ethnography as an investigative tool is linked epistemologically to the research question at hand. The video documents verbal and non-verbal behavior of participants in their environments. It portrays communication, interaction, and emotions. Video is also an effective way to show the nuances of human interaction, styles of expression, body movements, gestures, and sense of a place. Pink argues that "the video interview allows informants the opportunity to use established narratives that depend on visual as well as spoken experience to structure their performance of self" (2004, p. 63). Using video ethnography in this research helped us capture movement in original form and contextualize the behavior. This contextualization was crucial in detecting complex nuances in the participant's direct or indirect experience of the Institute as a place and how he or she moves through places, interacts with others, etc.

There is no question that using video generates data beyond other approaches because of the performance that video engenders. Also, there is no question that using video produces data that would otherwise, in the heat of the moment, be lost. We have used an example of a tear in an eye. We know that we did not notice this tear when we were there in the moment.

Having said this, we also recognize that we do not know just what to do with this sort of nuance. This uncertainty bridges between video as a mode of research inquiry and video as an artistic expression. We want to continue to work across this division and in fact, it is nice to have this challenge. Being immersed in editing helps us see things but it doesn't tell us what to do with them.

Finally, What's Different about Doing Video from Audience Perspective?

Just as participants are capable to immediately take familiar roles in view of a video camera, so too are audiences immediately competent at reading the situation in view. This contemporary view of audiences is well described by Sturken and Cartwright (2001), especially in chapters titled "Viewers Make Meaning" and "Spectatorship, Power and Knowledge." In a certain sense, audiences are participants, also.

Because video editing happens over time, there is an opportunity for audience previewing. We regularly ask people who are unfamiliar with our work to view our rough cuts and discuss their reactions. We do this, first, because even at the crudest level of editing we want to know what an audience "gets." Part of the art of editing is for the editor to become more and more skillful at predicting an audience reaction, but even the most skillful editor continues to learn from an audience's reaction[2]. We emphasize that digital video editing makes it easy to have an audience review.

Of course, more traditional forms of social science publication such as journal articles are also subject to review. Research authors themselves may have gone through years of mentoring as well as the experience of submitting articles for review by journal editors and book chapter editors. One of the differences between these traditional revues and "previewing" video at various stages of editing is that the traditional forms are usually open only to a narrow band of experts.

---

[2] Ralph Rosenblum and Robert Karen (1979) explain this beautifully in *When the Shooting Stops…The Cutting Begins: A Film Editor's History.*

A second reason for asking audiences to preview our work is that people who are willing to perform as an audience automatically take on a critical stance. The reaction to early drafts is often difficult for a researcher to endure. In fact, we sense that many videographers tend to be unwilling to show their work until they consider it to be complete and beyond change. We, on the other hand, see showing our incomplete work as an opportunity to engage in yet another narrative and yet another form of immersion.

It's a Wrap

In this chapter, we presented the advantages of using video in social science research and the processes of video-editing. It is not our intention, however, to suggest that video is a superior research method to other available methods. For that, in our concluding remarks, we want to leave you, our reader, with an example that will question the applicability of video in research on the role of objects in displaced peoples lives mentioned earlier in this chapter. The example comes from a discussion of the work *Objects of Legacy* (Turan, 2008) in a Visual Research Methods class. The students were asked to compare how they would react to two different presentations of the same data. They were first asked to listen to a clip from an interview read by the interviewer. They, then, were asked to watch the video of the same snippet. In the two-minute video, a middle-aged woman whose family experienced displacement tells the story of her grandmother and the ring she inherited from her. She explains the meaning of the ring, and how she took care of it until the ring was stolen when her apartment was burglarized. In the classroom discussion following the reading of the text and watching the video, some students said they preferred the video because they could see the emotional state of the woman, which enriched their understanding of the loss she experienced. One student, on the other hand, had a different reaction. She said she preferred the text to the video. She found the video distracting with the background music, the woman's beauty, her make-up, and the surrounding environment—her personal things in the apartment. We think the student's comment was invaluable in considering video research because it challenges the use of video in the presentation of research data to an audience. As it is developing, video vision research needs to address issues like this one by focusing on different case studies. Even though we start our next project with the questions of applicability and presentation, we argue that digital video has at least one advantage over other social science research methods: the opportunity for immersion, meaning, that is, the maximum involvement with the data.

References

Altman, I. & Low, S. (Eds.). (1992). *Place attachment.* New York: Plenum Press.

Collier, J., Jr. (1947). *Visual anthropology: Photography as a research method.* US: Holt, Rinehart, and Winston.

Guba, E. G. & Lincoln, Y. S. (2005). Paradigmatic controversies, contradictions, and emerging confluences. In N. K. Denzin & Y. S. Lincoln (Eds.) *The sage handbook of qualitative research* (3rd ed, pp. 191-216). Thousands Oaks, CA: Sage.

Pink, S. (2004). Performance, self-representation and narrative: Interviewing with video. In C. J. Pole (Ed.) *Seeing is believing? Approaches to visual research* (pp. 61-77). Oxford: Elsevier.

Popper, K. R. (2002). *The open society and its enemies* (5th ed). New York: Routledge.

Rajiva, M. (2006). Brown girls, white worlds: Adolescence and the making of racialized selves. *The Canadian Review of Sociology and Anthropology, 43*(2), 165-183.

Relieu, M., Zouinar, M. & La Valle, N. (2007). At home with video cameras. *Home Cultures, 4*(1), 45-68.

Rosenblum, R., & Karen, R. (1979). *When the shooting stops…The cutting begins: A film editor's history.* New York: Penguin Books.

Sturken, M. & Cartwright, L. (2001). *Practices of looking: An introduction to visual culture.* Oxford: Oxford University Press.

Turan, Z. (2008). *Objects of legacy: Material objects of displaced people.* Unpublished doctoral dissertation, City University of New York, New York.

Turan, Z. & Chapin, Z. (Directors). (2005). *Living Salk Institute.* [Motion Picture]. New York.

Wheatley, E. E. (1994). How can we engender ethnography with a feminist imagination? *Women's Studies International Forum, 17*(4), 403-416.

PART II

ZOOM OUT: A WIDER PRAXIS

CHAPTER FIVE

WATCHING TRANSFORMATION
IN STUDENT-MADE VIDEOS

LARA MARGARET BEATY

Video has increasingly been used as a tool for social science research, yet the potential for video cameras to reveal the activity of the person standing *behind* the camera has been largely overlooked. The fact that videos provide a record of the willful intentions of camera operators as well as the events in front of the camera is more likely to be viewed as criticism of research than as a tool for furthering our understanding. This chapter reports on an approach to studying the actions of videographers as a way to understand learning, development, and social relations among high school students. It began with a simple premise first used by Worth and Adair (1972) and furthered by Bellman and Jules-Rosette (1977). They recognized that the decisions a person makes while creating a film or video reflect the person's relations to and understandings of the events being recorded:

> No matter how 'disinterested' the observer filmmaker or videoist is in the events taking place, he [or she] perceives them from an intentional perspective located in the 'here and now' of the recording situation. . . . The camera operator throughout the process of filming or taping makes definitive choices of what to shoot, when to turn the camera on and off, and where to use zoom, pan, dolly, crane, and follow shots. These decisions, whether they are made for aesthetic considerations or to posit a particular feature of the setting, are intentional choices. (Bellman & Jules-Rosette, 1977, p. 3)

The choices include all that videographers do with the camera as well as the selection of accessories to use, people to work with, and planning tools such as scripts and storyboards. Another set of choices then become available during the editing phase of production. These choices can emerge in the moment or result from careful planning but must involve the videographer's relationship to both the aims and context of production. They are indications of dynamic student-school relationships when the video production occurs as part of a school course. This chapter briefly presents my strategies for analyzing informant-made videos as a way to understand specific student-school relationships and to study "cognitive change" as a social process (Newman, Griffin, & Cole, 1989).

My methodology is based on and intended to elaborate upon a sociocultural perspective of development. As such, I assume that learning and development are not equivalent and that learning brings about development (Vygotsky, 1978). The problem is that learning and development are interwoven. Moreover, the necessarily social nature of these processes impacts learning and development in ways that were not considered by Vygotsky. Power, agency, resistance, cooperation, identity, alliances, and affections shape what and how learning and development occur (Diamondstone, 2002; Gutierrez, Baquedano-Lopez, & Tejada, 1999; Holland, Lachicotte, Skinner, & Cain,1998; Litowitz, 1993; 1997). The processes of learning, development, and social relations are thoroughly intertwined, challenging our capacity for description and explanation. Studying these processes and the relations between them requires a methodology that reveals situated activity over extended periods such that subjective experiences are available for analysis. Informant-made video offers this opportunity and many others for research.

Schools are actually making the use of informant-made videos easier for researchers by adopting video production as part of many school curriculums. Dozens of organizations and individuals are calling for the integration of video production in one form or another (i.e. Miller & Borowicz, 2003; Goodman, 2003; & the American Film Institute). Programs frequently pursue reforms for reaching disenfranchised youth including media education, multimedia literacy, technology integration, media arts, and vocational training. Goodman described three dominant strands of media education for youth: technology integration, media literacy, and community media arts (2003, p. 10). The changes in technology that allow new and cheaper uses of video, however, clearly contribute to the rise in programs. Regardless of how video production has entered a school, I have found that the activity necessarily shifts social relations so that students have increased power and the possibility of shifting long-standing relationships (Beaty, 2005). Most importantly, though not necessarily appreciated, the process of editing requires the kind of reflection that is a major goal of secondary and post-secondary education.

Simultaneously, researchers are already using video as a way of documenting school activity. Goldman-Segall (1998) pioneered video ethnography of schools as a way of accessing processes and giving students a voice in research, but she was typically still the one holding the camera. Teachers and the teachers who teach them are also using video as a way of demonstrating exemplary lessons and critiquing one's own practices (Schwartz & Hartman, 2007; Sherin, 2007). Video production has been introduced as part of education, and it has entered the classroom as a tool to document school activity for both researchers and practitioners. By combining these two uses, researchers can shift the focus from teacher practices to the reception and use of practices by students.

The first section of this chapter describes how video production can reveal learning and development. Then I shift the focus to the real-time events of the recording sessions and discuss my strategies for revealing social relations. The role of video cameras is taken up in the next section because the camera introduces changes that are fundamental to research with informant-made videos and help demonstrate the interdependence of learning, development, and social relations. In this section, Latour's (1996) challenge to view artifacts as participants or *actants* is placed squarely in the middle of the analysis. Finally, an analysis of a brief video segment will be presented. I have thus far conducted research in four schools under diverse circumstances and have begun exploring a new program. My analysis demonstrates the effectiveness of informant-made videos— particularly for revealing and shifting power relations—and indicates directions to be pursued. This chapter intends to demonstrate the value of informant-made videos for social science research and to highlight possible uses.

A Method For Seeing (And Hearing) Situated Learning And Development

My use of video was initially inspired by Worth and Adair (1972), who sought expressions of "cognitive styles" in informant-made films. They taught Navajo informants how to use movie cameras and edit film, seeking to use their informants' lack of experience with film as a way of capturing culturally specific ways of making films. The study was based on the premise that movies were in many ways like language and would reflect the culture of their makers, believing that the Sapir-Whorf hypothesis would be supported. Worth (1981) later backed away from asserting a strong resemblance between language and film, but the analysis nevertheless revealed patterns of usage that reflected cultural meanings and practices as well as the subjective experiences of individuals. Worth and Adair, for instance, found more movement in the Navajo films as well as a lack of close ups, yet one man's film—while sharing these characteristics—was distinct from the others because of his distinct relationship with the community. Their analysis examined their informants' choices in terms of *context* and *code*.

The contexts of video production programs vary enormously, creating subcultures of video production that relate in diverse ways to the larger cultures of video and schooling. The contexts that Worth and Adair (1972) studied, however, were specific to the productions: "Context" referred to the *process* of production and, applied to school programs, involves many types of characteristics that reflect program culture and individual or group differences. Video characteristics that I have considered include the recording location, the selection of equipment, the type and amount of planning, the choice of who to work with, the manner and level of labor division, and instances of instruction and imitation. The manner of participation has thus far revealed the most about cognitive change. Obviously, students will participate more or less, but the choices of *how* to participate provide more information than how much. Students find numerous ways of working with one another, and programs structure these relations in different ways. Students are sometimes required to select roles that imitate professional television studios, but some students will stick rigidly to their roles while others will compete for or more evenly share ownership and creative input. Similarly, many students will want to spend their time in front of the camera while others find joy in standing behind the camera (Beaty, 2005; Worth & Adair, 1972). Changes in participation are the most salient aspect of observable changes. The interest a student shows rarely remains consistent, and changes in participation—whether increasing, decreasing, or showing a shift in the type of activity—are the clearest indication of change. Often, obstacles to learning are revealed. One young man, for instance, recorded the entire project on his own and literally paced behind the students who were editing his work. He seemed to feel trapped by the division of labor and did not know how to negotiate continued participation. By contrast, many students shared all phases of the work, learning from one another on the way. The choice of how to participate defines the areas in which learning and development may occur, but participation itself often represents progress.

The similarity of video to language, which Worth and Adair (1972) discussed in terms of "code," is particularly meaningful for the study of learning and development. The most important similarity is that language and video production are ways of communicating; they are expressions of our experiences and thoughts. Both have the potential for being more or less planned—more or less "intentional"—and analysis can focus on overt characteristics such as subject matter and more abstruse characteristics such as the patterns of camera actions that resemble grammar (Worth and Adair, 1972, p. 45). Video production is less like language, though, than it is like writing. Teaching media literacy is increasingly a priority for schools, and the endeavor resembles and compliments traditional literacy (Hobbes, 2004). There are multiple points at which writers and videographers can choose to act spontaneously or to engage in careful planning, but the writing/recording phase can usually be distinguished from the rewriting/editing phase. In video, these phases are more distinct because they use different tools and involve different actions (Beaty, 2005, p. 188). Videographers initially record shots, referred to as "cademes" by Worth and Adair (1972), and then transform these into "edemes" when they sit down at a computer to capture video clips for editing. Edemes are created by trimming, dividing, or otherwise altering cademes. The techniques used, whether used in the original cademe or inserted during the editing process, and the connections between edemes give the edited video a meaningful structure. While Worth (1981) decided that this did not truly qualify as grammar, understanding the use and meaning of different techniques clearly requires learning and development. I argue that learning becomes development when techniques that were taught or observed are successfully used to communicate—when they become an established part of a videographer's repertoire. The shift from a pan being a simple movement of the camera that shows the other side of the room to something that carries meaning and furthers the message of the project is development. Video production thus enables researchers to trace the use of techniques and allows broad involvement in defining when its use has been mastered.

My forays into examining the learning and development of high school students have not yet systematically traced techniques into final projects. My explorations have thus far taken three different approaches: The first examines interview techniques over time, the second compares different projects according to an array of qualities, and the third makes use of the connections between cademes and edemes. The examination of changes in interviewing actions is the most straight forward and the clearest application of following a technique over time. Of my completed research (Beaty, 2005), only one group had a series of interviews, and despite a wide range of contexts for the interviews, the questions and camera work varied little. Because the project was never edited, there was no opportunity to consider their selection of utterances from interviews. In short, there was no observable transformation in relation to interviewing. In a new analysis of projects with interviews as a central part of their activity, I am finding that some refinement of questions is common, and I will examine the edited work to consider whether students' selection of interview segments shows an understanding of their meaning.

My second approach employed an exploration of the following characteristics in both cademes and edemes: the clarity of the message, coherence between shots, agency in initiating and influencing events, technological proficiency, aesthetics, and self-expression (Beaty, 2005). My conclusion was that the strength of a characteristic is highly dependent on the context. I had initially expected to find a closer resemblance between edemes and cademes in the strongest projects but discovered that there are two distinct approaches to video production: one with extensive planning and one that involves exploration or experimentation, and then selects and connects disparate clips during the editing phase. Many projects mix the processes to varying extents. While both approaches have clear merits[1], the level of exploration changed the relations between cademes and edemes. Cademes tended to be altered more when there was considerable exploration, and their number was larger.

Projects in all contexts showed self-expression, but the expression of other characteristics were so connected to assignments, topics, locations, and equipment that they reflected little about what one might consider the "abilities" of the students. Students showed a clear shift in priorities as the contexts changed. The only opportunity I had to compare multiple projects by the same videographers demonstrated most clearly that some qualities will become the focus and others will drop to the background depending on the topic the students choose and the context of the production. With

---

[1] Exploration seemed to lead some students to have more agency and more awareness of the effect of camera techniques, while planning made the process easier and faster as well as having students work on traditional literacy skills.

more consistency across projects or more projects, some form of "literacy development" is likely to be observable, but the connection to the contexts will continue to shape the meaning of changes. In theory, expertise leads to less dependence on the context, and therefore, greater consistency across contexts.

My third analysis examines the events within cademes and the subsequent selection of edemes (Beaty, 2007), but the actual application of the method is dependent on the project. In the project to which I have applied it, two Native-American youth wandered their school, engaging in entirely spontaneous recording and later transforming a small selection of unrelated images into a digital art project with a message about power. The transformation of cademes into edemes and their placement in the completed project demonstrate meaning-making as it occurred. Furthermore, the full meaning of the final project was only evident in an examination of the cademes. This analysis provides evidence that concepts arose in moments but developed in the act of connecting otherwise distinct events, much as Vygotsky (1994) described. The images were intentionally connected and set to music by the students. The way that concrete events were meaningfully associated would not otherwise have been observable. The cademes captured real-time events in a way that allowed me to trace them from their origin to the point at which they became a sharable artifact. Video affords the observation of meaning-making as videographers select events from their cademes, connect them, and present them as parts of a whole.

Cademes and edemes, however, are not the only artifacts created during production that give researchers entry into cognitive processes. Storyboards, scripts, and early edits reveal the videographers' actions, intentions, and changes in both. I am currently exploring an analysis of different points in the editing phase as well as the selection and placement of cademes as a way to evaluate student and course progress. Though concept formation is not visible in these projects, they are audible as students struggle with how best to use other people's statements to assert their own understanding of the topic. As I continue this analysis, I will collect written work. The processes of planning, recording, and editing a video thus allow multiple points for researchers to enter into the production process and therefore into activity that is not easily observed.

The dynamic relationship between learning and development (Vygotsky, 1978) within the social and material contexts of production are revealed by tracing the choices students make during video production. Video is a form of literacy that documents many stages and steps in the composition process—without distracting or costly research procedures—making learning and development uniquely visible and audible. This use of student-made videos reveals many actions during the process of composing a video. The greatest value of pursuing this methodology, however, is in how videography maintains a visible and audible connection to the "real" world while recording the actual flow of time. If, as Bakhtin (1986) suggests, the words of others become our own, then videos have the ability to demonstrate this literally as the words and actions of a friend, teacher, or principal are reshaped to tell the videographer's message. Moreover, the work must involve some relation to and negotiation with the community as a student or students pursue activity within school that is not normally part of their schooling.

The Real-World, Real-Time Meaning Of Video

Video literacy is different from traditional literacy in important and useful ways. "Moving images" in any format are closer to our experiences of the world (Gibson, 1986) and therefore do not have the same level of structure imposed upon them. There is no real grammar to constrain camera use, though there are many other structures to constrain actions. Videographers are in many ways making a record of their experience of events, and by shifting our focus from the communicative function of video to the implicit messages within the recording context, we can examine the actions of the videographer as part of a dialogue with the events occurring around the camera. Bellman and Jules-Rosette (1977) took up this potential and shifted the analysis from questions about cognition to questions about social relations. They used film and video with Kpelle and Bapostolo communities in Africa and stressed the actions of the camera operators as a way to capture the informant's understanding of and relationship to the events being recorded. In short, culture as experienced by informants was revealed in how they related to and displayed cultural practices. Bellman and Jules-Rosette compared their use to photographic elicitation (p. 15), a method of using photographs to stimulate an informant's conceptions of what is portrayed. With video, however, informants can demonstrate attitudes and concepts in how they use the camera that they may not entirely be aware of or that would be less likely or more difficult to talk about. Photographic elicitation draws forth comments that might not arise in a standard interview because it provides people with something to relate to, but by putting people behind the camera, their relationships with what is in front of the camera are displayed in real time as the structures of events and places lead to particular recording choices. The material reality of bodies, furniture, and walls becomes part of an analyzable dialogue, facilitating an ecological perspective (Barab & Roth, 2006). Every explicit and implicit choice the videographer makes as well as reactions to the videographer become available for analysis. Additionally, one can still return, as I have, to have videographers describe their reasoning and reflect on why they made particular choices. The major challenge for this analysis becomes one of selecting from and interpreting the many choices that occur.

The key to structuring my exploration of social relations was obtained from de Certeau's (1984) distinction between *strategies* and *tactics*. Accordingly, a *strategy* is activity from a position of power, and it is associated with the designation and ownership of places. Power arises in defining what is appropriate behavior within a particular *place*. A place and its power are "borrowed" when one aligns oneself with the activity structure of the place. A *tactic*, on the other hand, is activity from a position of weakness and is associated with time in that a tactic must take advantage of moments in time to either use the structure to achieve alternate ends or to subvert the meaning of a context entirely. I have found that the video camera has a tactical ability to change the meaning of places, providing new ways for people with less power in the social structure, such as students, to have an enhanced status and new opportunities to designate meanings and exploit structures (Beaty, 2005). This power will be discussed further in the next section, but the result is that students can choose between strategic or tactical uses of the camera. De Certeau, moreover, offers an ecological interpretation that equates dialogues with people and dialogues with the material environment that facilitate a systematic analysis and draws forth the role of places and artifacts in shaping events. The difference is exemplified by a comparison of standing atop the World Trade Center versus walking through the streets.

> To be lifted to the summit of the World Trade Center is to be lifted out of the city's grasp. One's body is no longer clasped by the streets that turn and return it according to an anonymous law; nor is it possessed, whether as player or played, by the rumble of so many differences and by the nervousness of New York traffic. When one goes up there, he [or she] leaves behind the mass that carries off and mixes up in itself any identity of authors or spectators. (de Certeau, 1984, p. 92)

A video camera, like a skyscraper, gives the spectator access to the plan—to the structure—underlying a place if the videographer chooses to use it.

The example of looking out over the city versus walking in the streets has guided my interpretation of videos as much as the consideration of power. The use of power is clear when students use cameras to establish topics and control who can speak, but de Certeau's (1984) more symbolic analysis creates a clear difference between displaying a scene and recording the subjective experience in terms of power. A videographer can literally constrain the actions of an individual or symbolically assert power by turning the camera away or inserting a defining narration. He or she could show their lack of power by following the instructions of the person in front of the camera or by distorting how the unknowing person looks. This is less about how much power a student has than in how they express the power they have or that the camera has lent them. Strategies and tactics offer the tool of comparing diverse actions according to a single dimension.

The distinction between constraining actions and more symbolic uses of power, nevertheless, creates the need for an additional dimension: A strategic view of a school has a very different impact in the moment than turning the camera away from someone who is talking. Similarly, a student acting from a position of weakness who resists an authority uses their power quite differently from a student who chooses to cooperate with the authority. Hodge and Kress (1988) examined the messages of *power* and solidarity in their social semiotics, and I find that the added dimension furthers the analysis. It provided a solution when I first attempted an analysis of three young men who used the camera to relate to people in very different ways. One was aggressive and dominating as he challenged his classmates in on-camera conversations. His use of power was high and his solidarity low. Another young man shifted his position more often, but it was particularly an interview of a vice principal that caught my attention. He had written the questions down and handed the paper to the administrator silently and then proceeded to record his answers in an extreme close-up shot, with parts of his face drifting in and out of the frame. He recorded the interview from what was clearly a position of weakness, but the awkward image asserted a mocking critique, thus his use of power was low as was his solidarity. The third young man was quite different. When the first student was aggressively asking him about who he was, he turned his answers into ways of sharing qualities with the first youth. He so effectively diffused the aggression of his interviewer that I sought a category to draw out these differences.

I, therefore, define solidarity as drawing on similarities or the accepted meanings of a place, while accentuating differences or opposing some structural influence suggests a lack of solidarity. This added dimension structures the distinction between the power of benevolent leadership and that of tyranny on the side of power, and from a position of weakness, it distinguishes between cooperation and resistance. For instance, a student recorded from a distance as another student ran from school security. The overarching view of the student and security was strategic but no one's behavior was constrained, and solidarity was expressed simply in the videographer not revealing the hiding student. On the other hand, the videographer turned to the school security as they walked across the distant lawn and referred to them as "bozos," thus clearly expressing with whom he was and was not in solidarity. Another videographer showed both his lack of power and high solidarity when he followed a teacher's instructions to move closer to his interviewee or another who turned the camera to look at what someone was indicating should be recorded, while others have ignored or refused such suggestions.

Power and solidarity thus offer a framework for the analysis of social relations that has guided my interpretation of student-made video, and I have found it a useful lens for viewing student-school relationships among diverse videos. I had originally planned, however, a systematic application—conceived of as codes for each "event" in terms of their use of power and solidarity—but found that establishing specific actions that carried a clear meaning was more complicated than anticipated. For instance, a slow pan, in theory, suggests an overarching view that is strategic and shows solidarity with the structure of the place in that in reinforces what the place already contains. A walk with the camera down a school hallway, on the other hand, captures the odd movements of a pedestrian and is tactical in how it demonstrates the experience of the place yet simultaneously affirms the structure by using the walls to shape its path. The problem is in applying this distinction in a way that is consistent and meaningful. When, for instance, is a movement of the camera to the left or right a "pan" with strategic implications and when is it more of a shift or turn to look at something, thus recording the experience of the videographer? Would even asking the student make the original intentions clear? And what of the walking through a hallway? One student, when defining his rather strange walk, indicated that he was showing what it was like to be drunk. The camera turned from wall to wall and across a drinking fountain in what was clearly a tactic, but was it expressing high or low solidarity? With the additional information from the student and the information that students were routinely sent home from this boarding school for alcohol usage, he seems to express a lack of solidarity as the walls cause visual confusion rather than organization. Additionally, the idea of a camera tilt has clear symbolic significance: Looking up shows a lack of power and looking down dominates, but when none of the students seem to actively seek a tilt and do so only because they are above or below (taller or shorter) than what or whom they are recording, the apparent lack of intent suggests a lack of meaning. Meaning could still exist in its effect and it may still reflect social relations, but can this be treated as equivalent to actions that are clearly intentional? A whole range of experiments seem possible to remove some of this ambiguity, yet the fact remains that the meaning of a particular action is defined by the context and those involved in it, such that the meaning may not be consistent and should not be assumed to be so.

Many events, furthermore, contain contradictory actions. These demonstrate that contradictions seem to be a routine part of social relations. Take the striking example of teasing, which is common among adolescents and which is raised to new heights when a video camera is exploited for this purpose. Youth tease one another to flirt, to get to know someone, and to humiliate, but it is not always clear what the effect is and is certainly not clear what the intentions are. A. Marjanovic-Shane (personal communication, March 24, 2008) suggested that teasing involves negotiation between the participants about whether the "frame" (Goffman, 1974) is defined as play or not, but I would argue that the ambiguity itself is purposeful. One of my future plans is to use such shots to stimulate a conversation with the videographer as well as gather additional instances of teasing to document patterns. I will present the analysis of one instance of teasing in more detail as a way to demonstrate the analysis, but first the camera itself requires further attention.

Putting The Camera Into The Analysis

The power of video cameras was alluded to but not discussed above, yet it is an essential part of the analysis because the videos are not a recording of how people normally interact within their communities. The existence of the camera and the act of recording fundamentally changes a person's actions. Cameras become additional *participants* in school activities (Latour, 1996). They mediate activity and are often the cause of the particular events being recorded. As a participant that is often overlooked, artifacts like video cameras carry their own histories and assert their own ideologies (Latour, 1996). At their most basic, cameras have particular *affordances* (Gibson, 1986) that limit what can be done while promoting some actions (for a discussion of how development is both constrained and promoted, see Valsiner's (1997) descriptions of the *zone of free movement* and the *zone of promoted action*). Latour argued that people and artifacts equally participate in events—that both are *actants*, capable of action only through the other. Viewing the camera as an actant conceptualizes the agency of a video production as an emergent property of the interaction between videographer and video camera. The interdependence of actants is particularly clear in video production. First, the video production could not occur without having both a camera and a camera operator. Even if the camera is placed on a tripod, someone had to put it there and turn it on. The volition behind video activity therefore requires all the participating actants; the events to be recorded are equally essential. By taking the position that video cameras, videographers, actors, sets, and props are all actants in the video production, we are roused to interrogate the data—to question what it really means—given that we have not in anyway captured "normal" activity. We are no longer studying students but *camera-student entities*.

Latour (1996) stressed that artifacts have the ability to bring the actions of distant people into the immediate interaction, thus connecting macro and micro social relations. Distant actions are embodied and therefore participate in the immediate ones. In schools, the furniture that establishes seating and work patterns was chosen with some idea of how classes function, and the video equipment was selected with a particular conception of video production. Even posters on the walls maintain the presence of other activities and the ideologies behind them. Artifacts thus maintain the connection to the world outside the immediate context. They further maintain a stability over time because most materials do not frequently change.

Video cameras, however, are actants that change activities and relationships in particularly noticeable ways because they are not routinely present. They also have the power to reveal the participation of other artifacts. Video production courses are often designed to bring about change, and I have found that fundamental changes in school activity arise (Beaty, 2005; Beaty, in preparation). Students must get up out of their seats and are granted permission, because of the camera, to move around the classroom and campus and even into the streets in ways that they are never allowed at other times. This movement alone offers opportunities to create new relationships and to change old ones. The camera and student form an entity as they are empowered to interact with the school in new ways: going places, asking questions, or focusing on details never observed before. This new found freedom can, however, stress teachers and school staff who are not comfortable with their loss of control, and it can be uncomfortable for students or even make them more aware of their usual passivity.

A student videographer has the power to ask questions and designate topics. The student can choose who speaks and when. The videographer is often the center of attention, disrupting routines and teachers' plans. Rooms can be rearranged. Most importantly, videographers must become visibly active—sitting at a desk simply does not suffice—and can choose to use the power of the camera to shift the social structure, to change their position within the social structure, or to affirm the way things are usually done. Nevertheless, some decisions constrain students' exploitation of cameras. Tripods, for instance, limit the formation of camera-student entities. Similarly, the use of lights, sets, and microphones further distribute agency and constrain the affordances of camera-student entities. Even the size of a camera can change the ease of forming a pair. Thus the video camera is an actant that, like all actants, is constrained by its context and local meanings.

The potential for and promotion of change reveals the constraints on typical social relations as well as suggesting individual differences in the use of power and solidarity. Students in actuality rarely misuse cameras, and teachers can effectively mediate or more directly constrain use. One established teacher of a vocational program emphasized safety and protection of the equipment, which was accepted by students so that they limited their own production activity. Nevertheless conflicts do emerge and boundaries are tested and occasionally crossed. There are the relatively minor or symbolic uses of power that cause tension. One set of students used the camera to insist that a teacher reveal his first name when he clearly did not want to. The same set of students filmed through the windows of locked doors to exceed the environmental constraints. Cameras were used as hallpasses by students and teachers alike, replacing written excuses to be out of the classroom. These reveal patterns of normal student-school relationships by drawing out recognition of what has changed. The more serious problems and those that relate more to specific student-school relationships also hint at how severe the misuses of video cameras could be: A prop gun led to a conflict with school security that could have led to a tragedy; a male student "violated" a female student by recording inside her shirt; and one student's act of pointing a camera at another student led to a fight, which in the end led to the expulsion of both students.

Serious problems are possible but rare; these examples serve as a warning for teachers and researchers alike. From the researcher's perspective, Bradley (2007) has documented his struggle with gaining permission from one human subjects protection committee because of an institutional concern with "protecting" youth from themselves. I circumvented this problem by studying programs that already existed, being in the role entirely as researcher, but ideally, I will not be limited to this position in future studies. The merit to video production programs is that they promote new kinds of relationships, helping youth find power they did not know they had. People always have the potential to cross boundaries, break laws, and violate the rights of others, and situations with these potentials need to be studied. What is the limit to what a researcher can ethically analyze? These concerns are not unique to video production. Protocols for addressing and preventing serious problems are needed, but if the power of video is to be utilized, these ought to avoid controlling and silencing mechanisms. Bradley argues for involving participants in the process of establishing such protocols and protections, not only as part of planning but as part of the IRB process.

These problems demonstrate what it means for an artifact to be an actant that co-creates events without losing the impact of the student also being an actant. Actions of camera-student entities emerge from the joining of two actants and the context in which they become active. Emergent conflicts reveal the structures that normally constrain student activity. Most of the time, for instance, students are not allowed to get out of their seats and wander the building; students are limited in where and when they can go. The camera gives students a basic freedom of movement, which holds the potential for other constraints to be loosened. I have observed students occupying the teacher's position in the class, both materially and socially, and students have used the camera to raise uncomfortable topics. The most revealing part of the conflict over the prop gun was not that security became alarmed about a toy gun but that the teachers grasped onto this conflict as a way to halt all video productions, even though there were no dangers with the other projects. The teachers openly defended their decision because they feared the subject matter of the student projects: crime, drugs, and teenage pregnancies, might offend someone, sounding a lot like the IRB of which Bradley (2007) wrote. They seemed to want to keep the problems of the community out of the school. Thus the response of teachers and other school staff to student videographers serves as evidence of normal practices and the ideologies behind them.

An Application Of The Analysis

In developing an approach to understanding informant-made videos, several theories have been applied. This analysis is obviously not the only possible approach, but it has enabled entry into student-school relationships that took different directions with different projects, depending on what was relevant to a particular project. This approach enables descriptions of projects such that they could be compared to radically different projects. A more detailed analysis of a small piece of one cademe demonstrates the issues that have been discussed and then will be described in terms of its role in the project. I selected an excerpt from the explorations of two Native American youth that spanned only two days, a week apart. The section is short and not the most meaningful in terms of the project, but it shows how the camera serves as an actant in restructuring student-school relationships.

The camera operator, who chose the pseudonym "Wicket," stood with his partner, "Jerome," in the doorway to the "on-campus suspension" classroom. Wicket and Jerome immediately began to tease the suspended students. Illustrations of stills from the video follow.

Jerome says, "Hey, no cussing."

A girl is shown. Two girls laugh, and one says, "No." Someone walks between the girl and the camera.

Wicket says, "Oh, we got a Choice Dorm." [The dorm is where students who are being disciplined live temporarily and is written on the back of the student's shirt.] Wicket continues, "We're in for saying Choice Dorm." The female student turns toward the camera. She returns to hiding behind her notebook.

Wicket says, "Eh." Jerome says, "Eh! Quiet little boy."

Wicket says, "Oh man, I'm recording her folder." He laughs.

Jerome says, "Zoom in. See what all's written on there." But Wicket has already zoomed in. Wicket begins to read it out loud, "Off limits fucker."

Wicket and Jerome both laugh. . . .

The notebook is shown again. The girl holding it extends her middle finger toward the camera by holding the notebook such that only her middle finger is extended.

Wicket says, "Oh, she's flipping us off too."

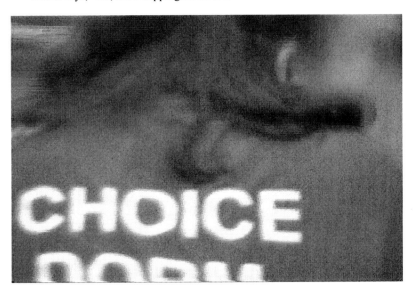

Fig. 5-1: The female student's shirt is visible.

Fig. 5-2: Female student shielding herself from being recorded.

Fig. 5-3: Female student extending her middle fingers toward the camera as she hides.

The shot continues, switching to focus on the female student's shoes being off and then a teacher is heard yelling and Wicket and Jerome leave. It is a typical example of the teasing that occurs during video production and alludes to some of the ethical considerations discussed above. The videographers express their increased power by forcing people to be on camera when they do not want to be and use the camera to emphasize or document some embarrassing situation. In this case, the fun comes from asserting an important difference: The students in the class are being disciplined, and one young woman was so thoroughly in trouble that she was placed in "Choice Dorm." Wicket's actions with the camera assert his power in being able to document her punishment. She shielded herself from the camera, offering a tactical message through the words on her notebook, but even these are exploited. The camera-student entity acts strategically, using its omniscient powers to read her note, and simultaneously acts tactically as the youth take joy in the defiance embodied in the notebook's message. The student continues to hide and sends another message with her middle fingers, resulting in more laughter. At some level, the laughter shows solidarity with the students being punished, even while playfully mocking them for it. And while Wicket emphasizes the differences in his position as compared to those being punished, Wicket and Jerome show high solidarity with one another in this and many shots. Wicket and Jerome routinely work together as part of the camera in shaping the events and playing with the power they have gained through their solidarity with the camera.

The events are not important—the youth are simply playing—but they take on importance because they represent a pattern. First, Wicket and Jerome record the OCS room three times in their two days. The proximity of the room near their starting point clearly affords this frequency, but they also have fun when they stop there. And the room has meaning, which ties in with the second significance: These events are part of a pattern of playing with power that becomes the focus of their final project. A few events respectfully display student and faculty art work or students playing instruments, but most involve some play with status or direct commentary on power structures. The OCS classroom is a monument to the power the authorities hold over the students. Third, these events, like many, were recorded entirely from the doorway. Doorways and hallways are places that are not *owned* by anyone (de Certeau, 1984; Lefebvre, 1974)—they are in-between places—and as such offer temporary freedoms; they are the spaces between places that can be tactically exploited (de Certeau, 1984). Hemmings (2000) described a "corridor curriculum" that exploited such spaces to assert a student hierarchy outside the institution's control, particularly when teachers were afraid to venture outside the safety of their classrooms, but my observations suggest that even when discipline is maintained, students find freedom from assigned activities in these places, which they use to pursue their own interests. This usage of doorways and hallways has occurred at every school I have thus far studied and indicates the position in which students find themselves. Few students have occupied the teachers' position in a classroom or traveled to administrative offices, but when they did, it was through their solidarity with the camera—by doing interviews mostly. Lastly, the cademe is important because it shows how camera techniques are meaningfully used by the students. Wicket and Jerome zoom in and out a lot, but it serves very clearly here as a way to read the text on the notebook. Similarly, Wicket turns the camera from one person to another and zooms in and out according to what he is focused upon. By contrast, many students were observed to use camera techniques without apparent purpose. The amount of play in Wicket and Jerome's cademes as well as the emphasis on art are likely to have facilitated what appears to be a more developed use of visual techniques. Based primarily on the work from this school, I would like to investigate what more freedom to explore and experiment would do for video literacy.

This excerpt was selected because it contains many of the issues that have been discussed, but it does not, by itself, reveal much about student-school relationships. That requires many more cademes and information about the context: Wicket and Jerome's videos show their school through their eyes in a way that I never would have been able to access through an interview. The college interns, who worked with the students at this school, and I had several conversations about the awkwardness of the work because students were so thoroughly uncommunicative. The students were quiet and respectful in our presence. If not for the video with its playfulness and social critique, I would have known nothing about these youth. Wicket was explicit about his beliefs during his narration of the scenes. Jerome, by contrast, struggled with his narration, leaving long silences. This suggests that Wicket dominated in the work, but Jerome's participation in the cademes revealed that he was not simply along for the ride. In short, I got to know Wicket and Jerome through their video.

Conclusion

The contribution of a detailed visual realm to the study of social relations should not be underestimated. Images provide concrete data, the meaning of which may remain contested as audiences share the analysis but for which patterns can be sought to resolve disputes. I have pursued the ability of "images [to] not only carry information in the constant battle over meaning but . . . to mediate power relations" (Fischman, 2001, p. 31) and to reflect the connections between people as they are drawn and severed. Power and solidarity are rarely spoken about concretely or consciously acted upon, but its role can be revealed in semiotically rich informant-made videos. A wealth of new information becomes available that is untouched in standard discourse analyses or video recordings.

As data, informant-made videos have five significant advantages over videos made by a researcher. First, individual positions—both material and metaphorical—are uniquely demonstrated by informant actions and the reactions they provoke. This provides the opportunity to view social relations in great detail. Second, the actions of the videographer are in dialogue with the people, places, and objects that are a meaningful and ongoing part of their lives. The material environment is made particularly salient by the nature of video production because it is visual and does not necessitate reflection. Third, changes in videography over time are documented. Whether the time span is half an hour or months or several years, differences in the choices the videographer made can be analyzed. Fourth, the camera promotes change. Students in particular have opportunities to look at and relate to the world differently. And lastly, videographers can be asked to reflect on their work. I have asked a small sample of students to narrate their work, and in future studies, I would like to extend this reflection to specifically ask students the same questions I am asking of the data—to ask if they see in their own work what I see.

Informant-made videos are important beyond their use as data collection, however, video production changes student-school relationships in ways that frequently remain unnoticed but that could be further exploited. Video cameras are actants along with students and contribute to activities in meaningful ways. Video production changes student activity in big ways such as in providing students with greater voice in school, in making their work more relevant, and in stimulating more active participation. It also changes school in small but important ways that are really about the camera itself. Movement, for one, becomes possible for students who normally must remain in their seats. This has profound implications for student agency as students have increasing affordances for directing their own education. Related to this are the new opportunities for interacting with people and environments. From possibilities for interviewing to affordances for seeing artifacts and places in new ways, camera-student entities shape the events that compose student-school relationships, thus video cameras afford new ways of being a student.

References

American Film Institute. (n.d.). *AFI screen education.* Retrieved June 13, 2008 from http://www.afi.edu

Bakhtin, M. M. (1986). *Speech genres and other late essays* (V. W. McGee, Trans.). Austin: University of Texas.

Barab, S., & Roth, W. M. (2006). Curriculum-based ecosystems: Supporting knowing from an ecological perspective. *Educational Researcher, 35*(5), 3-13.

Beaty. L. M. (in preparation). Video Cameras As Tools For Transforming Student-School Relationships In High School.

—. (2005). *"Give Me Space!" Situated Video Production And High School Social Relations.* Unpublished doctoral dissertation. Graduate School And University Center, City University of New York. Available: http://lbeaty.freeshell.org.

—. (2007). Concept development in action: Adolescent development in one student-made video from a Vygotskian perspective. 2007 Annual Meeting of the American Educational Research Association, Chicago, IL. Available at http://lbeaty.freeshell.org.

Bellman, B. L., & Jules-Rosette, B. (1977). *A paradigm for looking: Cross-cultural research with visual media.* Norwood, NJ: Ablex Publishing Corporation.

Bradley, M. (2007). Silence for their own protection: How the IRB marginalizes those it feigns to protect. *ACME: An International E-Journal for Critical Geographies, 6*(3), 339-349. Available at: http://www.acme-journal.org/vol6/MB.pdf.

De Certeau, M. (1984). *The practice of everyday life* (S. Rendall, Trans.). Berkeley: University of California Press.

Diamondstone, J. (2002). Keeping resistance in view in an activity theory analysis. *Mind, Culture, and Activity: An International Journal, 9*(1), 2-21.

Fischman, G. E. (2001). Reflections about images, visual culture, and educational research. *Educational Researcher, 30*(8), 28-33.

Gibson, J. J. (1986). *The ecological approach to visual perception.* Hillsdale, NJ: Lawrence Erlbaum Associates.

Goffman, E. (1974). *Frame analysis.* New York: Harper Colophon Books.

Goldman-Segall, R. (1998). *Points of viewing children's thinking: A digital ethnographer's journey.* Mahwah, NJ: Lawrence Erlbaum Associates.

Goodman, S. (2003). *Teaching youth media: A critical guide to literacy, video production, and social change.* New York: Teacher's College Press.

Gutierrez, K. D., Baquedano-Lopez, P., & Tejada, C. (1999). Rethinking diversity: Hybridity and hybrid language practices in the third space. *Mind, Culture, and Activity: An International Journal, 6*(4), 286-303.

Hemmings, A. (2000). The "hidden" corridor curriculum. *The High School Journal, 83,* 1-10.

Hobbes, R. (2004). A review of school-based initiatives in media literacy education. *American Behavioral Scientist, 48*(1), 42-59.

Hodge, R., & Kress, G. (1988). *Social semiotics.* Ithaca, NY: Cornell University Press.

Holland, D., Lachicotte, W., Jr., Skinner, D., & Cain, C. (1998). *Identity and agency in cultural worlds.* Cambridge: Harvard University Press.

Latour, B. (1996). On interobjectivity. *Mind, Culture, and Activity: An International Journal, 3*(4), 228-245.

Lefebvre, H. (1974). *The production of space* (D. Nicholson-Smith, Trans.). Oxford, UK: Blackwell.

Litowitz, B. E. (1993). Deconstruction in the zone of proximal development. In E. A. Forman, N. Minick, & C. A. Stone (Eds.), *Contexts for learning: Sociocultural dynamics in children's development* (pp. 184-196). New York: Oxford University Press.

—. (1997). Just say no: Responsibility and resistance. In M. Cole, Y. Engström, & O. Vasquez (Eds.), *Mind, culture, and activity: Seminal papers from the laboratory of comparative human cognition* (pp. 473-484). Cambridge: Cambridge University Press.

Miller, S. M., & Borowicz, S. (2003). City voice, city visions: Digital video as literacy/learning supertool in urban classrooms. Paper presented at the Annual Conference of the American Education Research Association, Chicago.

Newman, D., Griffin, P., & Cole, M. (1989). *The construction zone: Working for cognitive change in school.* New York: Cambridge University Press.

Schwartz, D. L., & Hartman, K. (2007). It's not television anymore: Designing digital video for learning and assessment. In R. Goldman, R.

Pea, B. Barron, & S. J. Derry (Eds.), *Video research in the learning sciences* (pp. 335-348). Mahwah, NJ: Lawrence Erlbaum Associates.

Sherin, M. G. (2007). The development of teachers' professional vision in video clubs. In R. Goldman, R. Pea, B. Barron, & S. J. Derry (Eds.), *Video research in the learning sciences* (pp. 383-395). Mahwah, NJ: Lawrence Erlbaum Associates.

Valsiner, J. (1997). *Culture and the development of children's action: A theory of human development.* New York: John Wiley & Sons.

Vygotsky, L. (1994). The development of thinking and concept formation in adolescence. In R. van der Veer & J. Valsiner (Eds.), *The Vygotsky reader* (pp. 185-265). Oxford: Blackwell.

—. (1978). Interaction between learning and development. In M. Cole, V. John-Steiner, S. Scribner, and E. Souberman (Eds.), *Mind in society: The development of higher psychological processes* (pp. 79-91).

Worth, S. (1981). *Studying visual communication.* Philadelphia: University of Pennsylvania Press.

Worth, S., & Adair, J. (1972). *Through Navajo eyes: An exploration in film communication and anthropology.* Bloomington, IN: Indiana University Press.

CHAPTER SIX

ETHNOGRAPHY, VIDEO AND THE AESTHETICS OF ENGAGEMENT

JASON PINE

Introduction

In Naples, I used video to carry out an ethnographic study of a peculiarly "underground" vocal music industry. This industry is comprised of tax-evading recording studios, pirated TV stations and a performance circuit at local baptism and wedding celebrations and piazza festivals. The songs, performed by solo vocal artists, are melodramatic pop ballads about love and betrayal and humble life among the Neapolitan popular classes. Quite spectacularly, a few of these ballads recount, sometimes with regret and sometimes with exaltation, the entanglements of ordinary individuals with organized crime.

I conducted several months of videotaping before learning that these entanglements are not merely lyrical performances. The music itself emerges from actual, variegated affiliations between industry participants and the *camorra*, the region's organized crime networks.[1] These affiliations can be extremely complex, ranging from tolerant coexistence to amorphous complicity, from temporary alliances to full-on collusion.[2]

---

[1] Organized crime in Naples, unlike the typically vertical hierarchy of the Sicilian mafia, is comprised of horizontal federations of tens of crime clans and thousands of individual affiliates. See, for example, Sales, Isaia and Ravveduto, Marcello (2006) *Le strade della violenza: malviventi e bande di camorra a Napoli*. Napoli: L'ancora del Mediterraneo.

[2] These can be described as multiple entanglements of affects and interests that generate a "contact zone" of wider, indeterminate forms of "everyday" participation

Despite, or rather because of, the overt musical melodramatizations of this particular local reality, the participants of the music industry and its tens of thousands of fans deftly manage their own and/or others' secrets.

Therefore, I had unknowingly been videotaping in a social environment rife with fear, dissimulation, irony and, above all, secrecy. This is because of the skill with which they give their peculiar social world over to an outwardly melodramatic form that often employs video. Music industry participants shoot music videos, produce live pirated TV performances, and they even appear on national television programs. To their critics, they perform an "excess" of melodramatized sentiment indicative of the excesses of a corrupt "Southern Italian" political economy.[3] In the sections that follow, I suggest that they engage in acts of "intimate melodramatization" that aestheticize a shared moral economic life and possibly generate an entirely new aesthetic.[4]

When I appeared on this scene with my video camera, the people I encountered avidly sought my attention while attempting to refract it. As I discuss in this chapter, singers, songwriters, producers and fans used their unique melodramatic performance aesthetic to incite in me a range of senses that undermined the dominance and "sovereignty" of my "gaze" (Foucault, 1972). They emphasized the camera's ability not to (re)present,

---

in organized crime. See Pine, Jason (2008) "Contact, Complicity, Conspiracy: Affective Communities and Economies of Affect in Naples" *Law, Culture and the Humanities* 4.2.

[3] Criminal anthropologist Cesare Lombroso and his students, beginning in the late 19th century, asserted that existence of a largely "congenital" "violent criminal type," found principally in the Italian "South," who harbors "primitive instincts, like passions for orgies and vendettas" Lombroso, Cesare (2006)[1884, 3rd edition] *Criminal Man*, by Mary Gibson and Nicole Hahn Rafter transls., Durham: Duke University Press, p.217. See also the well-known argument that capitalism was made possible by the regulation of human passions, including the channeling of "avarice" toward productivity and accumulation: Hirschmann, Albert O. (1997) *The Passions and the Interests: Political Arguments for Capitalism before Its Triumph*, Princeton: Princeton University Press.

[4] This Neapolitan music scene uses pirated TV as one would use a web cam, which "has the promise for a new aesthetics which does not have any precursors: the aesthetics which will combine fiction and telecommunication. How can telecommunication and fictional narrative go together? Is it possible to make art out of video surveillance, out of real-time – rather than pre-scripted – signal?" Manovich, Lev (2001) "Reality Media" http://www.manovich.net/DOCS/reality_media_final.doc, p.14.

but to provoke and intensify, social engagement. Indeed, even after many months in the field and many hours of video footage, I found that my lens had not and would not "capture" anything meaningful about everyday life in this Neapolitan milieu. It was only by adopting their particular "aesthetics of use" (Dunne, 1999; 2001) that I could productively and sensitively engage a secretive social world inhabited by people who fear and resist "capture."

Paying attention to the unique ways people in an underground music scene in Naples use video taught me to pay closer attention to my own use of video while in the field. My experiences in Naples demonstrate that the digital video camera, when it is used to document "reality," ultimately misrecognizes it as footage, artifactualizing it (Kirschenblatt-Gimblett, 1998). In the Neapolitan contexts described here, video emerges as a far more effective ethnographic tool when it is used to mediate "live" social entanglements on both sides of the lens (Pink, 2006).

Fig. 6-1: Singer lip-syncs his song on his live TV transmission.

Dramatized Intimacy and Intimate Dramatizations

My research in Naples began in the summer of 1998 when I was flipping through the regional TV channels. I came across four or five live transmissions, each hosted by a young male singer who lip-synced his songs upon request when viewers dialed the phone number at the bottom of the screen. The songs were melodramatic pop-ballads about love and betrayal, the praiseworthy humble life of the popular classes, and mournful family fissures caused by fugitive or imprisoned fathers. The lyrics were often unabashedly sentimental and, seemingly, intensely private. In fact, the more I watched and listened, the more I sensed the traces of a uniquely intimate social world.

When viewers called in to request songs, they greeted the singer and held, in the Neapolitan language, lengthy on-the-air conversations with him. One caller dedicated *"Napule mia"* (My Naples) and a kiss to grandma Cristina of Ponticelli. Another caller dedicated *"Scugnizza"* (Street Urchin) to his girlfriend Lucia. A third caller dedicated *"Innamorato"* (In Love) to Salvatore, wishing him "a swift return home because *unfortunately* he is not here with us now" (i.e., he is imprisoned). Many talked and joked with the singer about recent events and people they knew in common. They praised him, wished him success and sent him *un bacione grande, grande* (a big, big kiss).

Most people who called the live TV show knew the singer from either previous on-the-air contact or everyday "real" life. Callers and singers appeared as comfortable in this televised environment as they would in their everyday world. In fact, the shows teemed with a certain kind of everyday life that no one made much effort to "present." Whether they were lip-synching songs or fielding phone calls, the young singers paid minimal attention to what might be called "presentation style." On one show, the singer stopped mouthing lyrics and gesturing expressively well before the station manager faded out the digital recording of his song. On another, the singer conversed in a range of formal and informal registers with viewers and silent, invisible interlocutors standing somewhere off-camera, to his left. Twice, the arm of one such interlocutor reached into the frame to hand the singer a sheet of paper, which the singer unhurriedly accepted. On yet another transmission, the camera swept all around the small studio, sighting two middle-aged men engaged in an animated discussion, a child running up a staircase, and a sleepy woman who sat slumped in a rumpled armchair beside a stack of VHS recordings of Hollywood blockbusters.

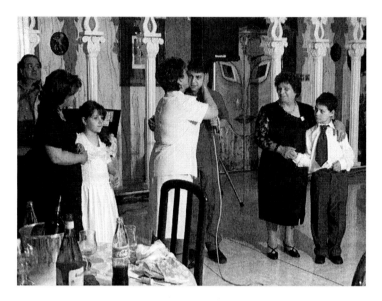

Fig. 6-2: Woman kisses singer at the baptism celebration of her grandson in a rented hall.

Fig. 6-3: Singer reads song dedications and messages phoned-in by viewers.

The programs are at once banal and enigmatic. They are not like the displays of dramatized intimacy that are performed among strangers on nationally broadcast reality TV shows such as *Big Brother*.[5] Instead, these transmissions are narrowcasts of an intimately dramatized social world *tout court*. They are dramatizations with a signature melodramatic aesthetic (Brooks, 1976). Ironically, the mediation of pirated television makes the intimacy of these dramatizations possible. But why dramatize and why narrowcast?

Anti-Aesthetics

For participants of this Neapolitan music scene, the unique aesthetic of intimate, sentimental melodrama provides a mediated space for interaction. For many non-participants, I learned after a few months of ethnographic fieldwork, this aesthetic is actually the "anti-aesthetic" (Foster, 1998). That is, they perceive it as undermining cherished ideologies concerning law and authority and regional, national and "European" identity.

Fig. 6-4: View of Vesuvius and the Bay of Naples.

---

[5] *Big Brother* continues to be the most successful reality TV show in Italy.

This is evident in the genre's very name, *la musica neomelodica,* or neo-melodic music. There are varying assertions as to who coined the name, but all agree it was a figure of the wider public media.[6] On its face, the term "neo-melodic" signifies a contemporary revision of the world-famous Neapolitan melodic song tradition, of which the performer Enrico Caruso and the song *'O Sole Mio* are probably the most well known. Two of the most notable features of the melodic tradition are found in its lyrics: they were composed in the "high-poetic" strain of the Neapolitan language and they were performed in the vocal style called *fronne 'e limone* (leaves of a lemon) (Scialo, 1996). "High-poetic" refers to non-vernacular language forms reserved for the expression of extraordinary sentiments. To sing in the style of *fronne 'e limone* means to elongate a lyrical syllable with a melisma composed of microtones, producing the *frisson* reminiscent of "Arab" music.[7] These features of melodic song lyrics are revived by *neomelodica* song.

However, the name "neo-melodic" is also enunciated and interpreted in unflattering ways. This is because *neomelodica* song is not merely a revival of the melodic song tradition; it is also a revision of it. The lyrics of *neomelodica* song are composed in the Neapolitan language, but in *napoletano stretto* or "street Neapolitan."[8] The vocal style of *neomelodica* music performers is *fronne 'e limone,* but they make "unrestrained" and "excessive" use of it.[9] In other words, to their critics, *neomelodica*

---

[6] Some claim it was Maurizo Costanzo, the national prime time talk show host on Rai 1; others claim it was music critic Federico Vacalebre of the southern Italian newspaper *Il Mattino.*

[7] Both fans and critics describe *neomelodica* music as "Arab" music. *Neomelodica* music is saturated with microtones arranged as expressive ornamentation with modal accents. Microtones may be a combination of quartertones and semitones. Consecutive semitones, the basis of chromatics, have long been considered... "irrational" and "feminine" in western music aesthetic ideologies. See, for example, Taruskin, R. (1993) 'Entoiling the faconet': Russian musical orientalism in context. in J. Bellman (Ed.) *The exotic in western music.* Boston, MA: Northeastern University Press. He writes that, in the Russian imaginary, melismatic and chromatic music "evoke[d] not just the East, but the seductive East that emasculates, enslaves, renders passive" (p.202). See also Weiss, P. & Taruskin, R. (Eds). (1984). *Music in the western world: A history in documents.* New York: Schirmer.

[8] *Stretto* literally means "narrow."

[9] When, for example, a contemporary *neomelodica* singer performs a classical Neapolitan song (composed between the late 19th century and the early 20th century), in most cases, he will embellish a strikingly greater number of notes with

performers sing in a "vulgar" language while drawing too much attention to themselves. Moreover, critics complain, this "unseemly" lyrical form is used to recount the "sordid" tales of imprisoned fathers and family fissures.

The initial response of the wider public to the *neomelodica* aesthetic was folklorization. In the local and national media, there was talk of a new curiosity from the ever-inventive Neapolitan bricoleur: *la musica del vicolo* (music of the alley).[10] Other romantics embraced its "underground" qualities and celebrated the politicization of an "urban subproletariat" (Vacalebre, 1999), inadvertently recuperating the perceived anti-aesthetic (Hebdige, 1979). Eventually, as we will see, *neomelodica* music emphasized for many people the alleged premodern marginality of the "Italian South," piggybacking on the denigrating orientalization of the region that has persisted since pre-unification Italy (Moe, 2002; Schneider, 1998).

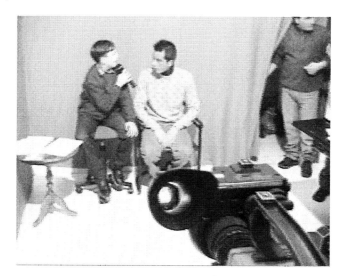

Fig. 6-5: Singers talk to man off-camera during live TV transmission.

---

melismas than would the song's original interpreters.
[10] 0 *vicoli* (plural of *vicolo*) are the historic neighborhoods' narrow and shadowy cobblestone streets, which serve as an extended living space for the inhabitants of the cramped, dark ground-level dwellings that flank them. See De Simone, G. (2000). "La città indifferente". http://www.konsequenz.it/c02.htm

Narrowcast Secrecy

Neomelodica music aesthetics is not the only thing that causes it to be reviled; there is also the question of its economy. Indeed, the two are inextricably intertwined. Accordingly, after many months of fieldwork, my study of a music scene and its shadow media outlet encompassed a web of shadow enterprises.

Fig. 6-6: Singers and program manager chat with viewers who are phoning in to TV station.

The *neomelodica* music industry thrives in the indeterminate contact zone between the informal and illicit economies. It is amorphous, makeshift and rapidly changing. It consists of hundreds of Neapolitans who freelance as songwriters and composers, run tax-evading recording studios, operate pirated TV stations, shoot music videos, and sell CDs on card tables on the city's sidewalks. Moreover, the *neomelodica* music industry can be highly lucrative. For this reason, hundreds of underemployed families pour thousands of Euros into the industry in order to launch their sons' singing careers.

Fig. 6-7: Father stands off-camera while son performs on live TV.

Real success, I learned years later, goes only to singers who receive the backing of wealthy and influential impresarios with wide social networks. They send singers to lavish baptism and wedding parties, as many as ten in one day. Incredibly, these impresarios are bosses in the *camorra*, Naples' violent and extensive organized crime clans.

These details make *neomelodica* music shows on pirated TV still more enigmatic. *Neomelodica* music is enormously popular in Naples. Tens of thousands of fans sing along at high volume to the latest releases in their homes and cars with the windows wide open. Primary school students use their cell phones to share songs and serenade each other.[11] Fans lionize their favorite singers and tried, month after month, to get their photos in the monthly glossy magazine dedicated to them.[12] Lyrical tales of love,

---

[11] Insights gleaned from research conducted in 2006 with Simona Frasca in a Neapolitan middle school in the neighborhood of Capodimonte.
[12] The now out-of-print *Sciuè Sciuè* (Quick-Quick) was a highly popular *neomelodica* music star magazine that featured photos of singers and fans.

imprisoned fathers, and life in the housing projects or the *vicoli*,[13] have given shape to a melodramatized world (Williams, 1983). For many people, *neomelodica* music is like a soundtrack for life. And yet, they maintain a spectacularly public secret: *neomelodica* music is, in many instances, a polyphonic production of ordinary underemployed young men and powerful *camorristi*.[14]

Undoubtedly, maintaining a tenacious silence about facts and identities is essential to surviving in the contact zone where the informal and illicit economies meet in Naples (Pine, 2008). The question, therefore, remains: Why do people in this milieu televise their intimate social world?

Video Documents and Video Performances

Before going further, I should first back up in my story and explain why it ever occurred to me to use a video camera while conducting fieldwork in an environment rife with secrets and physical dangers. Why attempt to capture and document on video the everyday life of people who were clearly wary of facts and identifications? When I began my research, my focus was on musical performance on Neapolitan regional television. Because I was unaware of any connection between *neomelodica* music and the *camorra*, I did not imagine any reason to be afraid. This, in itself, convinced the people I was videotaping that they too had nothing to fear. Fear is contagious, but it is also true that self-assurance breeds reassurance.

Fig. 6-8: After reading incoming texts with song requests, singers pass cell phone to man off-camera.

---

[13] Plural of *vicolo* (alley).
[14] members of the *camorra* (pl. of *camorrista*).

Even when I began to hear rumors, within and outside of this scene, that the *camorra* "controlled" the *neomelodica* music industry, there was no clear way to go about confirming them. People "know" yet do not *know*. Organized crime is palpable but amorphous; much of its potency comes from evading identifications (front people, nicknames, money laundering) and spreading fear (repeated intimidation and spectacular violence). In Naples, the *camorra* cultivates its power by making itself indistinguishable from the economic "system" itself (Gribaudi, 1990; Saviano, 2006). Given the dual identity of economic enterprises encompassing virtually everything, from basic foodstuffs to public housing projects to a local music industry, "ordinary" Neapolitans tend to "know" but not really *know*.

Fig. 6-9: Singer blows anthropologist a kiss while he videotapes him during a live TV transmission.

That fact is that people welcomed my video camera on the *neomelodica* music scene, where digital video and television have always been organic. Every Sunday from May to July, videographers recorded families as they enjoyed *neomelodica* music performances at their weddings and baptisms. Without fail, they included shots of the family embracing, kissing and dancing with the singer. All year round, young singers and their associates shot rapid-fire music videos throughout the historic center and at any spot with a panoramic view. Without fail, they framed the singer's face so that it was at the center of nearly every shot. Every evening until the wee hours, in back-alley garages or the back bedrooms of humble family apartments, *neomelodica* music narrowcasters aimed their video cameras at anyone anywhere in the "studio." Without fail, they toggled freely between music videos, viewer telephone calls, off-camera guests and center-stage live lip-synced performances. My own video camera was welcomed in these contexts because, rather than an intrusion, it was received as an opportunity for interaction. People on the *neomelodica* music scene interact with video cameras (and TV) in ways that are consistent with their own performance aesthetics. Performance, for them, is less an act or artifact of (re)presentation than it is a mode of sociality. People in this milieu are comfortable with video cameras to the extent that they can subordinate them to their everyday social practices.

Although I shot from the sidelines, the people I sought to "capture" persistently drew me into their performances. Some singers looked in my direction while lip-syncing on live TV. Some announced to their viewers that I was in the studio and told the cameraperson to turn the shot on me. Other singers told me to put my camera down and join them center stage. It was impossible to remain on the sidelines, but my impulse was to resist their pull. My goal, I told them, was to document *neomelodica* music performances, not join them. Perhaps I sought what I perceived to be authentic pristine performances, unchanged by my intruding video camera. Was I guilty of attempted folklorization? It would take me many more months to realize that there was something significant about their performances that would remain unchanged *only if* I participated in them.

Performing

Televised *neomelodica* music performances aside, there was still the question of people's everyday performances. Would my video camera cause people to begin scripting their words and behaviors? Would it intimidate, irritate and silence them?

Up to that point, most of the people I approached without my video camera were immediately effusive. They expressed strong opinions about Neapolitan music and they were eager to buttress them with cultural analysis: "Neapolitan music is like the poetry of the popular classes. It's all that we have. We sing to forget our miseries" (functionalist explanation popular among those who are either old enough to remember postwar Naples or are familiar with its representations in nostalgic cinema, theater and literature); "Vesuvius reminds us that all we have is *today*, and so we sing" (environmental psychological explanation preferred among those wishing to invoke a 19th-century northern Italian view of the "volcanic south"[15]); "Our music is like an emotion. We sing because it's in our hearts" (biological determinist explanation for those who dare dredge up

---

[15] Giacomo Leopardi coined this phrase in his 1837 poem *La Ginestra* (cited in Moe, 2002).

the racial discourse embedded in the "Southern Question").[16]

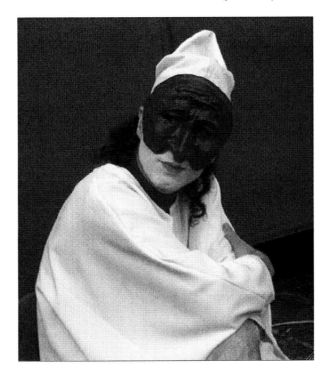

Fig. 6-10: Pulcinella, the Neapolitan character of the Commedia dell'arte.

In nearly all of my conversations about the *neomelodica* music industry, people rehearsed recitatives like these. They demonstrated that they too could play culture-as-text. They were more than familiar with the academic search for "meaning" behind the "signs" and "patterns" of cultural worlds. They trafficked in representations about themselves, and

[16] "The Southern Question," or the divergent histories, cultures, economies and paths of development of the Italian north and south was the focal point of Antonio Gramsci's   theory of hegemony. Naples has been the subject of denigrating othering ranging from the racializing discourse of the late 19th-century "father" of criminal anthropology, Cesare Lombroso, to the 1960's political scientist Edward C. Banfield's (1953) infamously influential assertion that southern Italians constitute a "backward society". Banfield, E. C. (1958). *The moral basis of a backward society*. Glencoe, IL: Free Press - University of Chicago.

like Pulcinella, the Neapolitan archetype of the *Commedia dell'arte* and the greatest of all folkloric invocations, they performed the oppressed Neapolitan with expert irony.[17]

Fig. 6-11: San Gennaro and pizza on the set of live national broadcast of Life Live.

This sort of self-folklorization is arguably a reaction to northern Italian (and European) desires for a pre-modern picturesque "South" dating as far back as pre-unification Italy (Moe, 2002; Schneider, 1998). An event I attended in 2003 may help to explain the reason for my claim. Upon the invitation of a Neapolitan journalist, I observed and videotaped the live national TV broadcast of the *Rai 1* entertainment program, *La vita in diretta* (Life Live). Each week, the host of the show tours a different Italian town. Naples was this week's highlight, coinciding with the city's annual *Pizzafest* competition. *Comme il faux*, the set was populated by proud *pizzaiuoli* (pizza-makers), donned in red t-shirts and clean white

---

[17] *Pulcinella* (variously defined as "little flea" and "little chick") is the archetype Neapolitan character who behaves as "the servant of two masters" – that is, quick to please others in order to please himself.

aprons, who presided over displays of ruby red San Marzano tomatoes, bowls of milky *mozzarella di bufala*, and an assortment of not-yet-baked pizzas. Resting on one of the displays was an ostentatiously framed image of Naples' patron saint, San Gennaro, whose blood annually de-coagulates, warding off the wrath of Vesuvius. When the cameras of *Rai 1* began rolling, three women walked onto the set to model 19th-century wedding dresses. Following them was a top *neomelodico*,[18] who began singing with maximum expressivity *T'amo t'amerò* (I Love You and Will Always Love You). At the refrain, five young *pizzaiuoli* encircled the singer as they spun large flat discs of pizza dough high above their heads.

Fig. 6-12: Popular Neapolitan singer lip-syncs for Life Live.

---

[18] A male performer of *neomelodica* music.

Fig. 6-13: Avid fan rushes on-camera during Life Live broadcast.

"This is what people in the north know about Naples, and so this is what they find: pizza, singing and weddings," the Neapolitan journalist later said to my camera with a sneer. And yet, he and everyone else in the *neomelodica* scene were willing to partake in the spectacle, including the music's Neapolitan fans. The very moment the *neomelodico* finished his song, a 30-something female fan rushed onto the set. She embraced the singer and for just a moment, they were on national television together. Afterwards, I asked her if she enjoyed herself. Victoriously, she looked directly into my camera lens and declared, "Now I'm satisfied. Now everyone will know that I did it and that I matter." The fan was referring not to "Italians," but to the Neapolitans in her milieu. Many people in the *neomelodica* scene regard the "Italian" national media as an opportunity to perform for other Neapolitans their "mastery of form" (Baker, 1992). That is, they demonstrate to each other their deft execution of the self-folklorizing performances that the national "Italian" media often expects of them. Appearances in "Italian" media spaces may not win them success among national publics (quite the opposite), but it certainly affords them cultural capital among others in their Neapolitan milieu.[19] By wearing the mask of Pulcinella, people in the *neomelodica* scene create an ironic "space of habitation" and room to maneuver.[20] In this space, they communicate with each other, transforming "Italian" national media into Neapolitan narrowcasting.

Performing Performing

Neomelodica music industry participants may want publicity, but they certainly do not want exposure (Dean, 2001). In 2001, the one *neomelodico* who had managed to sign a contract with BMG was investigated for receiving money from members of the *camorra*. In response, scathing criticisms and denigrating epithets began to circulate. The attacks have been simultaneously aesthetic and economic in nature: Why should unprofessional, improvising, approximating, Neapolitan con-artists get away with suddenly becoming, for all intents and purposes, true pop stars? For such critics, the problem is discursive: *neomelodica* music cannot be simultaneously "underground" and popular. "Italy" can either recuperate it as folk art or criminalize it as con-art (Hebdige 1979). As "Italians" and Neapolitans turned accusatory, the *neomelodica* scene got jumpy.

In fact, the more I videotaped people in this milieu, the more they anxiously deflected my lens. Many of them expressed exaggerated disappointment with my choice to study *neomelodica* music. Some tried to hijack my conversations with others by haranguing me with boisterous talk. They tugged at my arms and forcibly steered me towards other singers and genres, such as the jazz-influenced Pino Daniele and the folk

---

[19] In 1996, when the national media first noted the popularity of *neomelodica* music among Neapolitans, the top prime time talk show, *The Maurizio Costanzo Show*, invited five of the genre's star performers to appear. The broadcast subsequently inspired derisive television skits and articles about *neomelodica* music in magazines such as *l'Espresso* and newspapers such as *Corriere della Sera*. Moreover on the local level, a popular Neapolitan radio show host launched a *neomelodica* music awards ceremony that he called the Neapolitan Melogrammy to emphasize the music's perceived overwrought sentimentality and to instruct performers "not to take themselves too seriously."
[20] Baker (1992) writes that, during the Harlem Renaissance, black people appropriated the blackface mask and transformed it into an art form (p. 33). Similarly, Neapolitans engage in the essentially ironic practice of self-folklorization and, in so doing, perform for their peers their mastery of the form.

form the *tarantella*.[21] "Forget *neomelodica* music!" they shouted, "Neapolitan music has a long history, and back then there was *real* music." They talked fast, put an arm around my shoulder and walked me aside for a confidential conference. Sometimes, vaunting their status as Neapolitan music "experts" and "virtuosi," they took the camera from my hands and interviewed each other.

Fig. 6-14: Singer lip-syncs his song on a live TV transmission.

Others, sensing just how much I "know," made pointed efforts to distinguish themselves as "true" performers of "real" *neomelodica* music. They are artists and the "others" are con-artists. They are all about aesthetics while those "others" are all about business, dirty business. They are performing, while the "others" are performing performing. They waved their arms and shouted with dramatized disgust, "To accomplish anything in Naples, you have to leave Naples!" In a last-ditch effort to

---

[21] The *tarantella* is a "ritual" dance that was believed to remedy the tarantula bite. Ironically, "to do a tarantella" is a colloquialism meaning "to make much ado about nothing."

maintain mastery of form, people began unmasking each other. My lens, like that of the "Italian" media, was a provocation.

Aesthetic Engagements

After an 18-month-long hike through thickets of drama, dissimulation and fearful silence, I still could not find a clearing in the secrets I sensed all around me. Things began to change, however, once I pursued a new tack. If people in the *neomelodica* music scene were continually drawing me and my video camera into their social world, why not make it a regular practice, a job? I decided to begin promoting myself as a *neomelodica* music video director. Following the advice of a research associate from the *neomelodica* scene, I started to build a portfolio by creating for a young singer a music video, free of charge.

The song for which I made my first video was called "*Siente a me*" (Listen to Me). Acting as a sort of lyrical rehabilitation of Naples for Neapolitans, the song tells Neapolitan audiences not to "pay any mind to anyone" because "you're like me, you're a child of Naples." It declares that "those boys in the street" actually have jobs and tells us to "look at those mothers who are struggling to get by." Because of its numerous images of life among the popular classes, I decided to gather B-roll footage in the streets of the poorer (and somewhat infamous) neighborhoods of the *Quartieri Spagnoli* (Spanish Quarters). I asked a resident and friend to accompany me and act as my "ambassador," as it is called. I might have lost the video camera and use of the limb that held it had I done the shoot without one. While we videotaped, we caught the glance of several of the neighborhood's residents. Many of them gestured to us by pulling down the lower eyelid of one eye with an index finger: "Occhio!" (Eye!). They pronounced the word with a strangely perfunctory emphasis, as if indicating an ever-present yet unlocatable danger. The word seemed to bounce from one utterer to the next in endless, anxious deferment like a secret they wished they could tell.

When we were done shooting, I pieced together a rich montage of street scenes and shots of the young boy, whom I had previously videotaped lip-syncing his song in a busy piazza. When I presented the completed music video to the singer and his father, they didn't like it. Politely, they described it as documentary style.[22] Although I was aware of

---

[22] The completed music video can be viewed at:

the prevailing aesthetic in *neomelodica* music videos, I wanted to introduce new style to the genre. "Everyone is doing the same thing all the time," I told the boy's father, trying to convince him the video was good, "What you need is to make your son stand out." The father, however, could not be convinced. "They want to see only the singer close-up and all the time," an associate explained to me. "Only the singer," he repeated. Recorded video, like live video, is intended, in some way, to augment social interaction. *Neomelodica* music videos, like the live pirated TV narrowcasts that air them, are a source of face-time with the singer.

Fig. 6-15: *Vicolo* (narrow street) called Spaccanapoli (split Naples) dating back to the ancient Greek city *Neapolis*.

As my video work advanced, I found myself engaged in a range of video-related tasks that simultaneously served my own needs and the needs of others.

On one occasion, I asked a veteran *neomelodica* music fan if she would like to interview a well-known *neomelodico* while I videotaped. "And try to get him to relax enough to 'really' talk with you," I said. "Oh, you mean ask for some gossip," she replied, not entirely comfortable with the task. For the most part, the interview went well. The singer enjoyed the potential publicity, the fan enjoyed the contact, and I was finally able to observe an interaction while recording it. In unison, they slipped back and forth from the kind of intimacy aired on pirated TV narrowcasts to the more formalized performance of "performer and interviewer." However, when the fan asked the singer flat out, "So, is there any gossip you want to tell me?" the conversation faltered. Neither interviewer nor interviewee was accustomed to this form of videotaped engagement. Luckily, it took little for their syntony to resume.

The fan was ecstatic when I offered her a copy of the videotaped interview. She invited me for dinner with her family at their home. While she was in the kitchen preparing the meal, I videotaped and chatted with her teenage son about *neomelodica* music. Having heard a lot about me from his mother, he is unusually candid. The young man tells me that he is a fan of *neomelodica* songs, but only if they are about love. "Then there are other songs...that talk about Naples," he added. "Like you have rap in America, where they show off their cars and their girls. Here, they show you who they know. Some put 'ugly faces' in their music videos in order to let you know who they are." The young man, I later confirmed, was referring to singers who are closely affiliated with the *camorra*.

The *camorra*, in fact, acquired an increasingly palpable presence as I continued to engage Neapolitans with my video camera. My mediated engagements seemed to intensify my off-camera relationships, and people felt confident enough to broach the taboo subject. Once, a singer warned me not to videotape his performance at a wedding and explained why: "Not here, not this gig. If something happens later, if the police raid their next party, they'll blame us." He told me that fugitives often come out of hiding to attend the weddings of their kin. The consequences would be grave if the police captured the fugitive after I had been spotted capturing him or her on video. Another singer for whom I did video work explained something similarly unsettling about the pirated TV enterprises. "Sometimes, when callers want to dedicate a song, they pass encoded messages to associates watching the show from prison." He said he did not know the contents of the messages or how they were encoded. "I don't need to know and I don't want to know," he said bluntly.

Knowing, yet not knowing is a mode of attention that dominates the *neomelodica* scene. Melodramatic songs, sentimental dedications and familiar conversation in the Neapolitan language reproduce, for many Neapolitans, a shared sensibility and social world. Many regard singers' business affiliations with the *camorra* merely as the means to perform this sensibility. For them, it is the aesthetic engagement that matters. For others, the *neomelodica* sensibility provides cover for the business of the *camorra*, from building reputation with "ugly faces" to maintaining communications across prison walls. To most of us, particularly if we are not from this milieu, the *neomelodica* music scene appears as a melodramatized, sentimental and oddly intimate social world.

Business Engagements

Although I at last understood the value of engaging, rather than capturing with video the *neomelodica* music scene, I still did not know how to interact with the *camorra*. I had certainly associated with numerous individuals of varying levels of affiliation with the *camorra*, but it was only after two years of fieldwork and video work that I managed to directly affiliate with a *camorra* boss. Antonio is his name and, as my confidante on the scene told me, "he comes from a family of killers." Despite his reputation, I met with the young man because he wanted to launch, in addition to his drug trade and extortion racket, his own talent agency. I offered to be his in-house music video director. Antonio, who is shrewd, confident and opportunistic, told me that I first had to show him what I can do. "Come back in a few days," he said. We arranged a time and, three days later, I returned. When I entered his studio, he looked at me and announced, "You're coming to my son's birthday party tonight and you're going to videotape it." Before I could respond, he added, "We'll leave in a half hour."

After a 15-minute drive through trash-strewn streets lined with laundry-cloaked buildings, Antonio stopped at what he called the neighborhood community center. "The party's in there. You go in. I got more errands to do," he said and waited for me to get out of the car. The interior of the one-story community center was a single, florescent-lit whitewashed room marked with a modest amount of graffiti. At the far end of the space stood ten adults, some of whom were laying out trays of fried pizzas and wilted mignon pastries. About twice as many children played with balloons or ogled the birthday cake. I announced myself, but none of the adults returned my greeting. They clearly expected me, but they were not enthusiastic about my presence.

When the party began, so did my videotaping. The children's shrieks reverberated from cement wall to cement floor and back again. Their mothers bellowed at them angrily when they popped balloons or hit one another. Antonio junior, the eight-year-old birthday boy, barely managed to evade the whizzing red shoe that his mother flung at him. The candle-blowing and happy-birthday singing went flawlessly, but whenever I approached Antonio junior's mother or grandmother, they scowled into the lens of my video camera. At home, I meticulously edited the footage. I omitted the scowls, slaps and shrieks, replacing most of the audio with a soundtrack (Stevie Wonder's *Isn't She Lovely*). Once the work was completed, I presented to the boss a sweet Hallmark videogram. To my dismay, I found that while Antonio was not displeased with the video, he wasn't entirely satisfied.

Fig. 6-16: Singer invites anthropologist to introduce his music video during live TV transmission.

When I later recounted for my associate, Ciro, how hard I worked to make the video presentable, he told me I should have emphasized, even showcased, the less nostalgic moments: "Damn! You could have inserted one of those talk bubbles with the word *BAM!* or *WHAM!* when the high-heeled shoe hit the wall. Antonio would've gotten a kick out of it." Immediately, I knew that Ciro was right. I might have even reached a new level of confidence with the boss had I not allowed my video representations to get in the way. Our engagements could be just as aesthetic as they were business oriented.

The next week, armed with this understanding, I spontaneously devised a new strategy. While hanging out one afternoon with Antonio and three of his associates, I switch on my camera and point it at them. "So you want to interview me? You want me to talk about our new agency?" one of the guys asks with unmasked irony. I already know plenty about their talent agency, and by now they know full well that I'm not interested in "interviews." Without missing a beat, I return with irony, "Yeah, tell me about your agency…I hear you're expanding, going national." We are sitting surrounded by overflowing red plastic ashtrays in a cramped recording studio on the ground floor of a two-story gray cement building. The entrance opens onto a narrow, oil-stained parking lot flanked by sagging, pockmarked apartment buildings. The neighborhood where we are located clings to the backside of the hill that dominates Naples, the side that does not see the glittering bay. The guys know from my irony that I know that when they give interviews, they give self-aggrandizing performances. This makes the interview much more entertaining for them. "Yes, we are. We're opening an office in Rome and another in Milan," one of the others joins in. Straight-faced, I continue with my own performance, "That's right! I saw you talking with the architects the other day…" Our mock interview continues like this for a few minutes, until one of the guys tells me to interview the agency's proprietor, Antonio.

My camera is still rolling as I move closer to the boss and say, "It would be an honor." Antonio has been enjoying our game, but he turns out not to be as playful as we are. Instead, he merely recounts for the camera the basic facts: he is launching a talent agency, it is located in Naples and it supplies Neapolitan singers for weddings and baptisms. His words disappoint; I had expected a more creative response. Hoping for more "play," I try a new provocation: "I hear there's some kind of American working with you?" Once again, Antonio answers me plainly: "That's right. There's someone called Jason working for us and he'll be making all of our music videos." Although he refers to me in the third person, it is still not the level of "play" that I am looking for. This time around, I try even harder: "Americans, in the end, are very crafty. Sure, they have that *faccia da scemo* (idiot face),[23] but behind it..." Before I can finish, Antonio laughs. He doesn't expect this. He and I had never addressed our rapport, be it business or otherwise. I, however, was greatly invested in knowing where I stood with Antonio and his associates. I had hours of video footage, some of it possibly incriminating. In fact, my closest confidante had twice "joked" with me about it: "You know what will happen to you if anyone sees you with some cop, sharing your footage, don't you?" I not only "know" about what buttresses the neomelodica music scene; my video documentation indicates that I may also *know*. After a moment just brief enough to reassure me, Antonio answers, continuing to refer to me in the third person: "Let's say he's neither stupid or crafty. Let's just say that he knows how to behave and that he knows how to do his job."

With this encounter, I entered with Antonio an enclosure, a space we created where we could talk in quotation marks. Sharing the awareness that "this is play," we engaged each other aesthetically. Sharing an aesthetic experience, we found the means to "really" communicate. My video camera enhanced our engagement. It not only emphasized our shared frame; it also provided me with a means for mediating my fear.

Conclusion

It is possible to say that the unusual Neapolitan context described above amplifies sensibilities that are found everywhere in all ethnographic contexts. What is experienced as secrecy in Naples may emerge elsewhere as the intimate, personal or private. The indeterminacies produced by and constituting all of these sensibilities may require new modes of attention that focus in places other than the "depths" of analysis. They serve, perhaps, as a reminder that people and social worlds are vulnerable when faced with "capture" by video or any other representational mode, including text and discourse more generally.[24] The engagements of field

---

[23] In *napoletano stretto* (street Neapolitan), it is common to hear references to the face such as *faccia dura* ("hard face" or a person who is seasoned) and *faccia da scemo* ("idiot face" or naïve).

[24] Deleuze, G., & Guattari, F. (1991). *A thousand plateaus: Capitalism and schizophrenia* (B. Massumi, Trans.). Minneapolis, MN: University of Minnesota Press; Foucault, M. (2002). *Archeology of knowledge* (A. M. Sheridan Smith,

research, from the subtlest to the most intense, call for equally engaging
methods of cultural poeisis in the academy (Stewart, 2003). This means
allowing the vitality of encounters to endure beyond the field, into
reflection and throughout their reproduction and circulation as
"knowledge." It also means committing to sharing a space of vulnerability
with the people and social worlds that are subject to research. Far more
than the analytic remove implied by the "documentation" of ethnographic
fieldwork with media such as text or video, it is aesthetic engagement, or
experiential ethnography,[25] that holds this potential.

Acknowledgements

This research was funded, in part, by the Wenner-Gren Foundation.
Many thanks to Halide Velioğlu, Ahmed Afzal, Katie Stewart, Shaka
McGlotten and Michelle Stewart for their helpful comments.

References

Baker, H. A., Jr. (1992). *Modernism and the Harlem renaissance.*
Chicago: University of Chicago Press.
Banfield, E. C. (1958). *The moral basis of a backward society.* Glencoe,
IL: Free Press.
Brooks, P. (1976). *The melodramatic imagination: Balzac, Henry James,
melodrama and the mode of excess.* New Haven, CT: Yale University
Press.

Trans.). New York: Routledge. Focusing on "capture" also "limits ethnography to
content or its reception and plays down the means by which technologies, through
their very form, impose new social relations. The role of the subject in this
tradition is submerged to the circuit of information," Ginsburg, F. D., Abu-Lughod,
L., & Larkin, B. (2002). *Media worlds: Anthropology on new terrain.* Berkeley:
University of California Press, p. 19.
[25] "For the production of knowledge and for epistemological reflection,
experiential ethnographers depend on how the 'self' of the anthropologist interacts
with experiences, people, and the flow of events in the field. This multi-level
reciprocal dynamic between anthropologist and the field is the source of the
proliferation of experiential ethnographies and genres" Poewe, K. (1996). Writing
culture and writing fieldwork: The proliferation of experimental and experiential
ethnographies. *Ethnos, 6*(1), 3-4. See also Denzin, N. K. (1997). *Interpretive
ethnography: Ethnographic practices for the 21st century.* Thousand Oaks, CA:
Sage.

De Simone, G. (2000). "La città indifferente." Retrieved on February 20, 2008 from http://www.konsequenz.it/c02.htm

Dean, J. (2001). Publicity's secret. *Political Theory, 29*(5), 624-650.

Deleuze, G., & Guattari, F. (1991). *A thousand plateaus: Capitalism and schizophrenia* (B. Massumi, Trans.). Minneapolis, MN: University of Minnesota Press.

Denzin, N. K. (1997). *Interpretive ethnography: Ethnographic practices for the 21st century.* Thousand Oaks, CA: Sage.

Dunne, A. (2001). *Design noir: The secret life of electronic objects.* Birkhäuser Basel.

—. (1999). *Hertzian tales: Electronic products, aesthetic experience and critical design.* London: RCA CRD Research Publications.

Foster, H. (1998). *The anti-aesthetic. Essays on postmodern culture.* New York: The New Press.

Foucault, M. (2002). *Archaeology of knowledge* (A. M. Sheridan Smith, Trans.). New York: Routledge.

—. (1972). *The birth of the clinic: An archaeology of medical perception* (A. M. Sheridan Smith, Trans.). London: Tavistock Publications.

Ginsburg, F. D., Abu-Lughod, L., & Larkin, B. (2002). *Media worlds: Anthropology on new terrain.* Berkeley: University of California Press.

Gribaudi, G. (1990). Mafia, culture e gruppi sociali. *Meridiana, 7-8.*

Hebdige, D. (1979). *Subculture and the meaning of style.* London: Methuen.

Hirschmann, A. O. (1997). *The passions and the interests: Political arguments for capitalism before its triumph.* Princeton, NJ: Princeton University Press.

Kirshenblatt-Gimblett, B. (1998). *Destination culture: tourism, museums, and heritage.* Berkeley, CA: University of California Press.

Lombroso, C. (2006). *Criminal man* (M. Gibson & N. H. Rafter, Trans., 3rd ed.). Durham, NC: Duke University Press. [Original work published 1884]

Manovich, L. (2001). "Reality media." Retrieved on June 10, 2008 from http://www.manovich.net/DOCS/reality_media_final.doc

Moe, N. (2002). *The view from Vesuvius: Italian culture and the southern question.* Berkeley, CA: University of California Press.

Pine, J. (2002). Contact, complicity, conspiracy: Affective communities and economies of affect in Naples. *Law, Culture and the Humanities, 4*(2), 201-223.

Pink, S. (2006). *Doing visual ethnography: Images, media and representation in research* (2nd ed.). Thousand Oaks, CA: Sage.

Poewe, K. (1996). Writing culture and writing fieldwork: The proliferation of experimental and experiential ethnographies. *Ethnos, 6*(1), 3-4.

Sales, I., & Ravveduto, M. (2006). *Le strade della violenza: malviventi e bande di camorra a Napoli.* Napoli: L'ancora del Mediterraneo.

Saviano, R. (2006). *Gomorra: Viaggio nell'impero economico e nel sogno di dominio della camorra.* Milano: Mondadori

Schneider, J. (Ed.). (1998). *Italy's "southern question": Orientalism in one country.* Oxford: Berg.

Scialo, P. (1996). *La canzone napoletana: dalle origini ai giorni nostri.* Roma: Newton & Compton editori s.r.l.

Stewart, K. (2003). Cultural poesis: The generativity of emergent things. In N. K. Denzin & Y. S. Lincoln (Eds.), *Handbook of qualitative research* (3rd ed.). Thousand Oaks, CA: Sage.

Taruskin, R. (1993). 'Entoiling the Faconet': Russian Musical Orientalism in Context. In J. Bellman (Ed.), *The exotic in western music.* Boston: Northeastern University Press.

Vacalebre, F. (1999). *Dentro il Vulcano: Racconti neomelodici e altre storie dal villaggio locale.* Napoli: Pironti.

Weiss, P., & Taruskin, R. (Eds.). (1984). *Music in the western world: A history in documents.* New York: Schirmer.

Williams, Raymond (1983) "Drama in a Dramatized Society" in *Writing in Society*, London: Verso.

CHAPTER SEVEN

CAPTURING THE HIKE EXPERIENCE ON VIDEO: AN ALTERNATIVE FRAMEWORK FOR STUDYING HUMAN RESPONSE TO NATURE

CLAUDIA MAUSNER

The impetus for this project originated with my review of the literature on theories of perception as related to landscape perception research, for my doctoral studies in environmental psychology. I reviewed phenomenological theories of perception (McConville, 1978) as well as theories from psychology (Banks & Krajicek, 1991) and human geography (Appleton, 1996; Seamon, 1979; Tuan, 1990).

Zube, Sell, and Taylor (1982) had classified landscape perception studies according to four paradigms: "expert", "experiential", "cognitive" and "psychophysical". Many "expert" studies had been conducted by landscape architects, and most empirical work was conducted by psychologists following the "cognitive" or "psychophysical" models. These studies were primarily conducted in laboratory settings using still photographs to simulate the natural environment. Subject responses to these images were typically evaluated with questionnaires and rating scales, or physiological measures such as galvanic skin response or blood pressure.

The predominant research techniques used to study landscape perception have implicitly conceptualized nature as a static landscape and perceivers as passive observers. These studies have focused almost exclusively on what people are looking at, with the visual mode of perception isolated from other sensory modalities such as hearing, touch, or smell. These studies have also reflected the prevailing assumption that the act of perceiving environmental simulations is comparable to real-world perception. Although much work has been done to demonstrate the validity of this assumption (Bosselman & Craik, 1989), my research direction was influenced by a group of ecological psychologists who spent their careers challenging this perspective (Brunswick, 1956; Gibson, 1979; Hochberg, 1966). Their work was also supported by empirical studies revealing significant differences between picture perception in the laboratory and reactions to the same natural landscapes in a field setting (Kroh & Gimblett, 1992).

In recent years video and computer-generated simulations have begun to replace still photographs (Orland, Budthimedhee, & Uusitalo, 2001), to replicate what observers see while moving through the landscape. Additional technologies have been designed to simulate immersion in the environment, reflecting changes in perception that result from shifts in the perceiver's physical orientation (Haq, 2002). Despite these advanced techniques, I would argue that the underlying theories and resulting research questions remain largely the same. For instance, studies rarely examine the impact of whole body movement on perception, the interaction effect between multiple sensory modalities, or changes in perception over time.

Over the past two decades, Stephen and Rachel Kaplan (1989) have been the most widely referenced and influential researchers in the study of human response to nature. Their seminal book outlines a "landscape preference framework" with categories based on psychological dimensions rather than physical attributes of the environment. This framework or "preference matrix" includes the dimensions of *coherence, complexity, legibility,* and *mystery,* and is based on the assumption that cognitive dimensions reflect perceptual information attended to by observers.

The Kaplans' research findings also indicated presence of "restorative" benefits when people observed natural environments, forming the basis of their Attention Restoration Theory (ART) (Kaplan, 1995). This theory explains how exposure to natural environments can reduce stress by promoting use of *involuntary* attention. This mode of attention was found to require little, if any, effort on the part of the perceiver. In contrast, they found that *directed* attention, used to perceive built environments, requires significant effort. Thus *involuntary* attention promoted by natural environments, can provide a "restorative effect" to counter the "mental fatigue" resulting from extended use of *directed* attention in built environments. Although this theory of restorative effect has generated a significant amount of empirical work across a wide variety of settings (Hartig, 2001), I was not convinced that the Kaplans' cognitive framework would be adequate for exploring the myriad dimensions of real-world nature experience.

I sought to make a contribution to this area of inquiry by developing a new research methodology to study perception of nature in a real-world setting. In pursuing this goal for my dissertation I also hoped to uncover key dimensions of nature experience not yet explored in the literature. Since theory and method are mutually reinforcing (Sommer & Sommer, 2002), I needed an alternative theoretical framework to guide development of this new methodology. Ittelson's (1973) environment perception framework provided the necessary foundation for this project. According to the tenets of this framework, the landscape would be re-conceptualized as a multisensory environment and, concomitantly, visual observers would be re-conceptualized as multimodal perceivers. Environment perception was conceptualized by Ittelson as a dynamic process, constantly unfolding over time. Perception could no longer be studied as a static moment reflected in the subject's response to photographic representations. Since the impact of motion on human perception would also be acknowledged within this framework, I would need to study embodied perceivers moving in and through the environment as well as their perceptual responses to movement of environmental features.

To achieve these objectives I chose to study hiking, an outdoor activity that fosters perceptual encounters with nature. During my initial review of the literature, I found only one study of hiking which incorporated tenets from Ittelson's (1973) framework. Hull and Stewart (1995) combined "visitor-employed photography" with the "experience sampling method" (Csikszentmihalyi & Larson, 1987) to study the relationship between hike experience and natural features encountered on the trail. Participants were given cameras at the trailhead and instructed to photograph whatever they were looking at when a randomly-timed beeper sounded. Hull and Stewart were mostly interested in studying the relationship between nature experience and the distance of features encountered. Although this research design made significant progress toward capturing real-world experience, the use of still photography reflected the traditional concept of a static, visual landscape and might help to explain limitations in the study's research findings.

Developing An Innovative Videographic Methodology

As I developed a methodology to address the limitations of previous research, I sought an approach that would be relatively unobtrusive, preserving the integrity and ecological validity (Winkel, 1985) of the hike experience. Videography seemed to have significant potential as a medium for studying human response to nature in a real-world setting.

For my first pre-test with a video methodology, I mounted a camcorder on an external frame backpack worn by the research participant. I accompanied the hiker on the trail and encouraged him to talk about environmental features, which caught his attention. Although the camcorder captured the participant's whole body movements as he hiked along the trail, it did not track his head movements and therefore failed to record many natural features that had his attention. For this reason, the video equipment was completely redesigned for the next pre-test.

I purchased a 2" x 2" microvideo camera for the second pre-test, mounting it on the elastic headband from a hiker's headlamp (with headlamp removed). The headband would be placed on the hiker's forehead and fastened with hair clips to prevent slippage (Fig. 7-1). The forehead-mounted microvideo camera would be attached by cable to a camcorder carried inside the hiker's backpack, and the camcorder would operate in Video Tape Recorder (VTR) or playback mode. I chose to use a microvideo camera with moderately wide-angle lens (4mm) rather than the extremely wide-angle fish-eye lens (8-10 mm).

Although the latter type of lens would have replicated the hiker's 180-degree field of view, it would have produced distorted video images with a convex appearance. Use of the microvideo camera was preferable to the previous equipment design because it would track both head and body movements, more accurately capturing the participant's perceptual encounters along the trail.

The biggest challenge associated with this new technique was finding the appropriate angle for the mounted microvideo camera. It quickly became apparent that hikers lean forward, especially while climbing uphill. Without compensating for this forward-leaning posture, the camera focused downward more often than not, and videotaped the ground more than the surrounding environs. I eventually developed a hinge mechanism that allowed me to adjust the camera's angle upward, accommodating each hiker's unique posture.

Fig. 7-1: Researcher wearing microvideo camera and shotgun microphone

In order to capture naturalistic observation, I recruited 6 pairs of hike partners from the Appalachian Mountain Club's New York-North Jersey Chapter to capture companions' conversation in a naturalistic manner. Each pair of participants was scheduled for a separate hike along a 2 ½ mile section of the Appalachian Trail in New York's Sterling Forest State Park. Hikes were scheduled between September and November of 1999 to avoid the summer's heat and to end before the beginning of hunting season. Participants were informed that hikes would cancel due to inclement weather since neither the microvideo camera nor the microphones were waterproof. Unfortunately, this schedule did not consider the challenge of hiking during the fall season when leaves cover the trail's surface. Luckily, no one was injured despite a considerable amount of slipping and sliding, and the equipment was not damaged even when hikers fell and knocked the backpack against the ground.

This project required full review by the Institutional Review Board

(IRB), and was considered "Intermediate Level Risk" because of the usual risks associated with hiking. On the application I described my recruitment strategy, criteria for selecting participants, and methodological procedures. In addition to approving the project, the IRB approved two Informed Consent Forms. The first form was mailed to participants prior to the hike. It described the research procedure and equipment and requested permission to show the hike videotapes to members of my dissertation committee; a photograph of the equipment was mailed to participants along with this Consent Form. A second Informed Consent Form was used after each follow-up interview, asking hikers for permission to use images from the video excerpts they had just reviewed, in public presentations or publications.

Each hike lasted approximately 4 hours and was videotaped continuously from beginning to end, with a 1-hour break for lunch. This research design differed significantly from that typically used in visual and sociological anthropology (Banks, 2001), since participants did not have the opportunity to intentionally select visual images to tell the story of their hike. Instead, images were captured continuously and unobtrusively, and each hike story unfolded on tape in real time.

Hike partners were instructed to speak with one another as they normally did when hiking together. They were encouraged to discuss anything along the trail that caught their attention "in a special way", especially things they heard, touched, smelled or saw. I selected participants who had hiked together previously to ensure that they were compatible vis-á-vis pace and decision-making, and to ensure that they knew one another well enough to engage in frequent, spontaneous, and uninhibited conversation. I also chose participants who had not previously hiked the section of trail chosen for this research project, since familiarity may have altered their perceptions (Gibson, 1991).

Since the camcorder would be in VTR mode, as mentioned earlier, neither its camera nor microphone would be operational. Although the microvideo camera came equipped with a miniature microphone, it did not have sufficient pick-up for research purposes. Instead, I mounted a shotgun microphone on the straps of the hiker's backpack to capture distant nature sounds, and a wireless microphone was attached to each hiker's jacket to record individual comments as well as shared conversation whether participants were walking side by side or far apart.

With each hike lasting approximately 4 hours, it would be necessary to change both the camcorder tape and microphone batteries half-way through. In order to accomplish this task I decided to accompany each pair of hike partners from a distance, staying outside their range of sight and sound until a pre-arranged meeting time. Since participants would be able to contact me via walkie talkie, this research design meant I would also be available in case of technical difficulties or medical emergencies.

This naturalistic method of videography would make it possible to enter each hike experience by accessing participants' emotions, thoughts and actions in real time, while retaining the links between each strand of experience. However, secondary data would be needed to validate and augment my interpretations of these data. I chose to devise a brief questionnaire and to conduct follow-up interviews within two weeks of each hike. The brief questionnaires were distributed immediately after each hike, when recall would presumably be most comprehensive and accurate. Questionnaires were designed to gather information about the perceived sequence of events and temporal dimensions of the hike. Participants were also instructed to list hike highlights, which were subsequently included in video excerpts used for the follow-up interview. Participants watched a 30-minute tape of video excerpts during their follow-up interview. This afforded them the opportunity to provide detailed explanations of perceptual encounters they had on the trail, as well as additional reflections and insights gleaned with the passage of time.

Challenges of Data Analysis

Data collected for this research project included 24 hours of videotaped hikes, 12 hours of tape-recorded follow-up interviews, and 12 questionnaires. Transcription of the video and interview data was extremely time-consuming and presented significant challenges. Video transcriptions included both verbal comments and non-lexical sounds that were relevant to the hike experience such as deep sighs, labored breathing, and laughter. Body movements such as head turning, pointing, and changes in tempo or pace were transcribed when they appeared to reflect shifts in environmental awareness.

When transcribing follow-up interviews, it was necessary to link participants' comments to the video excerpts being discussed. In part I relied on handwritten interview notes, which included timecode numbers from the videotapes. More precise identification of video segments was at times retrieved by listening to the background sounds from the tape-recorded interviews.

Upon completion of data transcription, I used content analysis (Holsti, 1969; Weber, 1990) as the primary method of data analysis. In its first phase, this analysis was guided by theoretical perspectives from studies in environment perception, environmental experience, landscape perception, and trail design. The second phase of analysis was accomplished with a variation of Glaser and Straus' (1967) grounded theory approach, whereby data were re-categorized and thematized to more directly reflect participants' hike experiences.

During data analysis I discovered two additional studies of hiking that had used innovative video methodologies. In Ohno, Hata, and Kondo (1997), researchers walked behind participants who had been recruited to traverse a 1/4-mile circuit path around a lake. Although researchers videotaped both the hikers and the lake environment, they focused primarily on head movements as indicators of where participants were looking and, by extension, what they were noticing. In the other study, Murray and Aspinall (2001) recruited hikers to videotape the trail environment as they walked approximately 2 miles through a forested area in Scotland. Participants were given a camcorder at the trailhead and instructed to film whatever caught their attention while hiking. They were also asked to comment about the natural elements being filmed.

Although the videographic techniques in Ohno et al. (1997) and Murray and Aspinall (2001) were completely different, both studies used graphic notation to facilitate data analysis. After reviewing these studies, I concluded that graphic representations would be needed in my study as well, to condense and organize the extensive amount of data I had collected. Moreover, I was not convinced that discursive text in written transcripts would do justice to the full complexity of nature experience captured on video.

Although there already existed a comprehensive notation system for landscape design (Thiel, 1997), this system did not meet key tenets of Ittelson's (1973) environment perception framework and was therefore not suitable for my research project. I proceeded to develop a new system of notation, which I named Hiker's Experiential Notation (HIKEN™; Appendix B-1 & B-2). I created one set of symbols to represent the Hiker, and another to represent the Environment. Symbols were scored on two separate staffs, one on top of the other, much like a music or dance score. Symbols for the Hiker were inspired by choreographic and anthropological notation systems (Eshkol, Melvin, Michl, Von Foerster, & Wachmann, 1970; Hall, 1963), and many Environment symbols were adapted or borrowed from the sport of orienteering (Bratt, 2002). A special Orienteering "IOF" font was used to print these symbols on the notation (© 1990-94 Martin Minow). Hikers' emotions, thoughts and sensory modalities (visual, auditory, tactile, olfactory) were represented with colors and design patterns. In contrast with written transcripts, HIKEN™ would "tell a story" by communicating these multiple relations at a single glance (Tufte, 1983, p. 30).

The HIKEN™ notation required geographic placement markers to score the hike experience – actions, thoughts, and emotions – in relation to the trail environment. Markers were also needed to score perceptual encounters in proper sequence (although not reflecting real-time). To achieve this objective I identified a single set of 111 environmental features across all 6 hike videos, including elements such as trees, painted blazes marking the trail's path, and boulders. With these markers it was also possible to locate participants at any point in their hike and to compare hikers' responses to the same natural features hiking into or out of Sterling Forest.

Additional work is needed to refine the HIKEN™ symbol set and to evaluate the validity and reliability of this notation system for future data analysis. Even in its preliminary form, however, HIKEN™ has attracted the interest of design professionals since they are accustomed to using non-lexical symbols with software such as Computer-Assisted-Design (CAD). For example, HIKEN™ was included in a review of various notation systems by a landscape architect writing about commonalities between "linear paths" in music and architecture for the 2006 conference on Architecture, Music and Acoustics (Hanoch-Roe, 2007).

I chose to use the unregistered trademark symbol rather than formally register HIKEN™ with the United States Patent and Trademark Office, since that process would have required a significant fee and much work still remained to make this a viable notation system. Although use of the ™ symbol does not provide legal protection, it does alert the public to my claim of ownership through "legitimate use of the mark" (USPTO, 2003).

Effectiveness of the Research Methodology

The follow-up interviews proved extremely effective for deepening my understanding of each hike experience. By watching their video excerpts, participants were able to re-live their hikes and in so doing, corroborate and expand upon my initial interpretation of the video data. One woman provided an apt description of this experience while watching herself climb the steep ascent in the video: "You do feel like you're climbing it [now, as we watch the film]. Like we're climbing it as we speak, as we look at the video, because it's so close." Another person identified with the motion of head bobbing apparent from the video's scenery moving up and down: "It's interesting to see on camera the way you look and see where the trail is . . . the video technique works . . . cause it's more real. It's such a natural motion, you're looking where you're going. Seeing it on tape makes you go, 'Oh yea, that's what you do.' You look at your feet, now I can see where I'm going to next." The videos were such effective prompts that on occasion people remembered events or natural features that had not yet appeared in the excerpts: "We're just getting psychic here I guess, in that we foresaw what we actually said on [the video] tape. I mean, we were just discussing in this interview everything that is now showing on the videotape."

The effectiveness of this multi-method approach was also confirmed through preliminary data analysis. Most importantly, the videographic technique successfully incorporated tenets of Ittelson's (1973) environment perception framework without significantly altering the hike experience. As reported by participants in the follow-up interviews, the microvideo and microphone equipment was minimally intrusive, and hikers rarely found it uncomfortable or distracting. In the words of one individual, wearing the microvideo camera was akin to "carrying a second person. It's like the watcher watches. Like you notice what you noticed." He proceeded to explain that "It's weird [to wear the microvideo]. In the upper range of my vision I can *just* see the camera. It's sort of like the bill of your cap. I forget that I'm even carrying the shotgun mike at this point. It's sort of in the corner of my peripheral vision, but I've stopped seeing it." The microvideo camera reminded another participant of the movie Clockwork Orange: "[It's] like I'm forced to watch nature. Have your eyes pried open."

Although wearing the equipment was clearly an out-of-the-ordinary experience, participants only seemed self-conscious when they encountered other people on the trail. After passing a family with a little girl in tears, one woman joked to her husband, "You probably scared her with all your equipment." He laughingly agreed, describing himself as a "cyclops. . . or triclops . . . [with] three eyes."

The inability to remove this gear without my assistance seemed a more serious problem. Some people did manage to disconnect the cables and take off the backpack when they wanted to remove sweaters or jackets after warming up. However, most people left the equipment on even when they would have liked to "take a separation" because "nature was calling." Instead they waited until our planned rendezvous at the lunch break, when I would be present to assist in this endeavor. I would recommend that the equipment be re-designed so that hikers could more easily turn the camera off and remove the equipment on their own.

Although the original reason for my presence on each hike was purely logistical, it proved advantageous for building rapport and facilitating data analysis. My relationship with hikers became more comfortable as we got acquainted over lunch; we chatted about hiking in general and casually discussed our reactions to this section of the Appalachian Trail. Since I hiked the trail on the same day(s) as the research participants and became very familiar with trail features after hiking the same trail more than six times, I was better qualified to comprehend and interpret hikers' videotaped comments and reactions.

Participants knew I would eventually review their videotaped hikes, but they rarely focused on this fact while hiking. For most people this knowledge had little, if any, impact on their conversation or behavior. When this realization did occur, it was usually fleeting. For example, one participant mused to her partner, "I wonder if we can get a copy of our video. We can ask for one." To which her partner replied, "We just *did* ask." Another person assumed that the microphones might not record her comments if they were made in a hushed tone. Feeling slightly embarrassed by her boyfriend's behavior, she laughingly whispered, "You're being recorded! Don't sing! Don't let them hear you sing!"

During the follow-up interview, one participant acknowledged her awareness of the privacy invasion as she was hiking, and explained her reaction as follows: "During the hike I did think about the fact that I'm sharing a personal part of my life, that otherwise would be very private. I didn't feel like I had to guard my conversation I guess, but on the way back when I stopped to think about it I thought, well, someone's going to be watching me hiking and listening to everything that I'm saying and that just seemed like kind of an odd experience." To respect hikers' privacy needs, I did not include in the video excerpts any potentially embarrassing material such as intimate conversation or body sounds and "silly" behavior unrelated to their encounters with nature.

Theoretical Contributions from a Videographic Methodology

The videographic technique used in this project produced a wealth of data. Preliminary data analysis suggested that this new methodology could make a significant contribution to the literature on human response to nature. Traditional theory and methods have imposed serious constraints on the research agenda, and may need to be adapted to retain their validity in a real-world context.

The research design for this study successfully met the tenets of Ittelson's (1973) environment perception framework. Most importantly, the microvideo camera and externally-mounted shotgun microphone successfully captured multisensory attributes of the natural environment. The videotapes recorded sights and sounds encountered by participants along the trail, as well as indirect data about the tactile environment. Videotapes contained hiker reactions to ephemeral features such as clouds and sunlight reflecting off the lake, and their exclamations of delight upon reaching the summit of Buchanan Mountain with its panoramic vista. The videos also showed close-up features such as moss or mushrooms, with hikers reaching out to stroke the soft surfaces. The microvideo camera captured hikers as embodied perceivers, with data such as pace and tempo indicating shifts in their focus of attention or level of environmental awareness.

The importance of touch and whole body movement was especially evident in videotaped images of the steep rock scramble. This trail section required more varied and challenging body movements such as "lower[ing] yourself down", "pull[ing] yourself up", and climbing "hand over hand . . . like [on] a jungle gym." For this reason, many hikers reported having an *optimal* or *flow* experience (Csikszentmihalyi, 1990) as they ascended or descended the boulders. According to Csikszentmihalyi, this state occurs most often when people are engaged in a physical activity and concentrating intensely on meeting a measurable goal associated with that activity. In the words of one hiker, "It's about getting dirty and touching more . . . this [steep descent] forces you [to be aware] in a way that a beautiful scene forces you to be aware of it."

With my video methodology it was also possible to capture changes in perceptual encounters from morning to afternoon, and to compare perceptions for the hike into and out of Sterling Forest. Changing patterns of sunlight such as shadows, reflections in the lake and "dappled" light shining through the trees were often mentioned as highlights on the questionnaires and in the follow-up interviews, thus confirming the importance of studying perception over time. Moreover, fleeting features or *ephemerals* such as these have received short shrift in the existing literature. Perhaps this tendency to focus on the permanent landscape can be explained by the need to understand human response to features more readily influenced by landscape design practices or natural resource management.

Data analysis also revealed dimensions of the hike as a sequence of events with beginning, middle, and ending. The beginning of the hike was usually associated with increased awareness of natural features and fading away of the built world (i.e. sounds of cars). The beginning was also associated with changes in body state, as participants felt their heart rate increase and body temperature rise when they began the initial ascent. The end of the hike was more closely identified with shifts in mindset, as participants' thoughts began to focus on post-hike plans instead of the natural features around them. Changes in body state accompanied this shift in thought patterns as hikers grew increasingly tired, sore, or hungry. Final indication of the hike's ending came when hikers once again heard cars and saw the road at the end of the trail.

Data analysis also revealed a sense of *insideness*, a dimension that seemed to define the middle section of each hike. As described by one person, being "inside" the hike involved "that feeling like you're in it, away from everything." When they entered this phase of the hike, participants seemed to have heightened perceptual awareness of natural features, felt a bodily connection with nature, and were no longer thinking about their day-to-day lives. Although the concept of *insideness* has been explored in architectural phenomenology (Norberg-Schulz, 1980) and the urban design principles of Pattern Language (Alexander, Ishikawa, & Silverstein, 1977), it had not previously been used to explain landscape perception or nature experience. Perhaps future research will reveal a correlation between *insideness* and the cognitive-perceptual category of *mystery* (Kaplan & Kaplans, 1989) or the experiential state of *flow* (Csikszentmihalyi, 1990).

Conclusion

As might be expected, this video methodology has primarily been of interest to recreation professionals and natural resource managers. In one study for instance, researchers in the Division of Forestry at West Virginia University had planned to videotape a trail and ask hikers in a laboratory setting to rate trail conditions using Continuous Audience Response Technology as they watched the videos. Originally the methodology involved use of a hand-held camcorder; but when the researchers learned about the microvideo technique they hoped to incorporate this method instead, given their expectation that the microvideo camera would capture more realistic images and thus elicit more accurate rating responses (Pierskalla, C., personal communication, May 9, 2005).

This project demonstrates that videographic methods have great potential to deepen our understanding of nature experience and in so doing, to strengthen our connection with nature. In contrast, I would argue that traditional methods have reflected and reinforced a dis-connection with the non-human world. Using videography to capture real-world data, landscape perception researchers can work with practitioners to more effectively preserve and protect landscapes that are both perceptually varied and experientially meaningful.

References

Alexander, C., Ishikawa, S., & Silverstein, M. (1977). *A pattern language.* New York: Oxford University Press.

Appleton, J. (1996). *The experience of landscape* (rev. ed.). New York: John Wiley & Sons.

Banks, M. (2001). *Visual methods in social research.* Thousand Oaks, CA: Sage Publications.

Banks, W. P., & Krajicek, D. (1991). Perception. *Annual Review of Psychology, 42,* 305-331.

Bosselmann, P., & Craik, K. H. (1989). Perceptual simulations of environments. In R. Bechtel, R. Marans, & W. Michelson (Eds.), *Methods in environmental and behavioral research* (pp. 162-190). New York: Van Nostrand Reinhold.

Bratt, I. (2002). *Orienteering*. Mechanicsburg, PA: Stackpole Books.

Brunswik, E. (1956). *Perception and the representative design of psychological experiments* (2nd ed.). Berkeley: University of California Press.

Csikszentmihalyi, M. (1990). *Flow. The psychology of optimal experience.* New York: Harper & Row.

Csikszentmihalyi, M., & Larson, R. (1987). Validity and reliability of the experience-sampling method. *Journal of Nervous and Mental Disease, 175*, 526-536.

Eshkol, N., Melvin, P., Michl, J., Von Foerster, H., & Wachmann, A. (1970). *Notation of movement* (Biological Computer Laboratory Report 10.0). Urban, IL: University of Illinois.

Gibson, E. J. (1991). Trends in perceptual development. In E. J. Gibson (Ed.), *An odyssey in learning and perception* (pp. 365-385). Cambridge: MIT Press. (Reprinted from Gibson, E. J. (1969). *Principles of perceptual learning and development.* Englewood Cliffs, NJ: Prentice-Hall.)

Gibson, J. J. (1979). *The ecological approach to visual perception.* Boston: Houghton Mifflin.

Glaser, B. G., & Strauss, A. L. (1967). *The discovery of grounded theory. Strategies for qualitative research.* New York: Aldine.

Hall, E. T. (1963). A system for the notation of proxemic behavior. *American Anthropologist, 65*, 1003-1026.

Hanoch-Roe, Galia (2007). Scoring the path: Linear sequences in music and space. In M. W. Muecke & M. S. Zach (Eds.), *Resonance: Essays on the intersection of music and architecture* (pp. 77-144). Ames, Iowa: Culicidae Architectural Press.

Haq, S. (2002). *Role of VIE (Virtual Immersive Environments) for the study of movement.* Lecture presented for EDRAMOVE Workshop, Environmental Design Research Association Conference, Philadelphia, PA.

Hartig, T. (Ed.). (2001). Restorative environments [Special issue]. *Environment and Behavior, 33* (4).

Hochberg, J. (1966). Representative sampling and the purpose of perceptual research: Pictures of the world, and the world of pictures. In K. R. Hammond (Ed.), *The psychology of Egon Brunswik* (pp. 361-381). New York: Holt, Rinehart and Winston.

Holsti, O. R. (1969). *Content analysis for the social sciences and humanities.* London: Addison-Wesley   Publishing Co.

Hull, R. B. IV, & Stewart, W. P. (1995). The landscape encountered and experienced while hiking. *Environment and Behavior, 27*, 404-426.

Ittelson, W. H. (1973). Environment perception and contemporary perceptual theory. In W. H. Ittelson (Ed.), *Environment and cognition* (pp. 1-20). New York: Seminar Press.

Kaplan, S. (1995). The restorative benefits of nature: Toward an integrative framework. *Journal of Environmental Psychology, 15*, 169-182.

Kaplan, S., & Kaplan, R. (1989). *The experience of nature: A psychological perspective*. NY: Plenum Press.

Kroh, D. P., & Gimblett, R. H. (1992). Comparing live experience with pictures in articulating landscape preference. *Landscape Research, 17*, 58-69.

McConville, M. (1978). The phenomenological approach to perception. In R. Valle & M. King (Eds.), *Existential-phenomenological alternatives for psychology* (pp. 94-119). NY: Oxford University Press.

Murray, J., & Aspinall, P. (2001). The experience of forests. In T. Sievänen, C. C. Konijnendijk, L. Langner, & K. Nilsson (Eds.), *Forest and social services. The role of research* (Finnish Forest Research Institute Research Paper 815, pp. 79-94).

Norberg-Schulz, C. (1980). *Genius loci. Toward a phenomenology of architecture*. NY: Rizzoli International Publications, Inc.

Ohno, R., Hata, T., & Kondo, M. (1997). Experiencing Japanese gardens. In S. Wapner, J. Demick, T. Yamamoto, & T. Takahashi (Eds.), *Handbook of Japan-United States environment-behavior research: Toward a transactional approach* (pp. 163-182). NY: Plenum Press.

Orland, B., Budthimedhee, K., & Uusitalo, J. (2001). Considering virtual worlds as representations of landscape realities and as tools for landscape planning. *Landscape and Urban Planning, 54*, 139-148.

Seamon, D. (1979). *A geography of the lifeworld: Movement, rest, and encounter*. New York: St. Martin's Press.

Sommer, R., & Sommer, B. (2002). *A practical guide to behavioral research* (5th ed.). New York: Oxford University Press.

Thiel, P. (1997). *People, paths, and purposes. Notations for a participatory envirotecture*. Seattle: University of Washington Press.

Tuan, Y. (1990). *Topophilia. A study of environmental perception, attitudes, and values*. New York: Columbia University Press. [Original work published 1974]

Tufte, E. R. (1983). *The visual display of quantitative information*. Cheshire, CT: Graphics Press.

United States Patent and Trademark Office (2003). Should I register my mark? Retrieved December 25, 2003, from http://www.uspto.gov/web/offices/tac/doc/basic/register.htm

Weber, R. P. (1990). *Basic content analysis* (2nd ed.). Newbury Park, CA: Sage Publications.

Winkel, G. H. (1985). Ecological validity issues in field research settings. In A. Baum, J. E. Singer, & J. L. Singer (Series Eds.) & A. Baum & J. E. Singer (Vol. Ed.), *Advances in environmental psychology: Vol. 5. Methods and environmental psychology* (pp. 1-41). Hillsdale, NJ: Lawrence Erlbaum Associates.

Zube, E.H., Sell, J.L., & Taylor, J. G. (1982). Landscape perception: Research, application, and theory. *Landscape Planning, 9*, 1-33.

CHAPTER EIGHT

REMEMBER TO PRESS RECORD:
A PRACTICAL GUIDE FOR USING VIDEO
IN RESEARCH

AUTUMN BECKMAN

As an artist and an academic I have a tendency to combine art and research. This was something I did in the years I volunteered at the Houston Zoological Gardens, often bringing animals into my artwork and artwork into zoology, and it's something I continue today in my psychology research with Hurricane Katrina survivors[1]. My most recent project involved interviews with nine survivors in New Orleans and three in Houston about their stories and experiences since the hurricane, each of which I videotaped for the purposes of data analysis, short research films to be presented in academic settings, and a feature length documentary to be given to participants. In this chapter I utilize this experience in order to provide a practical guide for the use of video in academic research, something I wish I'd had while working on my project. Despite a life-long artistic background, including a year and a half studying animation production, this was my first attempt at creating a live-action film. I entered the project with confidence in my artistic abilities but found that I had a lot to learn along the way. For this reason, my chapter is aimed at researchers new to video but I hope it will be useful to others as well. I begin with ideas about what I found beneficial in using video in research, then offer advice on equipment, filming, and editing. Following the text I provide a checklist of equipment needed for a video project.

---

[1] For more information on this work see http://autumnbeckman.com/research.aspx

Benefits of Using Video in Research

The first question to ask when contemplating the use of video in research is the same for contemplating the use of any other methodology: why use it? What benefits will video add to the research, the participants, and the final project? I chose to use video for several reasons. First, I knew I would be conducting qualitative interviews and video provides the most complete record possible of them. When I was ready to begin transcription and analysis, I had not only my interview notes but also audio and video documentation of body language and every word, inflection, and facial expression emitted by participants. This is not to say that video data is always objective, in fact it's often very subjective and open to interpretation (Mackay, n.d., Pink, 2004), but it was infinitely helpful in the transcription process because, if a word or phrase was inaudible, watching lip movement enabled me to more accurately determine words that were unclear through audio alone. It was also helpful in analysis and write-up because once I had interviews transcribed I tended to rely on the written word but as time passed I found that I had interjected my own inflections on participants' stories. Referring back to the video footage opened my eyes to moments I had missed or misinterpreted (for example, a statement made with sarcasm instead of seriousness or with anger instead of sadness) and allowed me to recompose my analysis based on (I hoped) participants' intentions as opposed to my own inventions.

Second, the use of video in research intersects well with ideologies of qualitative, participatory action, and feminist methodologies; specifically the desire to create a platform for participants (who might not otherwise be heard) to construct and voice their stories and perspectives (Pink, 2004). In the case of video this voice is quite literal, though it can easily be squashed or misinterpreted in the hands of careless or unethical editors. Another benefit for participants is that, through this medium, they can be provided with video documentation of their own stories which they can keep for themselves, share with others, or even pass down through generations.

Third, using video specifically as a product of research (in addition to or instead of a written piece) has its advantages. One is that video has the potential to reach a wider, more general audience (as opposed to the traditional academic audience) who is accustomed to visual media as a primary source of information (Masur, 2007). Another is the richness and complexity that video has to offer through comprehensible layers of sound intertwined with still and moving imagery in a concise manner. For example, in a just few seconds of one of my research films viewers digest images of severely damaged New Orleans housing, which is then overlaid with text giving statistics of how many applications versus closings have been made by the Road Home Program (a government program financing home rebuilding along the Gulf Coast) and they hear the researcher's (my) analysis of the program followed by an interview clip of a participant explaining how Road Home affects her life. To present the same information in as powerful a way would be much more difficult to accomplish in a written or oral presentation, at least from my artistic perspective (see also Mackay, n.d.).

Finally, and this may be more specific to my project than to others, Hurricane Katrina was an event that most of us (myself included) experienced through film in the days following the storm, a medium through which representations of those affected by the storm were constructed and skewed (Garfield, 2007; Kasinitz, 2006; Masur, 2007; Sommers, Apfelbaum, Dukes, Toosi, & Wang, 2006; Tierney, Bevc, & Kuligowski, 2006). It seems only logical then that presentations focusing on a follow-up to this event should utilize the same medium, particularly if the intent is to construct survivors in ethical and truthful ways.

Video and Institutional Review Boards

At first, I was daunted by the task of getting a video project approved by my university's Institutional Review Board (IRB) but, following the advice of our IRB administrator, the addition of a simple permissions form to the consent document was all I needed. For my study I asked for participants' permission to record their interviews in either audio or both audio and video formats then for permission to use those recordings in all the contexts I could foresee wanting to use it (a research film to be viewed by myself and my professors only, a research film to be viewed by academic audiences, and a film to be viewed by the general public). A separate question for permission was given for each of these uses[2]. Once all interviews were complete I burned DVDs of them and sent each participant a copy of his or her own uncut interview footage with a note thanking them for their participation and updating them on the progress of the research. I hoped this note would make them feel included and valued, instead of like a stranger had taken a few hours of their time for

---

[2] For an interesting discussion of the ethics of video, see Mackay, n.d, as well as Lauren Tenney and Patricia MacCubbin (Chapter 2 of this volume).

professional gain and then forgotten about them. The footage I sent doubled both as compensation for their participation (I was unable to compensate them financially) and as an opportunity for them to review their footage and change their minds about how I could use it (e.g. Mackay, n.d.). Pink (2004) uses an alternate method. She does not give copies of the footage to participants but, rather, reviews clips with them both a few minutes into the interview and immediately after the interview so that they may see how they are both coming across and being represented on video. Ultimately, I also mailed all participants a copy of the final feature length film once it was complete. This occurred nearly a year after the interviews were conducted.

Equipment

Video camera. One of the most daunting tasks in beginning a study with video is the decision about what equipment is needed (see the *Equipment Checklist* at the end of this chapter), particularly if you must purchase it and are working within a tight budget. I started from scratch with very limited funds and was able to obtain what I needed for under $1,000. The most minimal equipment required is, of course, the video camera, which is also the most intimidating of the purchase decisions to be made because there are so many cameras available in so many price ranges (from around $100 to many thousands). It was especially daunting to me because I had never purchased and had barely even used a video camera before. My advice is simple: shop around. I checked the internet first to learn about differences between cameras; to decide what features I needed, wanted, and didn't need or want; and to read customer reviews. I then narrowed it down to a few select cameras and took my list to stores to try the cameras out, paying attention to weight, picture quality, and user-friendliness. With some reluctance to advertise for *any* company, I reveal that I decided on the Sony Handycam HDD (hard disk drive) model DCR-S40 and have been extremely happy with it. A sturdy and well-padded carrying case is also essential to protect this investment. Personal preference will determine if you want a case that fits only the camera or one that will hold the camera and its accessories (i.e. batteries, cables, and lenses) as well. I prefer the latter.

Immediately, I knew I wanted a hard disk drive camera because they store digital video to an internal hard drive instead of to media such as DVDs, CDs, or videotapes. This option is the most economical since you don't have to purchase media or film/video tape editing equipment; you just upload the video to your computer and edit with digital video editing software. My camera has 30 Gigs of hard drive space and, for the most part, that was more than sufficient for the interviews I conducted (which were about one hour each). I also wanted the highest optical zoom I could afford, which is important for zooming into things at great distances; and I purchased a separate wide-angle lens which, if you are in a tight space, allows you to see more of the space than would be possible with the built-in camera lens. The desire for high zoom capabilities is a personal preference. It's important to me because I've often found it useful in photography, specifically when shooting close-ups of zoo animals from behind the boundary of a fence (I used to photograph them for paintings); in other words, in situations where there is a physical limit to how close I can get to a subject. In my Hurricane Katrina research I used the zoom feature for environmental shots, such as in obtaining close-ups of levees from distances. One warning about using video zoom: the quality of the image is reduced slightly and, if you are shooting with the handheld technique (as opposed to on a tripod), the camera will accentuate the slightest movement you make, causing the image to be jumpy and difficult to watch; so use it sparingly.

My camera came with night vision, an option I never expected to use but which actually came in handy a few times in low-light conditions (although the picture was washed out and tinted green). Other camera features that may be of interest include recording in standard or widescreen modes; recording in color, black and white, or sepia tones; and shooting still images. These effects can usually be achieved through editing software so I did not find them necessary in a video camera. I also found the built-in still camera to be disappointingly low resolution and grainy so I recommend using a separate still camera for photographs that you might want to include in presentations and publications of the research. The video itself had a similar low resolution, grainy appearance but I suspect this would be the case with any consumer grade camcorder and that the only way around it would be to spend thousands of dollars on a professional camera.

Battery and Tripod. Video cameras come equipped with a battery but I *highly* recommend purchasing a second, long-life battery and using the included, shorter-life battery as a back-up. My longest interviews ran for two hours and the included battery would not have lasted that long. I also recommend having a camera tripod at your disposal. I have not found a significant difference in tripods based on price so I recommend going with the cheapest you can find as long as it's sturdy and allows you to raise and lower the camera height and to swivel the camera both vertically and horizontally.

Light. It is also extremely helpful to have a portable light in case you run into a low-light situation (which can happen indoors during the brightest part of the day, not just at night). I conducted the Hurricane Katrina interviews inside the homes or businesses of survivors except one that was done on the outside porch of a participants' home. When the time and space were available to do so, I attached a clip-on light to a second tripod and positioned it about two feet to the left or right of the camera. Having the light shine on the participant at a different angle than the camera is important to prevent that awful, straight-on, washed-out effect you get when you use a flash on a still camera. I also loosely placed a white garbage bag over the light as a filter so it wouldn't be so harsh and I brought an extension cord in case the plug wouldn't reach where I was filming. A wireless light would be ideal so as not to use participants' electricity and more than one light would be optimal under some low-light circumstances.

Microphone. Audio recording was one of my biggest concerns. I wanted a camera with the option of attaching an external microphone but the one with this feature was several hundred dollars more than the one I purchased and I didn't have the budget for it, not to mention the $200 for the microphone itself, so I opted for the cheaper model with a built-in mic. It worked much better than I expected but the sound was still only adequate at times, especially when recording outdoors where traffic, wind, and other noises interfere. I tried recording both with a handheld digital voice recorder and with a microphone plugged directly into my laptop but neither attempt worked well. The first provided very poor sound quality and the second gave me compatibility problems. If your budget permits, I highly recommend purchasing a camera that enables you to attach an external mic. I also recommend a clip-on mic (as opposed to a shotgun or handheld mic) as it will allow close proximity to participants' voices, as well as visual discreteness.

Assistant. One of the most important things I needed while filming was an assistant. An assistant can save both your time and your participants' time by helping set up and take down equipment, and s/he can even help save the research itself. For example, during one interview the camera's low-battery warning signal began flashing and I couldn't see it from where

I was sitting but, luckily, my assistant caught it in time to interrupt the interview and change batteries. If he hadn't been there the entire interview (one of the best, of course) would have been lost and I wouldn't have known it until I went back to review the footage.

Back-up Storage. Following each interview I connected the camera to my computer and downloaded footage to the hard drive. This process varies depending on your camera (keep in mind that my camera records to an internal digital hard drive, not to tapes or DVDs which require a different process for digital conversion; a process I know nothing about) and depending on your computer, so in order to do this just follow the instructions included with your camera. When I returned home (the research was done out of town in New Orleans and Houston but I lived in New York at the time) I backed up the interviews on both an external hard drive and on DVDs. It is a good idea to back up your data in more than one medium (i.e. hard drive and DVDs) in case one medium fails and also to store data in more than one location (i.e. work and home) in case one is destroyed. I also recommend back-ups of original data because if you accidentally delete something in the editing process you can restore the file from this data. The amount of storage space you will need varies by the length of your project. One DVD usually holds about two hours of video. When shopping for an external hard drive I recommend purchasing the largest amount of storage you can afford because video takes up an incredibly large amount of space. I had about twenty-four hours of raw data and created several short films and one two-hour film and by the time the project was finished I had filled a 250 Gig hard drive and had to purchase another. I will speak in more detail about software and editing equipment in the *Editing* section.

Filming

Setup. I conducted most interviews in participants' homes or places of business because I wanted their own environments behind them in each shot.

Fig. 8-1: Beckman interviewing Hurricane Katrina survivor, Becker, in her New Orleans home. 2007.

Even with my assistant, it took several minutes to set up our equipment (especially the first few times). It was after one participant complained about this that I stopped using an external back-up mic (which I was having trouble with anyway) that I had plugged directly into my laptop computer and relied only on the camera and, when necessary, the portable light. In most cases, I mounted the camera on a tripod so that it was positioned at participants' eye level. The tripod stood a little to the left or right of me so the camera would capture them at a ¾ angle instead of straight on or in profile (participants sometimes looked at the camera anyway). The light, again, was placed about two feet to the left or right of the camera. The limited space at one interview location required that I stand while the participant sat, so I positioned the camera in front of me at his eye level. In this case, I and the camera were close enough within the participants' line of vision that he kept looking back and forth between us. He also seemed to be more aware of the presence of the camera than most other participants, which seemed to affect his ability to speak as comfortably and freely as he did when the camera was off. It's common for people's behavior to change when they know they are being videotaped

(Mackay, n.d.; Pink, 2004).

Composition. The composition of the frame is vital to the visual appeal of the film, especially if it is intended to be a product of the research (as opposed to being used only for analysis). I composed my frames so that participants were seen from the waist or chest up and positioned them on one half of the screen with their line of vision directed toward the other half. This way, if they leaned forward or moved their arms it would all be captured in the frame. The background is also important, particularly if it is of significance to participants. In my first few interviews I placed participants near walls, usually with some colors, textures, or objects (i.e. photographs, curtains, or plants) to break up the space and make it more interesting. Upon reviewing the footage, however, I found that it resembled bad public access television (e.g. poor lighting, low image quality, figures positioned against a flat background) so I watched a few documentary and media interviews to see how they accomplished a more professional look. Besides using higher quality film equipment, the secret seems to be to position interviewees near the center of the room, as far from walls as possible, so that a larger amount of the room can be seen behind them in the frame.

Tripod versus Handheld. I conducted one interview on the spur of the moment without access to my tripod so I was forced to hold the camera by hand as this participant spoke. I was worried that the camera movement, caused mostly by my unsteadiness as a human tripod, would ruin the footage but to my surprise it actually turned out to be much more visually dynamic than other interviews. The handheld camera technique provides the freedom of being able to follow participants as they move. In this interview, the participant was a candy shop owner working in her kitchen while we spoke and, hence, she moved around the room a lot. I was easily able to follow her, which I could not have done with a tripod, and it made for much more interesting footage. While she moved I also zoomed in and out to both keep her in the frame and keep the composition interesting. I was afraid to do this at first because it felt amateur but it actually worked very well. I recommend using the zoom occasionally but caution to do so slowly and somewhat sparingly (quick and constant zooming in and out can make a film difficult to watch). Obviously, it would be best to practice all of these techniques prior to the project in order to gain skill and confidence. If you use a moving camera technique, especially if you are moving quickly, it's also a good idea to check your footage immediately after filming to be sure it is legible. For example, I filmed damaged housing from a moving car and had to reshoot after watching the too-fast, too-blurry footage. In this case it also helped to shoot the environment from an angle instead of straight on because the shot then contains elements of visual perspective, offering reference points from which viewers can stabilize their gaze and better understand the images passing across the screen (this was my experience in viewing the footage, at least).

There are a few benefits to shooting with a tripod. First, the footage is steady and consistent; second, once you have the camera set up, you can leave it and not have to think about it during the interview. This makes it easier for the participant to forget it's there and is also less distracting to the researcher who would otherwise be forced to take on two jobs (interviewer and cinematographer) at once. This was my biggest struggle with the handheld method. Though I was confident about my interview technique at the point at which I shot with the handheld, I found myself paying more attention to what I was filming than to what I was hearing. I was conscious to make as much eye contact as I could to show the participant that I was paying attention and interested in her story but I didn't feel quite as attentive to her as in other interviews, and I felt it wasn't as fair to her as the tripod technique was to other participants. That said, the dynamic footage resulting from this technique did her more justice than the static footage from the tripod technique did for other participants. To help solve this dilemma I recommend two solutions: 1) a second camera to capture a second angle, providing a more dynamic wealth of footage from which to edit and 2) a competent and trusted person to do the handheld filming for you.

More Tips. A few more quick tips for filming: 1) the absolute most important thing to remember is to be sure you press the record button when you want to film and to be sure the camera says it is recording after you press that button! I learned that the hard way. While in the midst of editing, I was searching for footage of one participant's house and neighborhood (to use as establishing shots), which I distinctly remembered filming but was unable to find. I finally came to the dismal conclusion that I must not have pressed record. 2) Check the camera regularly during interviews to be sure it is *still* recording (or have your assistant do this for you). The camera could be giving you a low battery, low disk space, or other visual warning (it won't give you an audio warning because that would show up on your audio track) that you won't know about until you review the footage only to discover that the camera stopped filming halfway through. 3) Be careful about backlighting and having windows in the frame, especially if you don't have your own light source directly on the interviewee. Even if the participant looks well-enough lit on the camera's display screen, it might still be too dark when you view the footage from a computer or television. 4) Recharge the battery after every interview so it's always ready for the next one. 5) If you have a digital camera that records to an internal hard drive, upload the video to a computer as soon as possible after an interview in order to free the camera's hard drive space for your next interview. 6) For editing purposes, it's a good idea to film establishing shots (footage of the exterior of the space in which you are filming, which you would show in the film prior to shots inside that space) to ground viewers in a particular location. For example, when introducing a new survivor in my Hurricane Katrina film I wanted to first provide images of their home or business and the surrounding neighborhood to give viewers some semblance of the varying degrees of destruction within which that particular survivor was currently living. This would also allow viewers to compare environments and living conditions across participants. 7) Following each interview you might want to turn the camera on yourself to record your reflections. I did this (though I didn't end up using the footage) with the idea that it would not only help during analysis but could also make for interesting footage in a film product. 8) Check out (probably any edition of) Bordwell and Thompson's (1979) *Film Art*, touted as *the* textbook on filmmaking.

Editing

Software. Since all my video files were digital I was able to edit footage on my home computer, sparing me the huge expense of film or video tape editing machinery. The professional standard for digital video editing software is Final Cut Pro (for Apple computers) but I have a PC so I purchased the inexpensive ($120) Sony Vegas Movie Studio Platinum, which met my needs almost perfectly and includes Sony DVD Architect allowing you to create DVD menus. The biggest advantages to Vegas were that it was cheap and easy to learn (I taught it to myself) but I also encountered two big problems: first, Vegas unexpectedly shut down several times causing me to lose the work I did since I last saved the file. This was easily rectified by saving my work more often, which is a good idea anyway. The second problem was that once I had completed the two-hour version of my film and was ready to burn it to DVD through DVD Architect I repeatedly received error messages preventing me from completing the task. I was never able to fix this problem (neither was technical support) and I finally had to pay to upgrade to a newer version of the software and split the file into two parts, consequently burning the film on two DVDs instead of one in order to complete the project. After a year's worth of work, that was a very disappointing end. I'm not sure what suggestions I can offer towards avoiding this disaster in the future as it was a technical matter that I never figured out but my personal solution (I hope it will be a solution, anyway) is to switch to a Mac as soon as possible and to their Final Cut Pro editing software. Again, I'm not trying to advertise for any company and, in fact, it's been a decade since I last used a Mac and I have never used Final Cut Pro so I'm basing this hope completely on recommendations of my Mac-using friends, one friend in particular who runs his professional recording studio on Macs.

Computer. One major challenge in digital editing is how the large size of video files drastically decreases the speed at which a computer works. Due to this, I recommend a computer with the highest processing speed and memory you can afford. I worked with a 2.19 GHz processor and 1 Gig RAM and often found the editing software to run very slowly. This occurred particularly while opening, saving, converting, and burning files, the last two of which sometimes ran twice as long as the length of the film! Since I was unable to use my computer while these processes were running I often wished I had two computers so I could work on one while the other was processing.

Ethics. Another challenge is the editing process itself, particularly when: 1) considering ethical obligations to participants, and 2) creating films for an academic audience. During interviews, participants often reveal intimate details about their lives, leaving researchers with the choice of which details to share with film audiences and which to (possibly) censor for reasons of privacy. I, too, was sensitive to this issue and to the fact that different people have different perceptions of what information counts as "personal" so I provided the Hurricane Katrina survivors with whom I spoke with several opportunities to censor their own work. First, prior to interviews they signed informed consent and permissions documents allowing me to film them and to use their images and words. Second, during interviews the camera was always clearly visible in close proximity of both participants and myself (at whom their gaze was usually directed) so that they might always be aware that what they were saying was being recorded. Finally, I sent a DVD copy of each participant's unedited interview to them within about a month of the interviews themselves so participants had a chance to review their footage and the opportunity to change their minds about its use (Mackay, n.d.).

Audience-Specific Editing Approaches. As with any product, films connected to research are often intended for a variety of audiences and must be created with those audiences in mind. I never intended to share this project with the general public but I did intend for it to be seen by select academic audiences (for presentations related to my doctoral program) and by the research participants themselves (as documentation of their experiences). Since the purposes of these screenings varied depending on the intended audience I decided to create two separate films: one fifteen minute research version and one two-hour documentary version. For the feature length film, *Ties That Bound After Levees That Broke: Collective Stories of Hurricane Katrina and New Orleans*, I told participants' collective experiences of the storm and its aftermath through only their words, organized in chronological, then topical, order. The film begins, for example, with accounts of the days leading up to the storm. One participant tells of how she heard of the storm approaching Florida; then another speaks of the same incident from her perspective; then a third speaks of how the storm passed Florida and entered the Gulf of Mexico; another speaks of it turning toward New Orleans, and so on. I gave a copy of this film to each person who participated in the study as well as to a select few people who assisted in the project (such as my film assistant and my professors). I have already explained my reasons for providing participants with a copy but it was also important to me that my assistant have a copy as a "thank you" because the project would not have been as successful without him and to my professors for the same reason and so that they would have a record of the work. I have not and will not attempt to distribute or sell the film to a general audience because I do not have permission from all participants to do so (Mackay, n.d.), and each of the non-participants who received a copy are also aware of these ethical restrictions and I trust them to follow the guidelines; otherwise they would not have received a copy.

After much trial and error I decided to edit the shorter research version of the film, created specifically to present my work to academic audiences, following the format of a traditional research article organized into four sections: theory, methods, results, and conclusions. I combined clips from interviews, footage of the local environment, photographs, illustrations, text, and voice-over narration (by me, the researcher/author) to report on the research in a rich but concise manner. I provided one example above (about the Road Home Program) of the layered richness available in film. Another example is the use of animated diagrams and illustrations to help explain theory. I didn't use "real" animation because I don't know how to do it digitally so I created illustrations that varied slightly and cross-faded them into one another to create (primitive) animation effects. I also used photographs of participants to illustrate the demographics section; first presenting a collage of all twelve people then showing them divided into groups based on gender, race, home ownership, and business ownership. From this particular sequence I have received much praise for both the clarity with which the demographic data is presented and for the resurfacing of a human component in what has too often become a mundane string of numbers within a written report. Such a presentation also captures the complexity of individual participants in that viewers are able to recognize that a particular person may belong to more than one category.

Fig. 8-2: Video still of Hurricane Katrina survivor, Bill, in his New Orleans home. 2007.

Conclusion

Research on its own is a tremendous task and the addition of video brings yet another complex and time-consuming element to the table but the end result can be well worth the extra effort and challenges. Not only were my videotaped interviews endlessly helpful in the transcription and analysis processes, but the film products also lent a human element to the research that is often missing from more traditional academic products (or so I have been told by viewers). I did receive a small amount of criticism, which I expected, for integrating this nontraditional method into research. There was some concern about the ethics of revealing participants' identities. I addressed this with the research and video consent documents they signed and with the fact that I provided each person a DVD copy of their footage to review, giving them the opportunity to change their minds about whether I could use any portion of it. There was also concern (possibly because I am still a student) about me giving video instead of oral presentations. I worried about this myself so in order to assuage my own concerns and attempt to nip any criticism in the bud about film presentations not being "academic" enough, I made sure to write a presentation/film script (which I used as the narration to the film) that included all the information (i.e. theory, methods, and results) that would be expected from any other oral presentation. I have since shown this piece twice, once for a school presentation and once at an academic conference on video in research (the one that inspired this book, in fact); and, despite these concerns, audience response was overwhelmingly positive and the films even seem to have inspired some viewers to take up video in their own research. If you are new to video or are contemplating its use in a project, I hope this advice will help you get started and save you a few of the learning curves I found myself navigating. I wish you the best of luck in your own work.

Equipment Checklist

Film Equipment

Required
    ___ video camera
    ___ video camera battery (charged)
    ___ video camera carrying case

Recommended
    ___ extra battery with long life (charged)
    ___ tripod
    ___ light
    ___ filter for light
    ___ tripod for light

___ extension cord
___ film assistant

Optional
___ second camera
___ external microphone, preferably clip-on
___ wide angle lens

Editing Equipment

___ digital video editing software
___ computer with high processor speed and memory
___ external hard drive (for storage)
___ DVDs (for backup storage)
___ (optional) second computer

Final Product Supplies

___ DVDs
___ DVD cases
___ DVD case inserts (for outside of case)
___ (optional) DVD case inserts (for inside of case)

References

Beckman, A. (Director). (2008). *Ties that bound after levees that broke: Collective stories of Hurricane Katrina and New Orleans* [Motion Picture]. United States.

Bordwell, D., & Thompson, K. (1979). *Film art: An introduction*. Boston, MA: McGraw Hill.

Garfield, G. (2007). Hurricane Katrina: The making of unworthy disaster victims. *Journal of African American Studies, 10*, 55-74.

Kasinitz, P. (2006, March). Katrina, the media and the American public sphere. *Sociological Forum, 21*(1), 145-146.

Mackay, W. E. (n.d.). Ethics, lies and videotape... Retrieved October 19, 2006 from http://delivery.acm.org/10.1145/230000/223922/p138-mackay.html?key1=223922&key2=5980721611&coll=GUIDE&dl=portal,ACM&CFID=11111111&CFTOKEN=2222222

Masur, L. P. (2007, November 23). How the truth gets framed by the camera. *The Chronicle of Higher Education*.

Sommers, S. R., Apfelbaum, E. P., Dukes, K. N., Toosi, N., & Wang, E. J. (2006). Race and media coverage of Hurricane Katrina: Analysis, implications, and future research questions. Analyses of Social Issues and Public Policy, 6(1), 39-55.

Tierney, K., Bevc, C., & Kuligowski, E. (2006, March). Metaphors matter: Disaster myths, media frames, and their consequences in Hurricane Katrina. *The Annals of The American Academy of Political and Social Sciences, 604*(1), 57-81.

Pink, S. (2004). Performance, self-representation and narrative: Interviewing with video. In C. Pole (Ed.). *Seeing is believing? Approaches to visual research: Studies in qualitative methodology*, Vol. 7, Amsterdam: Elsevier Ltd.

Chapter Nine

"Represent": Reframing Risk Through Participatory Video Research

Caitlin Cahill, Matt Bradley, Denise Castañeda, Larissa Esquivel, Naima Mohamed, Joel Organista, Jessica Sandberg, Maria Valerio, and Kanesha Winston

Introduction

By putting you as an "illegal" person they have stripped you of your humanity. And by taking away your humanity you are no longer allowed the same rights and even the same respect as you would give a stranger. Or I feel comfortable in saying, an animal. You know, people don't kick dogs, but they feel very comfortable kicking a person who has no humanity, or is "illegal," or is undocumented.
—David, an undocumented university student interviewed for *Easy Targets*.

Why is the exploitation of undocumented immigrants tolerated? And the education of their children jeopardized? Why are young people of color disappearing from our schools before they graduate? And, what is our role and responsibility as researchers (young and old) to address the social injustices in our communities? These questions, and others, structure our inquiry. Our research focuses upon what Robin D.G. Kelley identifies as "the culture wars in urban America": "the ongoing battle over representations that continue to rage each day in the streets of urban America" (Kelley, 1997, p. 8). For young people growing up in Salt Lake City, Utah, issues of representation are of the utmost concern. One of the critical insights that we identified in our research is that power lies in controlling how you are defined. Stereotypes of the "other" as "illegal," "drop out," and "uneducated" serve to blame, exclude, exploit, and legitimate social inequalities. Young people, and in particular young people of color, are too often framed as "at risk" and in need of surveillance and control. In our research we challenge this framing and instead reveal the very real risks we, our friends/peers, and our communities, face in our everyday lives negotiating institutional racism and trying to access higher education.

Using a participatory action research approach, we have created two documentaries that provide a "safe"—or at least a "safer"—space for students like David (above) to reach out to a larger public and narrate their stories of discrimination on their own terms. In this case, the video presents a shared social context for witnessing the pain David expresses and becomes part of its transmission. However this space is not without vulnerabilities. Here in this chapter we address the thorny relationship between risk and representation in participatory video research, touching upon four interrelated "risks": 1) the personal and emotional risks involved in doing research on topics that hit "close to home" (racism/immigration, etc.); 2) the question of re-presenting or reframing the ways that "at risk" youth or communities are understood; 3) the issue of "informed risk" and representation; and finally, 4) the risks involved in activist research/working towards social change. Along the way we will discuss the theory and practice of participatory video research, and the challenges and epiphanies of our collective video research process.

Growing Up in Salt Lake City

We represent members of a team of researchers who participated in a collaborative community-based research project entitled *Growing Up in Salt Lake City* (Gui SLC). Our partners included Salt Lake City West Side High School students/youth researchers, University of Utah faculty members and students, the Salt Lake City Mayor's YouthCity program, and University Neighborhood Partners, a community-university program[1].

[1] The Growing Up in Salt Lake City research project was initially funded by a community-based research grant from the University of Utah's Lowell Bennion Community Service Center and the American Association of Geographers. We are most grateful for the critical support of Dr. Octavio Villalpando, Assistant Vice President for Diversity, University of Utah; Dr. Theresa Martinez, Vice President, Office of Academic Outreach, University of Utah; Dr. Cheryl Wright, Chair,

The key research collective members/co-authors include high school youth research team members: Larissa Esquivel; Naima Mohamed; Joel Organista; Jessica Sandberg; Maria Valerio; Kanesha Winston; University student/ research assistant: Denise Castañeda, and University faculty members/mentors: Matt Bradley & Caitlin Cahill[2].

In this chapter, as we reflect upon our experiences working together and sharing our personal perspectives, sometimes we shift abruptly between voices. Despite our differences, most of the time we have decided to write collectively as a strategic "we" placing emphasis upon our collective "message." But at times we shift to our personal voices articulating our multiple positionalities and distinct points of view. This is reflective of our process that was rich with dissent and negotiation, while our shared perspective is a political stance of solidarity.

Growing Up in Salt Lake City is part of an international collaboration with UNESCO's (United Nations Educational, Scientific and Cultural Organization) Growing Up In Cities project which has actively engaged young people in community evaluation, action, and change in low income communities in over fifty sites around the world.

> The project is widely recognized as one of the most significant international initiatives for engaging children and youth in action research for community change, resulting in improvements to local communities as well as a wide range of publications and presentations that have helped inform and strengthen participatory practice with young people. (Driskell, 2002)

While the Growing Up in Cities projects have taken different shapes in various contexts, they adhere to a core set of principles which promote young people's participation and inclusion, action, and community-based partnership development. The Growing Up in Salt Lake City project consciously situates young people's perceptions of their own lives and communities at the center of the research. Central to our inquiry were the

---

Family & Consumer Studies, University of Utah; and University Neighborhood Partners, University of Utah.

[2] Other key members of our research team who we had the privilege to work with include Sonia Caraveo, Ariana Prazen, Angela Romero and Roberta Targino. We have been lucky to collaborate with the University of Utah's University Neighborhood Partners. We are most grateful to everyone else who has been involved in the Red Flags and Easy Targets projects as this includes many generous, interested, and courageous young and old people.

questions: What do we learn when we re-think our community from the perspectives of young people? What issues are of particular concern?

Salt Lake City, Utah is an interesting place to research young people's experiences of urban environments because it is on the cusp of major urban development and dramatic demographic changes. While Utah is still "A Big White State" (as we identify it in our video *Red Flags*) with almost 90% of the state population Caucasian, the dominant white majority is being challenged. Between 2000-2004, 41 % of Utah's population growth consisted of people of color, predominantly of Latino background. And during the same time period, 75% of the enrollment increase in Utah's public school system were students of color (Perlich, 2006). But what do these changes mean for young people? And young people of color in particular? Our project focuses on Salt Lake City's west side, which is the most diverse zipcode in the state, as almost 40% of the residents are ethnic minorities.

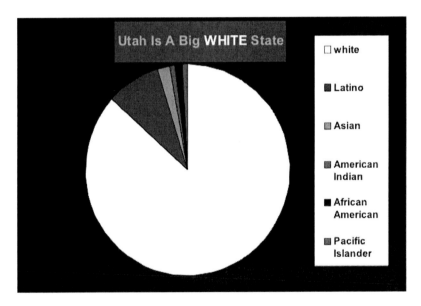

Fig. 9-1: The students created this chart for the video *Red Flags* to illustrate Utah's whiteness. Credit: © 2008 Growing Up in Salt Lake City.

There is, in fact, very little research about young people growing up in Salt Lake City and even less focused upon young people's own concerns. Our project addresses this lack of information while at the same time involving young people as agents of change in researching their own communities. The objective is not only to learn more about young people's concerns, but also to involve young people in developing proposals for action and social change. In a participatory action research (PAR) process, young people are repositioned as co-researchers as they identify priority issues affecting young people, and develop proposals for change (Cahill, 2007b).

PAR starts with "the understanding that people—especially those who have experienced historic oppression—hold deep knowledge about their lives and experiences, and should help shape the questions, [and] frame the interpretations" of research (Torre & Fine, 2006, p. 458). In a PAR project there is an emphasis upon process, a commitment to research contributing and 'giving back' to community collaborators, and a recognition of the power of knowledge produced in collaboration and action. Developed as part of a broad radical social agenda, PAR is rooted in grassroots liberationist, feminist, antiracist, activist, and social justice movements within an international context (Bell, 2001; Fals-Borda, 1979; Freire 1997/1970; Rahman, 2006; Smith, 1999). Participatory practices are widely used by youth rights advocates, critical educators, youth workers, and community organizers who work with young people to evaluate social issues/programs that are of concern such as problems of educational inequities, media portrayals of youth, violence in the community, police brutality, and discrimination based on sex/race/class [Youth Together (www.youthtogether.net); Kids as Self Advocates (www.fvkasa.org/); CAAAV Youth Leadership Project (http://www.caaav.org/projects/ylp); ESPINO (http://www.espinocoalition.net); Youth Organizing Communities (http://www.innercitystruggle.org); RedWire (http://www.redwiremag.com)]. There is also a small, but growing, group of researchers who are using PAR, working collectively with young people to study issues that matter to them. PAR offers a promising framework for researchers committed to social justice and change. The multiple benefits of engaging the perspectives of young people in research have served to challenge social exclusion, to democratize and redistribute power within the research process, and build the capacity of young people to analyze and transform their own lives and become partners in the building of more sound, democratic, communities (Cahill, 2007b; Cammarota & Fine, 2008; Ginwright et al., 2006).

Our participatory video project also builds upon, and contributes to, the field of youth media which places emphasis upon building young people's capacity to participate in social change movements (Goodman, 2003; www.evc.org; www.global-action.org; www.namac.org), as articulated by Meghan McDermott of the critical media literacy organization Global Action Project (GAP):

> We want to make young adults aware of their own agency in the world. When youth discover the power of their voices through making media, they find themselves, as Maxine Greene says, 'able to "name" and imagine how they might change their world. Critical literacy emerges as young people inquire into their lives and environment, produce a story that explores that life, reflect on the social and historical context of their experiences to understand root causes of inequities, and then become agents of positive change.
> (www.robertbownefoundation.org/ezine/vol3no4/wire.php)

Our Process

Our inquiry is youth-led and places emphasis upon the particular contribution and access young people bring to understanding their everyday lives. At the same time, our project embodies what Chavez & Soep identify as a "pedagogy of collegiality"—"a context in which young people and adults mutually depend on one another's skills, perspectives, and collaborative efforts to generate original, multitextual, professional quality work for outside audiences" (Chavez & Soep, 2005, p. 3). In our project, this involved the youth researchers working closely with others, young and old, to frame questions, collaborate on editorial decisions, and strategize how to represent their concerns most effectively to diverse audiences. Our process is characterized by exchange and collective negotiation. While we centered youth perspectives and concerns, the adult facilitators not only provided resources and training in research skills, but also critical perspectives on the research itself. We all—youth researchers and adult mentors—have a stake in the project, in terms of the integrity of the research, the personal and political implications involved in representation, the production of knowledge, and the potential impacts (p. 9).

Because participatory research is a practice of researching *with*, rather than *on* participants, the building of a community of researchers is critical to the success of a PAR process. This entails taking seriously processes of collaboration and community-building, and also involves the development of research proficiency among all participants. The development of 'skills' is significant because it creates space for the youth research team to take ownership over the process (Cahill, 2007b). The *Growing Up in Salt Lake City* project started by building upon the knowledge and experience of the young people involved. Through investigating their concerns and analyzing the contradictions of their everyday lives, the youth researchers 'learned through doing,' developing research skills in an applied way through the inquiry process. We engaged in multiple research methods including photography, field notes, mental maps, a guided tour of places of significance, interviews, and daily focus groups/brainstorming sessions. This preliminary training and collective research process in turn informed the focus of our research. The researchers identified two issues that were especially important to young people growing up on the west side of Salt Lake City:

1) Stereotyping and racism in schools (*Red Flags*); and
2) The challenges undocumented students face in trying to access higher education (*Easy Targets*).

The *Growing Up in Salt Lake City* research team divided into two teams, each project following its own messy, twisted, path of discovery and challenges. As part of this process we wrestled with questions of purpose and audience: What is the purpose of our research? To whom do we want to speak? If the goal of our research is to educate, how do we do this? And—how do we reach our intended audiences? How can we engage and provoke diverse audiences to act upon our research? Grappling with these questions informed our collective decision to create research video documentaries as a way to reach a broad public audience, to share our findings with other young people in particular, and, also, to create a platform for young people's voices to be heard. From the beginning, therefore, the youth research team articulated a desire to "make a difference" with their research and educate their community.

Our decision to create documentary research videos also had important ramifications for our research process as it involved learning new technical skills (how to use the camera/lighting/editing etc), and it changed the nature of the research (as conducting an interview for a camera poses different challenges). Significantly, using video also forced us to grapple with issues of representation and audience early on as part of our research process as we shall discuss in more detail with regards to each project below.

Our Projects

Fig. 9-2: Labels for *Easy Targets* and *Red Flags*. Credit: © 2008 Growing Up in Salt Lake City. Designed by Thomas Nelson.

For both documentary projects *Red Flags: Stereotyping and Racism in the Schools* and *Easy Targets* (Fig. 9-2) the youth researchers conducted interviews, focus groups, and attended legislative sessions and community meetings, filming over 20 hours of tape. Each documentary is approximately 25 minutes long. Labors of love and collective negotiation, each decision, from how to film a particular interview, or what clips to include (or cut), was made after much deliberation between the youth researchers, students, and their mentors. The two projects illuminate the politics of risk and representation that are at the heart of participatory video research. Questions we struggled with included (see Cahill & Torre, 2007, Cahill, 2007a): Who has the authority to represent a community's point of view? Is there a "we" within the community, or even within our research team, being represented? Who is made vulnerable by our research? What is safe to share and what isn't? Do we, for example, edit out stories of cutting school or dropping out because they feed into stereotypes about students of color (what Fine et al., 2000 identify as the 'bad stories', p. 126)? How can we contextualize the 'bad stories', and address the damaging consequences of globalization, structural racism, and exploitation (ibid)? And, how do we "represent" this context on film? How do we frame a critique of an educational system that is not meeting undocumented students' needs and still advocate for their inclusion? How do we contextualize the exploitation of undocumented communities in a larger conversation about structural racism and economic injustice and still hope to reach out to and engage decision-makers invested in meritocracy? Risk in this sense involves a careful consideration of the consequences of telling particular stories and how they could be used or potentially misinterpreted (Fine et al., 2000). And in this regard, there is also the question of how do we present our work so that it is 'received' and acted upon?

What are the calculated risks involved in activist research? And, is social change possible without risk? Do we have a responsibility to "protect" those individuals and communities most impacted by the injustices documented in the research? And, who, and how should the necessity and level of the risks involved be determined? These decisions are central to the ethical commitments of PAR and reflect our collective struggles around the politics of representation and, in turn the representation of political questions in our documentaries. We shall address these questions in our descriptions of each of the documentaries that follow.

Red Flags: Stereotyping & Racism in the Schools

We created the *Red Flags* video with the intention of ending the silence on race in our schools. The research question we investigated was "how does stereotyping and racism affect teens in schools?" We identified three main findings of our research: 1. Students feel unwelcome in school and like they don't belong; 2. Institutional racism; and, 3. Students lose motivation to succeed in school. These findings point to the risks that young people have to negotiate on an everyday basis. At the same time, our research challenges the representation of youth as "at risk." As Donald Macedo suggests there is a lack of pedagogical space for students to ask "who put these students at risk" and, what is the risk (Macedo, 1998, p. xxvi)? We are wary as to how the label "at risk" has been applied to young people of color who are stereotyped as less likely to succeed and become productive citizens. However, our research suggests that there are really risks for young people of color that need to be addressed for them to succeed in school[3].

With our documentary we hoped to jumpstart a conversation about the

---

[3] See also Downey, G., Eccles, J., & Chatman, C. M. (Eds.) (2005). *Navigating the future: Social identity, coping, and life tasks.* New York: Russell Sage Foundation.

proverbial elephant in the middle of the room that no one is really
addressing despite high drop out rates by students of color and ongoing
racial tensions in our schools (Aleman & Rorrer, 2007). While we realized
this conversation would not be easy, we think it is a necessary risk if we
hope to contribute to changing the situation. Racism and white privilege
are "dangerous" subjects that many Americans would rather avoid (for
different reasons). Discussing the personal violences of discrimination and
racial injustices is risky. It is rough emotional terrain. But as it is also part
of our everyday lives this is something we felt was necessary to address
with our research. One of our goals was to raise the awareness of the
administration, so, as Joel suggests: "they can see that racism is still
happening and there is something that needs to be done to make school a
better place for everyone." Naima explains that "they are showing what
people go through on a day to day basis...and hopes to increase the
awareness that students learn best when the teacher is able to link
materials learned to everyday life..." She hopes that "administrators will
make teaching about racial and ethnic backgrounds a required class so that
students will learn more about different cultures and races".

Personal risks. To answer our research question focusing on the
impacts of racism on students we decided to speak to other students about
their personal experiences of discrimination; however, finding people who
willingly wanted to do so—on camera—was challenging for us. Another
challenge was figuring out how to establish a trusting and safe
environment for other students to feel comfortable enough to talk about
racism and share their experiences with us as these discussions can be
personally very distressing. Although our research addresses the realities
that students of color are already confronting everyday, doing research to
consciously dig in deeper and probe sensitive areas...and sometimes we
didn't want to because it was too painful. And for us as researchers,
witnessing student after student share their stories of discrimination, and
their struggles to just get through high school "intact" was difficult and
often demoralizing. At times it was necessary for us to spend time
collectively reflecting, processing our findings, and expressing our outrage
together.

In turn, as part of the process of doing research we also had to come to
terms with how stereotypes and racism has affected each of us individually
and collectively, and the impact they have on our own everyday lives. This
was also painful. Our own process involved moving from personal
experience to social theorizing; that is moving from an initial emotional

response to a given situation (outrage/indignation/upsetment) to understanding this within a social and political context. Kanesha reflects:

> Racism is a big part of daily life in school. We decided to make our documentary on stereotyping and racism in school because we all experienced it in school. That is a huge part of our life and it's a huge problem in schools and it's really hard to deal with sometimes. As I look back on when we were in the documentary process, the things that stood out more to me was knowing that teenagers that are my age are going through the same things in school as me. They all want what we want: to let people see that racism has not stopped is still here and also let the adults know how it's affecting us, changes how we perform in school, and even makes us not want to go any more. Another thing that stands out was hearing from the people we interviewed their personal stories. The reason why it stands out to me is because I could relate to it and say hey, 'I am not the only one going through this'!!

The process of doing research was personally transformative and changed the way we understood our own experiences. As part of our research we found new "frames," or ways of making sense of, our everyday experiences of discrimination. For example, through one of our interviews we learned about institutional racism from a university student who was reflecting upon her experiences of tokenism in high school. The frame of institutional racism shifted the way that we interpreted our research and for that matter our own experiences of teachers neglecting us, or asking us to share our "Black Experience" to a White classroom, or the inequitable ways that White and Latino/a students were tracked in school. As Joel explains: "Now that I know the difference I can see it in my daily life and understand then explain to others." Now that we understand institutional racism, we see it everywhere. This has forced us to confront the structural ways that racism and White Privilege shape our educational experiences, and in turn we hope to educate our audience–in particular our peers, other teenagers of color—about this with our documentary. Here the risks involve the emotional distress that comes with identifying the power of oppressive structural forces on one's everyday life. We wondered will poking holes in the meritocracy—that if you work hard enough you will succeed—be a dangerous enterprise if you still have a few years of high school left. Or can it be liberatory? We think so. Pricking "the psychic amnesia of American racism" (Torre & Fine, 2006, p. 460) stings. But as Freire remarks "liberation is thus a childbirth, and a painful one" (Freire, 1997/1970, p. 31). It is this pain that pushes us forward, that motivates our personal and social transformation (Cahill, 2004; hooks, 1995).

After filming a focus group with other young women of color who shared their experiences of institutional racism, Kanesha decided she also wanted to be interviewed for the video and include her story in the research. Although this was really difficult, Kanesha made a conscious and courageous decision to share her experiences of discrimination in the classroom and offer a "counter story" to the dominant one that stereotypes young people of color as lazy or drop outs (Solórzano and Yosso, 2002). Kanesha took a personal risk with the hopes of emboldening others to speak out. Although telling her story was not easy, it was therapeutic for Kanesha, to come to terms with her pain, or at least release it in a supportive space. She felt empowered to reinterpret her private experience of being stereotyped by a teacher as not smart enough to succeed, and to speak back and name it as institutional racism.

Kanesha's brave decision to participate in the research inspired all of us. It was a turning point in our process. Knee deep in the process of doing research, it became clear how close this hit to home for all of us on an everyday basis. But how, we wondered, could we reach out to others with our stories? Would listening to us tell our stories inspire our audience? In particular we were concerned with reaching out to other students of color, as this was our primary audience of concern, although we also hoped to educate teachers and administrators about our situation. As part of the process of creating our video we attended to the interrelated questions of subject (stereotyping & racism), audience (students of color), purpose (to raise awareness of racism and challenge stereotypes) and voice/point of view (our own!) (see Fig. 9-3).

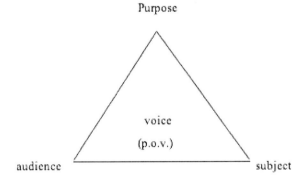

Fig. 9-3: Editing triangle. Credit: © 2008 Matt Bradley.

As a result, we decided that in order to engage our primary audience, other young people, it would be more powerful to "show" rather than just "tell" what we found out through our research. Performing our own experiences of racism would bring our research "to life" in a direct fashion. We each chose a particular story that reflected our research findings and related to the stories our respondents shared. Kanesha acted out her intimidating experience of being accused of bringing a knife to school by the principal, being aggressively interrogated and asked to empty her pockets and take down her hair. Joel shared his humiliating experience of having to take the ESL test every single year because, although he is a fluent English speaker and in an Advanced Placement (AP) English class, his family speaks Spanish at home. And Naima shared her experience of being laughed at and ostracized in the school hallway because she wears a hijab. These were our "secrets," our private stories of shame that we had hardly shared with anyone else before. But we took a risk stepping out of our comfort zone and re-enacting these humiliating and painful experiences with the goal of pushing others out of their own comfort zone as they witness our intimate humiliation. We hope to inspire others to be brave enough to talk about issues of racism and speak back to stereotyping.

Fig. 9-4: Still frame of Joel taking an ESL test as he narrates his own experience being required to take the test repeatedly year after year. Credit: © 2008 Growing Up in Salt Lake City.

The question of audience raises other issues of risk and vulnerability. In our project because we are attempting to communicate with both "insiders " and "outsiders" the issue of representation is critical. How, for example, might *Red Flags* be viewed in a predominantly White classroom? What conversations might it engender? These questions came up for us after presenting our video locally and being asked by White audience members to share more of our experiences and also to identify solutions for institutional racism. This was not a comfortable situation for us and we were concerned about how other students of color might be made more vulnerable by our documentary. We decided to confront this issue directly and at the end of our documentary we speak to the camera one at a time:

> Dear Audience, thank you for taking the time to watch our film. We ask that after watching the film you not ask the students of color to interpret their experience. Instead we ask that you all reflect upon your own responsibilities to address racism in your everyday lives. Thank you.

In this gesture we recognize the risks involved in doing participatory video research. We hope to also raise consciousness about the vulnerabilities and shift the question of responsibility.

The *Easy Targets* Project

The *Easy Targets* project also raises questions of representation and risk although in this case the risks have very literal legal, economic, and familial consequences. Undocumented students and their families constantly face the risk of being apprehended and deported back to their native countries or even physical violence[4]. When a young person or his or her family chooses to speak out about their experiences living in the U.S. as an undocumented person, this risk is amplified. When these voices are then publicly presented to policy makers, lawmakers, the media, and the general public, these risks become even greater. Yet many young students and their families did agree to share their experiences with us in our

---

[4] In 2006 a Salt Lake City Latino high school student was attacked and beaten by two White men while he walked to school. The young man reported his attackers called him a "stupid wetback" and told him, "go back to your country, you don't belong here" as they kicked and punched him. This is just one instance of physical violence that has been instigated against allegedly undocumented people in the U.S. For a report of other similar instances see "Immigration Backlash: Hate Crimes Against Latinos Flourish" (Mock, 2007).

documentary for a variety of reasons. David, quoted at the beginning of this paper, in fact, insisted that his face not be concealed or obscured in anyway. He made a specific and political decision to engage those who would deport him or pass laws that limit his opportunities and make them confront him as a human being. He often quotes the famous words of the revolutionary Mexican leader Emiliano Zapata: "It is better to die on one's feet than to live on one's knees" --"*Prefiero morir de pie que vivir siempre arrodillado!*"

The reasons undocumented young people and their families chose to share their experiences are varied, however, and so are the ways in which they were comfortable being represented. The video we created had various audiences and purposes, and as we approached each potential audience or purpose, we collectively reviewed how best to represent those who shared their experiences in a way that could effectively communicate their experiences while also not putting them at unnecessary risk.

H.B. 144. In the 2002 Utah State Legislative session Utah became one of only ten states in the U.S. to offer in-state tuition rates to public universities to undocumented students. To qualify for in-state tuition rates students must demonstrate residency in the state by attending and graduating from a Utah high school for at least three years, and they also must sign and submit an affidavit that they are pursuing legal status. Though only approximately 180-190 students statewide take advantage of this bill, it is a great benefit for those students who do. Many of them would not be able to attend college if they were required to pay the out-of-state tuition rates, which are approximately four times as much as in-state tuition rates.

Ever since 2002, however, a cohort of anti-immigrant legislators have pushed bills that would repeal H.B. 144. Fortunately none have been successful to date, but it is a heated battle each year. It was within the context of this debate that the Gui SLC team created *Easy Targets* in order to find out what obstacles undocumented students face in accessing higher education. As a team we interviewed many undocumented students and their families, both those still in high school as well as some who were already attending or had graduated from college. One of our primary findings was that although Utah is one of the few states to offer in-state tuition rates to undocumented students, relatively few undocumented students take advantage of it.

In the process of conducting the research and creating the documentary we realized the potential use of our research on a number of levels. First, recognizing that lack of information about H.B. 144 and how to access higher education are the primary obstacles that young undocumented students face, we saw the presentation of our research findings to high school students and their families as a primary means by which to address this issue and help students and families gain the knowledge they need to access higher education. Our college student/research assistant Denise Castañeda is currently compiling a college resource guide for parents and students that may accompany the documentary video and includes information about H.B. 144, private scholarships (undocumented students do not qualify for federal grants or loans), and how to prepare for and apply to college.

Second, we recognized that because of the risk involved in telling their stories, policy makers and lawmakers do not often hear from the actual students or families affected by bills such as H.B. 144. The voices of undocumented students and their families are often not heard in the halls of the capital or in the media. *Easy Targets* presented a means through which the voices of undocumented students could be heard by lawmakers and the media. Recognizing, however, that many lawmakers and media consumers are openly hostile towards undocumented families, we knew we would have to revise what we presented and how it was presented. Most of the students and their family members who we interviewed for our research chose to conceal their identities. We used lighting or blurred the footage in the editing to keep the faces of the undocumented students concealed. A few of the students interviewed for the original documentary, however, chose consciously to not conceal their identities. They wanted viewers to see their faces and recognize their humanity. As college graduate David expressed, "I'm not going to hide."

We revisited these decisions, however, when we decided to create a shortened five-minute version of *Easy Targets* that could be distributed to lawmakers and the press during the 2008 State Legislative session. During this session the Utah chapter of the Minutemen was especially active in lobbying for the repeal of H.B. 144. We collaborated with the activist organization Utahns for the American Dream (UAD), a coalition of groups that supported H.B. 144, to hold a press conference with educational and political leaders who voiced their support of in-state tuition rates for undocumented students. For the five-minute excerpt version of our documentary we dropped the focus on our research findings, and instead, focused on presenting the voices of undocumented students and their families. We wanted the legislators to hear these voices first hand.

We also, however, recognized that this put the undocumented young men and women who had shared their experiences at greater risk. After all, one of our own state legislators had called ICE (Immigration and Customs Enforcement) the previous year hoping they would come and detain the hundreds of immigrants who had shown up at the capital to rally against the repeal of drivers licenses for undocumented drivers[5]. We also recognized that if the press decided to air segments of the documentary then the broader general public would see and hear the young undocumented students. As a result we conferred with some of the students as to how they wanted to be represented in the video. All agreed that because the video was going to be made available to the press and state legislators they *did* want their identities obscured.

The question was how to best do this. All of the students did want their visual identities concealed which we did with lighting and pixilation. We had an even bigger discussion, however, regarding whether we needed to disguise the voices of the young people interviewed. Caitlin, concerned about the possible repercussions once the videos were made public, felt very strongly that the voices should be changed. So we experimented with a number of different options. We changed the pitch to try to disguise the voices, but it didn't do enough to change some of the speech patterns and other recognizable aspects of the way some of the young people who had been interviewed spoke. We transcribed the interviews and recorded other young people reading the transcripts but the interviews then sounded canned and artificial.

One of the challenges we faced was that with each step we took to protect the identity of the people who had shared their experiences, we also took a step towards further dehumanization. When we masked the students' faces and voices we eventually had only a hollow frame of a person left. There is a significant and challenging tension between protecting those with whom we conduct research and making them visible as human beings. By obscuring the faces of those we interviewed, we run

---

[5] Utah was one of the few states who issued drivers licenses to undocumented drivers. This law, however, was repealed and the drivers license was replaced with a "drivers privilege card" which cannot be used in the same way as an official ID in the same way the state drivers license could.

the risk of criminalizing them (Banks, 2005/2001). This became especially evident to us when we realized that the white cinderblock walls of the Boys and Girls Club in the background of two of our interviews had the look of a juvenile detention center or other penal institution.

Fig. 9-5: Still frame from *Easy Targets* of high school student at Boys & Girls club. Credit: © 2008 Growing Up in Salt Lake City.

Ultimately we followed the decisions of the young undocumented students themselves. As is stated by the "tips on informed consent" posted by the U.S. Department Health and Human Services "Informed consent is a process, not just a form"[6]. We presented them with the different edited versions of the five-minute excerpt piece and let them choose what they wanted to do. Part of the conversation revolved around what we call "informed risk." We recognize that risk is an inherent aspect of social justice action. While Institutional Review Boards (IRBs) seek to minimize risk, or at least ensure that the benefits outweigh the risks, we understand that individuals and the communities they represent should be empowered to make decisions about how to represent themselves, whether it be through the presentation of research findings in a paper, or in a more visible means such as a documentary video. In academic research IRBs

---

[6] http://www.hhs.gov/ohrp/humansubjects/guidance/ictips.htm

often insist on anonymity, and research projects that do not promise anonymity are often denied approval (see Bradley, 2007; Manzo and Brightbill 2007).

Using the concept of "informed risk" we assert that the co-researchers, interviewees, and/or community members should be able to make their own, informed decision, about how they want to be represented, with the understanding that in social justice work significant risk is often necessary to bring about the changes we seek. In our conversation with the young students we discussed a number of the possible implications of their voices becoming available to the general public through media outlets, including possible deportation or even violence. The students, however, chose to use their own voices without any type of editing or masking. They wanted their voices to be heard by the legislators. They recognized the risks, but they also recognized that change cannot come if we are not willing to take risks. As a result of the various conversations and requests from the undocumented students, we masked the physical identity of all of those who were included in the five-minute excerpt of *Easy Targets,* but did not alter their voices in any way.

Informed risk is a useful concept to frame the process of creating the video as well. One of the decisions we struggled with as a team was whether to use the personal story of a young undocumented woman to frame and structure *Easy Targets.* In fact, we wrote a script for the video that weaved her personal story in with the interviews and research findings. Not all of the research team thought this was an effective way to present our research and we hotly debated whether to use this structure. And although the personal story aptly framed the main themes, we were concerned again about the risk it posed for the young student and the student's family. She waivered about whether she was willing to take that risk, but at one point, when we wrote the script, she had decided that she did want to tell her story because she was tired of being afraid and not being able to do anything. Ultimately, however, as the project progressed she decided against this.

As a research team we had a specific intention to conduct research that could help us understand why more undocumented students weren't taking advantage of H.B. 144 in order to use that information to provide greater access to college for undocumented students. In the process of our research we found other uses for our work, specifically presenting excerpts of our documentary to lawmakers during the 2008 legislative session during which H.B. 144 was under attack. As a result we were able to use our research in direct and meaningful political engagement as we sought to provide greater access to higher education for undocumented students. This increased the risk, however, for those who were involved in our project as well, and we had to carefully consider our work and possible implications in light of the potential risks. IRB approval is often seen as a hurdle that academic researchers must go through in order to conduct research, but for the PAR practitioners, especially those using a highly visible media such as video, obtaining informed consent is not just a hoop to jump through, it is a process that needs to be consistently negotiated and considered depending on purpose and audience.

Conclusion

The *Red Flags* and *Easy Targets* videos raise the question of what risks are necessary to participate in social change, beyond an "armchair revolution" (Freire, 1997). Here we have tried to unfold some of the layers of risk and vulnerability that are embodied, felt, and grounded in everyday experiences, and positioned within a broader social, economic, political context of global injustices of structural racism and immigration. With this in mind the decision to take a risk, to share your story, can be understood as personal and political commitments to address the asymmetries of our unjust world. But at the same time, the contradictions of our research are apparent. On the one hand our projects reframe the question of risk and the responsibilities for risk. On the other hand, who is made vulnerable by our research, and upon whose back lies the burden of responsibility for social change are ethical questions we must contend with. Here we are inspired by the many brave people who decided to participate in our documentaries to speak out, enter the fray and be included in national dialogues on educational inequities and immigration rights that too often silence the stories of those who have the most to gain - and lose.

Acknowledgments

We are most grateful for the support of the Bennion Center of the University of Utah, the American Association of Geographers, Dr. Octavio Villalpando, Assistant Vice President for Diversity, University of Utah; Dr. Theresa Martinez, Vice President, Office of Academic Outreach, University of Utah; Dr. Cheryl Wright, Chair, Family & Consumer Studies, University of Utah; and University Neighborhood Partners, University of Utah.

Heartfelt thanks to Martin Downing and Lauren Tenney for their patience and persistence.

References

Alemán, E., & Rorrer, A. K. (2006). Closing educational gaps for Latino/a students in Utah: Initiating a policy discourse and framework. Utah Education Policy Center.

Banks, M. (2005/2001). *Visual methods in social research.* London: Sage.

Bell, E. E. (2001). Infusing race in the US discourse on action research. In P. Reason & H. Bradbury (Eds.) *Handbook of action research: Participative Inquiry and Practice* (pp. 48-58). London: Sage.

Bradley, M. (2007). Silenced for their own protection: How the IRB marginalizes those it feigns to protect. *ACME: An International E-Journal for Critical Geographies, 6.*

Cahill, C. (2004). Defying gravity? Raising consciousness through collective research. *Children's Geographies, 2*(2), 273-286.

—. (2007a). Repositioning ethical commitments: Participatory action research as a relational praxis of social change. *ACME: An International E-Journal for Critical Geographies, 6*, 360-373.

—. (2007b). Doing research *with* young people: Participatory research and the rituals of collective work. *Children's Geographies, 5*(3), 297-312.

Cahill, C., & Torre, M. (2007). Beyond the journal article: Representations, audience, and the presentation of participatory research. In S. Kindon, R. Pain, & M. Kesby (Eds.), *Connecting people, participation and place: Participatory action research approaches and methods* (pp. 196-205). London: Routledge.

Cammarota, J., & Fine, M. (Eds.) (1998). *Revolutionizing education: Youth participatory action research in motion.* London: Routledge.

Chavez, V., & Soep, E. (2005). Youth radio and the pedagogy of collegiality. *Harvard Educational Review, 75*(4), 1-23.

Driskell, D. (2002). *Creating better cities with children and youth: A manual for participation.* London: Earthscan.

Fals-Borda, O. (1979). Investigating the reality in order to transform it: The Colombian experience. *Dialectical Anthropology, 4*, 33-55.

Fine, M., Weis, L., Weseen, S., & Wong, L. (2000). For whom? Qualitative research, representations and social responsibilities. In N. Denzin & Y. Lincoln (Eds.), *The handbook of qualitative research* (pp. 107-132). Thousand Oaks, CA: Sage.

Freire, P. (1997). *Pedagogy of the oppressed.* Harmondsorth, Middlesex: Penguin Books.

Ginwright, S., Noguera, P., & Cammarota, J. (Eds.) (2006). *Beyond resistance! Youth activism and community change: New democratic possibilities for practice and policy for America's youth.* New York: Routledge.

Goodman, S. (2003). *Teaching youth media: A critical guide to literacy, video production, and social change.* New York: Teachers College Press.

hooks, b. (1995). *Killing rage. Ending racism.* New York: Henry Holt and Company.

Kelley, R. D. G. (1997). *Yo' mama's disfunktional! Fighting the culture wars in urban America.* Boston: Beacon Press.

Macedo, D. (1998). Forward to Paolo Freire, *Pedagogy of freedom.* New York and Oxford: Rowman and Littlefield Publishers, Inc.

Manzo, L., & Brightbill, N. (2007). Towards a participatory ethics. In S. Kindon, R. Pain, & M. Kesby (Eds.), *Connecting people, participation and place: Participatory action research approaches and methods* (pp. 33-40). London: Routledge.

Martin-Baró, I. (1994). *Writings for a liberation psychology.* Cambridge, MA: Harvard University Press.

Mock, B. (2008). "Immigration backlash: Hate crimes against Latinos flourish."
Intelligence Report. Southern Poverty Law Center. Retrieved on July 31, 2008 from
http://www.splcenter.org/intel/intelreport/article.jsp?aid=845

Perlich, P. (2006). Long term demographic trends impacting higher education in Utah. Prepared for the Board of Regents, May 2006.

Rahman, A. (2006). The praxis of participatory research. In P. Reason & H. Bradbury (Eds.), *Handbook of action research.* London: Sage.

Smith, L. T. (1999). *Decolonizing methodologies: Research and indigenous peoples.* New York: Zed Books, Ltd.

Solórzano, D. G., & Yosso, T. J. (2002). Critical race methodology: Counter-storytelling as an analytical framework for education research. *Qualitative Inquiry, 8*(1), 23-44.

Torre, M. E., & Fine, M. (2006). Participatory action research (PAR) by youth. In L. Sherrod (Ed.), *Youth activism: An international encyclopedia* (pp. 456-462). Westport, CT: Greenwood Publishing Group.

CONCLUSION

This work offers a multitude of bridges social scientists can walk across in choosing to go after data collection through video. In this volume, authors have explored multiple uses of video as a research tool that is changing the culture of social science research. This is a paradigm shift that began with the use of film and video in the late 1960s (Bellman & Jules-Rosette, 1977; Snowden, 1984; Worth & Adair, 1972). As technology has progressed, the medium of video makes the option of visually recording data more accessible and economically feasible, for some. Beckman, in this volume, presents insights to social scientists in how one chooses to purchase equipment. It is important for social scientists to understand that using video, as a research method is a skill and refining that skill can be as time consuming as carrying out multiple regressions by hand. As this volume has illustrated, video is an accepted qualitative method of data collection. Researchers using this valuable tool must ensure similar safeguards against personal bias as they would with any other methodology. This paradigm shift to the use of video in research affects a multitude of processes that some, such as the Congress for Qualitative Inquiry (2006) have already struggled with. When feminist (Libman and Fields), emancipatory (Tenney and MacCubbin), and participatory action (Beaty; GuiSLC) frameworks incorporate video, the challenges become more apparent as ethical and methodological issues bear a greater weight, particularly for those researchers who identify with conflicts in obtaining Institutional Review Board (IRB) approval (Bradley, 2007; Tenney, 2006).

Downing's position that video enhances qualitative research and strengthens our ability to produce knowledge should be at the heart of the discussion. He writes, "The visual had provided essential support to the audio, thereby rendering both elements mutually reinforcing" (p. 8). The benefits also include the ability for multiple reviewers to analyze data and release results to a wider audience.

Your path as a social scientist using video in research is long and begins with you deciding how to employ this method. Will you share the footage with others? Will you take footage of your own choosing? Will you record the same type of footage at every interview? Will you use lighting and external microphones? Will you ask the participant what imagery s/he would like to have recorded as data? Will you give the video camera to the participant to record his or her own data? Will you use a combination of these methods? This is a lot to think about as each question poses different types of data that could create layers of analysis. How much time do you have to analyze, edit and re-analyze the footage produced? How much support in terms of financing and access to participants do you have? Will you be using technology to protect the anonymity of participants such as blurring bodies or altering voices? Do you even know how to do this?

The planning of the IRB application ought to consider these and other questions that Tenney and MacCubbin have outlined. Many authors point to feared and real frustrations of gaining IRB approval for research with a visual component, but all agree that the data produced is worth the added levels of inspection a video research proposal will receive. Tenney's recounting of her own experiences attempting to get IRB approval for a participatory action research design with emancipatory underpinnings coupled with MacCubbin's historical understanding of the IRB process give a newcomer to research a grounded explanation of how to plan their own video vision.

Libman and Fields offer the technique of video messages as a creative solution for ethical dilemmas when using video. The authors are able to intertwine deep theoretical thought with action amidst the use of video. The undercurrent of social justice and the addressing of identity stereotypes is a significant contribution to the literature on field research methodologies in their research method, unrecorded focus groups were used to bring participants together and share their experiences. The final time in the focus group was spent offering participants the opportunity to choose to create a video message about their experiences to an audience of their choosing and given time to compose the message. In this way, particularly intimate moments in the focus group would not be missed because of participants awareness of the video camera and the indelible record of their experiences it creates, but did have the opportunity to consciously create the point they would like made.

Also of concern to Libman and Fields was how the data be presented. From a feminist standpoint, they make clear points about representation and ownership that deserve attention and address issues many researchers face concerning the limitations put on researchers by funding sources, organizations, and audience perceptions. As the adeptly pointed out a struggle and goal for all researchers has to be representing people as they represent themselves.

Turan and Chapin introduce readers to the significance of video editing and its relationship to data analysis. The authors present strong experiential analysis of the procedures, and are comfortable talking directly to readers. They have built a strong case for why thoughtfulness of editing first generation data through a process of immersion is essential within the use of video for field research. Offering stark comparisons of film and video, they give insight into just how accessible the technology has become. The analogy between "making soup" and editing video is visual and dynamic. It helps the reader shift their traditional modes of thinking, further changing the culture of social science research.

Beaty provides an excellent chapter regarding informant-made videos in a school setting. The author incorporates theory, research, and practical applications that contribute to the idea of video literacy for school-aged children. Her theme of transformation is evident and well received. Several points are made throughout her chapter, which speak to our message, particularly regarding awareness of the person behind the camera. The action-oriented work that she describes concerning evaluation of camera-student entities gives readers incite into the limitless opportunities video brings us. The technique of informant-made videos can easily translate to research anywhere there are informants. Beaty's positioning of young people as experts, informants of their own lives, in exploring transactions with others and environments is powerful. In fact, concepts of power can be found throughout the entire manuscript and it is important for social scientists to be aware of the power dynamics which video creates. The chapter alludes to pre-video, filming, reviewing, and editing techniques all of which can be useful to readers, especially those just starting out using this methodology.

Pine delivers an excellent communication of the potential dangers and benefits for using video in field research. The author highlights how a change in approach within his field encounters made for a much more productive experience, and the role that video played in this. The work holds readers in suspense and intrigue at several points, while maintaining a research context throughout. This article grounds the reader in the creative ways in which one goes about getting video footage and highlights some of the discomfort various groups may have with the idea of being captured on video. This is essential for the social scientist to understand and respect, particularly if your research is sensitive or intimate in nature.

Mausner explores using video in conjunction with research on participants' perceptions of natural settings. The author goes to great lengths to give readers a strong understanding of her methodology, while contributing practical tips for future endeavors. Her trials and tribulations with creating a way for participants to record what they saw without the camera being too cumbersome created an interesting technique of attaching a camera to hikers' heads, leaving the hands free. Think of all the possible ways this research can be replicated, to further our understanding of person-environment transactions. Her notation system is complex and gives evidence to how rich data gathered through video can be and the plethora of ways in which it can be analyzed.

Beckman offers a valuable piece that illustrates the humanity of video usage, both for participant and researcher. This chapter, reflecting work that is deeply psychological, gives strong experiential analysis of using video in field research. The author makes exceptional use of technical recommendations throughout, and builds a strong case for the importance of this technology. Her discussion of the IRB process illustrates strategies for social scientists to duplicate in their presentation of research designs to ethics committees. Also valuable to the social scientist is her discussion of equipment and choosing to work with a PC or a Mac. As indicated earlier, the use of video requires an entire set of skills that often researchers have to develop but the final product is worth the time and money invested. The benefits of video she recounts are not limited to the "richness and complexity that video has to offer through comprehensible layers of sound intertwined with still and moving imagery in a concise manner" (p. 178).

Growing Up In Salt Lake City Research Collective (Gui SLC). put forth the soul of participatory action research. Complicated realities that young people have to contend with in naming racism and other prejudices they encounter are explored in vivid and meaningful detail. Further challenging the role of young people and participants in conventional research, they introduce the concept of "informed risk", which paves an avenue for approaching research that has social justice and action at its base. It is clear when we listen to youth researchers voices that the definition of "at risk" needs to change. It is only once we privilege the voices of those who are affected by the problems we are seeking to remedy will we come close to finding answers that will effectively and efficiently solve problems. This collaboration proves not only that participatory action research with video is possible, but poignant, practical and warranted.

Final Thoughts

As two graduate students who were interested in learning more about the use of video in the social sciences, we have been inspired by what we learned. As more people begin to use this valuable method, more approaches for obtaining IRB approval, editing, analyzing, and presenting video will be available to us. The culture of social science research is rich, and adding video to your toolbox of methods is something that we deeply and strongly encourage. This work has given us many answers, but there are still more questions and future endeavors to explore.

We close this current work where Alinsky (1971) began his: "What follows is for those who want to change the world from what it is to what they believe it should be" (p. 1). What is your video vision?

References

Alinsky, S. (1971). *Rules for radicals: A pragmatic primer.* New York: Random House.

Bellman, B.L. & Jules-Rosette, B. (1977). *A paradigm for looking: Cross-cultural research with visual media.* Bellman, New Jersey: Ablex Publishing Corporation.

Bradley, M. (2007). Silenced for their own protection: How the IRB marginalizes those it feigns to protect. *ACME Editorial Collective.* Retrieved May 31, 2008 from http://www.acmejournal.org/vol6/MB.pdf.

Congress of Qualitative Inquiry. (2006). Position statement on qualitative research and IRBs discussion draft May 4-6, 2006. Retrieved on May 12, 2008 from http://www.c4qi.org/PositionStatement.pdf

Snowden, D. (1984). Eyes see; ears hear. Memorial University, Newfoundland, Canada download. Retrieved May 31, 2008 from www.fao.org/waicent/faoinfo/sustdev/cddirect/cdre0038.htm

Tenney, L. (2006). Who fancies to have a Revolution here? *The Opal* Revisited (1851-1860). *Journal of Radial Psychology. 5.*

Worth, S. & Adair, J. (1972). *Through Navajo eyes: An exploration in film communication and anthropology.* Bloomington: Indiana University Press.

APPENDICES

APPENDIX A

A Two-Step Consent and Release Process
for Video-taping

In our work at the Salk Institute for Biological Studies we were especially concerned that our participants were comfortable with the material we were creating (Turan & Chapin, 2005). The process we developed involved two steps; a Consent Form and a Release Form. The Consent Form was a form that we signed in the presence of the participant just before the interview. This was essentially a pledge from us--Zeynep and David--that we would *not* use any material that we taped without first having a signed Release Form from the participant. The participants agreed (by also signing the Consent Form) to be video taped upon our signing this pledge. Here is an example of a Consent Form (p. 221).

After taping, we produced a rough cut of the interview. This rough cut included everything that we thought might be used in the final project. We mailed a DVD copy of this rough cut to each participant. It was only after participants had reviewed their rough cut material that they were asked to approve its use by signing and returning the Release Form. If there was anything in the rough cut that the participant did not want to be included, we asked that the Release Form not be signed. Only after we produced an approved rough cut did we seek the participant's signature. Here is an example of a Release Form (p. 222):

Notice that these forms are *simple*. We believe that using long, complicated consent forms, with the excuse that, "No one reads them anyway," is just wrong-headed.

There are many examples of using video to catch people saying things that might be potentially embarrassing or even harmful. We think it is unethical and therefore chose to not take part in using video this way. We think that in making this choice clear we had additional rapport with our participants. There is also an important issue of power in using a video camera and producing and controlling imagery. We wanted to share this power with our participants.

The editing process of putting a person's image into context starting from a rough cut into a finished piece still remains problematic. We have not come up with a completely satisfactory way of doing this. However, as part of our process, we did send out early drafts of our DVD project so that all participants might see how they appeared in a context and then comment based on a real sense of how they were being portrayed.

LIVING
SALK
INSTITUTE
agreement
to be videotaped

Jacques Scorge :::

We want to videotape you as part of the Living Salk Institute project, as described on the opposite side of this form. Material will be used for scholarly, not commercial purposes. The times and place will be decided by mutual agreement. You may decide to stop videotaping at any time. We offer no rewards and hold no cudgel, whether you decide to be taped or not.

Our agreement process has two parts, this being the first. If you agree to being videotaped we will make a "rough cut" DVD for you to review. You may then decide to allow us to use the material as is, or you may decide that some material may not be used. We will not use any material in which you can be identified without your prior review and approval.

Date:
Signed: David Chapin
               Zeynep Turan
               dchapin@gc.cuny.edu
               zturan@gc.cuny.edu

PLEASE SEE THE OPPOSITE SIDE OF THIS FORM for information about the Living Salk Institute Project and for contact information.

With the understanding that no material in which I can be identified will be used without my prior review and approval, I agree to be videotaped.

Date:
Signed: Jacques Scorge
Contact information (where to send the DVD):

_____

LIVING
SALK
INSTITUTE
release form

I have received the DVD sent to me by David Chapin and Zeynep Turan titled "Jacques Scorge Rough Cut 1, 2005 January 15th." I agree that the material on this DVD may be used by them to document their "Living Salk Institute" video research project. I make this agreement with the understanding that this material will be used only for non-commercial audiences and purposes; dissemination may include scholarly journals, electronic media and non-commercial video. Further, I understand that in developing the project, editing decisions will be made about what material will be used and what will not.

For the project I will be identified as:

"Jacques Scorge
Salk Institute"
Date:
Signed: Jacques Scorge

PLEASE NOTE: If there is some part of the DVD that you do not agree to our use of, please DON"T SIGN THE RELEASE FORM. Discuss the issue with us and we will prepare a revised version for your approval. We will destroy (by over-recording the original tape) any material that you wish to have destroyed. PLEASE SEE THE OPPOSITE SIDE OF THIS FORM for information about the Living Salk Institute Project and for contact information.

Thank you for your participation! David Chapin and Zeynep Turan

APPENDIX B-1

Sample HIKEN™ KEY

Hiker Features

♂	up
⊸O	left
♀	down
i	point
⏐	stop
λ	walk
↳	stop and turn
⌐	action continues

Hiker Descriptors

><	near, up close
*	tempo: slow; slower
⌐↙	toward

Environment Features

Å	branch - conifer
△	cones - conifer
✩	sign of wildlife
ꙭ	snake

Environment Descriptors

#	small
H	Questionnaire Highlight

Emotions

	pleasure (pink)
	surprise (orange)
	worry (olive green)

Thoughts

	Aesthetic assessment
	Association
	Information-seeking; explanatory
	Expectation (yellow background)

Perceptual Information and Modality

	Auditory
	Olfactory
	Haptic-tactile
no shading	Visual - baseline

APPENDIX B-2

Sample HIKEN™ Notation

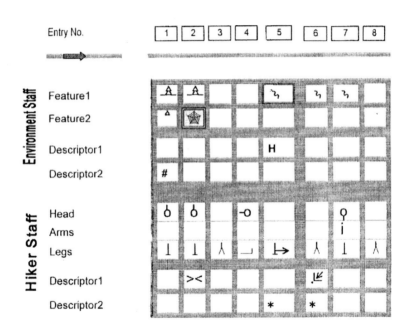

LIST OF CONTRIBUTORS

Martin Downing (Editor) is a Ph.D. Candidate in Environmental Psychology at the Graduate School and University Center of the City University of New York. He holds an M.S. degree in Research Psychology and has served as an Adjunct Lecturer in the Department of Social Sciences at both LaGuardia Community College and York College, in New York City.

His research interests reflect a commitment to understanding the human-environment relationship, particularly in the context of chronic illness. This interest has been informed by having worked with persons living with HIV/AIDS (PLWHA), both as a volunteer and a researcher. At this time he is completing his dissertation focusing on risk perceptions, sexual behavior, and HIV prevention in commercial and public sex environments. In addition, he has gained an appreciation for the use of video as a research methodology. His work in this area focuses on developing theory using an ecological model as well as issues of reflexivity. In the past he has utilized video as a means to understand how PLWHA come to know and interact with their homes. He is also a co-founder of Video Vision: A Conference for the Changing Culture of Social Science Research. Martin's work has appeared in the journals, *Counseling and Clinical Psychology Journal, Health & Place,* and *The Qualitative Report.*

Lauren Tenney (Editor) holds masters degrees in both psychology and public administration. She is a fifth year Provost Fellow in the PhD program in Environmental Psychology at the Graduate School and University Center of the City University of New York. She is currently an Adjunct Professor in the Department of Psychology at the College of Staten Island. She is also an artist and novelist. Miss Tenney (10e) is a co-founder of Video Vision: A Conference for the Changing Culture of Social Science Research. As a community organizer, her latest effort has been rallying people around Esmin Green's murder-by-neglect which was caught on surveillance tape at the Kings County Hospital Center Psychiatric Emergency Room in Brooklyn, NY. Thousands are calling for an end of torture and a commitment to human rights in psychiatric systems. Security guards, nurses, and other hospital personnel were captured on video looking at the woman on the floor and walking away as she died. This footage brought to life for her the use of video and its deep implications for all involved. For more information, www.theopalproject.org/vigil.html.

Her current research interest involves *The Opal*, edited by the patients of the Utica State Lunatic Asylum, circa 1851. In *The Opal*, 10e learned that the work she did while with the State was not new at all, but was part of a buried history of people trying to be liberated from oppressive systems and environments that have outrageous power differentials and rely on torture as a means to control. This finding has led her to intense historical inquiry concerning New York State's mental health system in its various forms since the early 19th century. Through this effort she conducted a participatory action research project using video as a research tool, where she asked current activists and advocates with psychiatric histories to confront *The Opal* and make suggestions on what if anything, ought to be done with its more than 3,000 pages. Six projects have stemmed out of this action research and can be found at www.theopalproject.org. She is preparing her Institutional Review Board application to conduct the next round of research, which uses video and asks people who make mental health policy and provide psychiatric treatments to confront and respond to *The Opal*.

Patricia MacCubbin is the Director of the Office of Research Conduct for The City University of New York (CUNY) and the Research Foundation of CUNY. She has many years of human research protections experience, as well as experience as a public health researcher and manager.

Over the past 15 years she has served in a variety of human research protections programs. Her experience covers both social and behavioral research institutions and biomedical research institutions. She served as the Director of the Institutional Review Boards (IRBs) at the New York State Department of Health in Albany and the University of Utah in Salt Lake City.

Her commitment to human research protections also extends to community service, as a volunteer on planning committees for the Public Responsibility in Medicine and Research (PRIM&R) annual meetings, as a community member and, later, a consultant for the Utah Department of Human Services IRB, and as a community member for the Weill Medical College of Cornell University IRB. She is currently a member of the Collaborative Institutional Training Initiative (CITI) Developers Group focusing on new social and behavioral training modules. She serves on the CITI Social and Behavioral Module Editorial Board and is the Team

Leader for Social and Behavioral Refresher Module Development. She serves on the Editorial Board of the *Journal of Public Health Management and Practice*. In that capacity she assembled a special issue focused on human subjects protection issues in public health. She published a chapter on human subjects protection issues in public health for a public health administration textbook. She had been a nominee for membership on the US Department of Health and Human Services Secretary's Advisory Committee for Human Research Protections (SACHRP).

Prior to working in the IRB world, she was an epidemiologist/ biostatistician and the Assistant Director of Chronic Disease Epidemiology and Surveillance at the New York State Department of Health. She has a Master's Degree in Applied Statistics and has supplemented that with additional graduate courses in Epidemiology, Biostatistics, and Public Health Law.

Kimberly Libman, MPH, is a doctoral candidate in Environmental Psychology at the Graduate Center of the City University of New York. Her research addresses structural and social determinants of health with special focus on food environments and housing. She has taught Urban Studies at Hunter College and Food Studies at the New School.

Desiree Fields is a doctoral candidate in environmental psychology at the Graduate Center of the City University of New York and a researcher for the Housing Environments Research Group at the Center for Human Environments. She received her B.A. in psychology from the University of California at Santa Barbara. She has studied the psychology of mortgage foreclosure as well as neighborhood belonging among residents of supportive housing for people with mental illness. Her current work concerns theories of urban governance, the use of the arts as an urban development strategy, and artists as spatial, social, economic and political actors.

Zeynep Turan received her Ph.D. in Environmental Psychology from the CUNY Graduate Center. She has two Masters degrees; one in Architectural Histories and Theories from the Architectural Association in London and one in Psychology from the CUNY Hunter College. She was awarded an Andrew W. Mellon dissertation fellowship in 2006-2007. She has written about material environments of displaced peoples and their role in shaping collective memories and narratives. She also co-created a video documentary of the Salk Institute of Biological Studies (built by

Louis I. Kahn), which looks at how people make meaning in their environments and how place attachment is constructed. Her research interests range from the meaning of place and of material environments, to issues of memory, identity, and culture. At present she is focused on Middle Eastern diasporas in the U.S. and video-ethnography, and most specifically the relation between material objects and remembering.

David Chapin is an architect and professor in the CUNY Graduate Center's Ph.D. Program in Environmental Psychology. "I spent lots of my childhood playing with an 8mm movie camera." In the 70s and 80s he was part of the ARC Group sponsored by the Ohio Department of Mental Health doing participatory research and collaborative redesign in the environments of total institutions. David worked with Zeynep Turan on the research video, "Living Salk Institute."

Lara Margaret Beaty has a Ph.D. in Developmental Psychology from the CUNY Graduate Center. She is currently an Assistant Professor of Psychology at LaGuardia Community College, City University of New York. Her current research focuses on in-school video-production programs as a context for understanding the connection between student-school relations and student development.

Jason Pine teaches anthropology and media studies at Purchase College, SUNY and The New School. He has conducted several years of research in Naples, where he studies the zone of contact zone where the *camorra*, the region's powerful and volatile organized crime networks, and more ordinary, underemployed families meet in day-to-day life. He studies how the moral economy of the camorra is inflected in various aesthetic forms ranging from music and musical theater, to pirated television, film and everyday linguistic performances. Additionally, he has been pursuing a research project on methamphetamine production and addiction in North America, and its relationship to the broader, more general everyday demands of optimal performance, productivity and expenditure that are encouraged by Big Pharma. Finally, he has been studying the aesthetics and political economy of virtual world-building in Second Life. He uses photography, video and machinima (virtual video) in all of his research projects.

Jason's work appears in the journals *Law, Culture and the Humanities*, *Public Culture* and the *Journal of Modern Italian Studies*, and the cultural pages of the Italian newspaper *Il Manifesto*. Currently, he is writing a monograph about Naples called *Contact* and producing a television program about Second Life for the indymedia collective Paper Tiger Television.

Claudia Mausner holds a doctorate in Environmental Psychology from the City University of New York. Her scholarly research has focused on how people conceptualize and experience natural environments. In her current position as Adjunct Professor of Environmental Studies at Pace University, Dr. Mausner has developed an interdisciplinary course on *Human Dimensions of Sustainability*. Dr. Mausner served as Field Research Coordinator for an environmental justice project funded by New York's Department of Environmental Conservation in Yonkers, New York, and has worked with ecologists and natural resource managers at the Institute of Ecosystem Studies, the Metropolitan Conservation Alliance, and the Appalachian Mountain Club. Dr. Mausner has presented at many professional conferences, including the Environmental Design Research Association Annual Conference and the Annual Northeastern Recreation Research Symposium. Most recently, findings from her video research on the hike experience were used in a training workshop for trail-building volunteers at the New York-New Jersey Trail Conference. Dr. Mausner hopes her work will inspire other social scientists to conduct videographic field research as they recognize the value in studying the lived experience of nature.

Autumn Beckman is a doctoral student of Social-Personality Psychology at The Graduate Center of The City University of New York. She is currently working on her dissertation examining the various ways women are rebuilding life in New Orleans following Hurricane Katrina and, as she often combines psychology with art, she hopes to publish a book of participants' narratives and photographs in conjunction with this work.

Autumn has taught courses in Social Psychology and The American Urban Experience at Brooklyn College and The Psychology of Women at Hunter College in New York City. She earned her Bachelor of Art in Psychology from the University of Houston where she simultaneously earned a Bachelor of Fine Arts in Studio Arts-Painting. Prior to this she studied traditional animation at the School of Visual Arts in New York and painting and photography at the High School for the Performing and Visual Arts in Houston.

In addition to her work in psychology and art Autumn has a passion for animals. She volunteered for three years in the bird department of the Houston Zoological Gardens, worked as a zookeeper for Moody Gardens in Galveston, TX, and has worked as a veterinary technician at animal clinics in Houston and New York. Autumn's most current paintings center on dogs and she currently lives in Houston with her African grey parrot, Vincent, and miniature dachshund, Sebastian.

For more information on Autumn's work in psychology and art please visit her website: www.autumnbeckman.com

The **Growing Up in Salt Lake City research collective** includes high school youth researchers: **Larissa Esquivel**; **Naima Mohamed**; **Joel Organista**; **Jessica Sandberg**; **Maria Valerio**; and **Kanesha Winston**; University of Utah research assistant, **Denise Castañeda**; and University of Utah professors, **Matt Bradley & Caitlin Cahill**. A labor of love, we collaborated on this project very intensely for over a year and learned much about our community, our aspirations, and each other. We invite you to watch our documentaries and to work with us to reframe the ways young people are represented.

INDEX

181, 182, 246
HIKEN™, 180, 181
hiker reactions, 184
historical, 3, 15, 16, 19, 25, 63, 230
HIV/AIDS, 2, 6, 7, 9, 10
hollow frame of a person, 223
home, 4, 7, 8, 9, 10, 11, 52, 192, 200
home computer, 200
home environment, 7, 10
home ownership, 203
home tour, 8
home visits, 8
homeowners, 3, 80, 81, 82, 83, 86, 88, 89, 90, 91, 92, 93, 94, 95, 96, 97
homeownership, 84, 93
homeownership education, 82
homeownership preservation initiatives, 82
housing policy, 3, 9
human being, 41, 221, 223
human component, 203
human geography, 173
human participant protections, 14, 60, 63
human research protections, 61
human rights, 51
human subject protections, 16, 24, 43, 44, 71
humanity, 3, 25, 222, 232
humanness, 53, 54
Hurricane Katrina, 192, 194, 195, 200
Hurricane Katrina survivors, 190, 201
hypothesis, 103, 123

I

ICE (Immigration and Customs Enforcement), 223
identifiable data, 23
identifiable information, 58
identifying information, 30, 52, 55
identities obscured, 223

image-based data, 6
immersed in data, 105
immersed in editing, 116
immersion, 105, 106, 113, 115, 117, 174, 231
immigrants, 223
incentives for participation, 39
inclusion/exclusion, 46
indirect data, 184
informant-made video, 3, 54, 121, 122, 135, 140, 231
informed, 20
informed choice, 16, 50, 55, 66, 68
informed consent, 1, 14, 15, 16, 19, 22, 24, 29, 35, 47, 50, 53, 54, 55, 56, 62, 66, 68, 71, 96, 201, 226
informed consent and release process, 51, 54, 58, 69
informed consent form, 57, 59, 68, 69, 178
informed consent process, 16, 27, 28, 29, 35, 45, 51, 55, 57, 62, 69, 73
informed consenting strategy, 69
informed risk, 208, 224, 225, 232
injustice, 48, 60, 90, 207, 214, 215, 216
injustices, 226
innovative techniques, 63, 70
insideness, 185, 186
insiders, 220
institutional racism, 46, 208, 215, 217, 218, 220
Institutional Review Board, 1, 3, 8, 16, 17, 24, 30, 31, 33, 39, 43, 47, 60, 61, 62, 64, 68, 177, 192, 224
Institutional Review Board approval, 15, 72, 229
interlocutor, 147
intermediate level risk, 178
internal narrative, 95, 97
interrogate the data, 132
interview(s)/ed/ing, 4, 7, 9, 10, 11, 15, 32, 41, 42, 55, 57, 69, 72, 83, 106, 107, 110, 111, 112, 113, 115, 117, 125, 129, 139, 141,

162, 165, 168, 180, 190, 192,
193, 194, 195, 196, 198, 199,
200, 201, 202, 204, 213, 214,
217, 221, 222, 223, 224, 225,
230, 237
interview clip, 192
interview data, 179
interview footage, 192
interview location, 197
interview methodologies, 84
interview notes, 179, 191
interview questions, 32, 107
interview segments, 125
interview techniques, 125, 199
interviewee, 2, 8, 130, 165, 198,
200, 225
interviewer, 2, 103, 117, 130, 165
interviewer and cinematographer,
199
interviews transcribed, 191
involuntary attention, 174
IRB(s), 3, 15, 16, 23, 31, 35, 41, 43,
44, 45, 47, 48, 49, 50, 55, 56, 58,
59, 60, 61, 62, 63, 64, 65, 66, 67,
68, 69, 70, 72, 73, 98, 99, 178,
224
IRB Administrator or Chair, 61, 65,
67, 192
IRB application, 23, 60, 66, 67, 71,
230
IRB approval, 3, 5, 15, 41, 43, 45,
49, 51, 57, 60, 61, 66, 67, 70, 73,
81, 226, 230, 233
IRB approved, 41, 46, 178
IRB members, 3, 28, 43, 50, 51, 60,
61, 63, 64, 65, 67, 68, 69, 70, 71,
73
IRB process, 45, 49, 50, 63, 65, 67,
134, 230, 232
IRB proposal revisal, 68

J

Jim Crow Era, 18
justice, 28, 38, 46, 47, 48, 52, 80,
81, 86, 88, 89, 92, 94, 98, 103,

180, 199, 211, 224, 225, 230,
232

L

laboratory, 7, 103, 173, 174, 186
lack of pedagogical space, 215
landscape, 173, 174, 175, 180, 185,
186
landscape architect, 173, 181
landscape design practices, 185
landscape of power, 3
landscape perception, 173, 180, 185
landscape perception research, 173
landscape perception researchers,
186
layers of analysis, 230
liberation, 36
liberatory, 217
lived experience, 2, 6, 11, 43, 58
Living Salk Institute, 109, 112, 238,
239
logical positivism, 103, 104
logical positivist tradition, 103

M

mandate, 44
mandated, 44
mandated reporter, 50
masking, 225
media, 14, 31, 91, 121, 152, 160,
161, 222
media consumers, 222
media interviews, 198
media literacy, 121, 124
media outlets, 225
media release, 49
melodrama, 149
melodramatic aesthetic, 149
melodramatic performance
aesthetic, 145
melodramatizations, 145
melodramatized, 145, 154, 166
mental health policy, 34, 36
mental institutions, 52
mental maps, 213

DATE DUE

AUG 2 6 2011	
NOV 1 0 2011 ILL# 82883797 ORZ	
JAN 2 1 2012 ILL# 85385614 WAU	